ADAM THE GARDENER

Written and edited by David Coltman

A pictorial calendar and guide to the year's work in the garden, showing how to grow vegetables, fruit and flowers.

With an introduction and contributions
by Max Davidson

A SUNDAY EXPRESS PUBLICATION

ISBN 0 85079 134 0

£1.35

CONTENTS

ENJOY YOUR GARDENING

There has never been a more exciting time for the gardener; never before has the opportunity to achieve perfection been so great. With all the modern aids and improved varieties of seeds and plants success is much easier to achieve.

Most gardens nowadays are fairly small and compact, but with careful planning even the smallest garden can give immense satisfaction. When laying out a garden, it is important to assess the good points and the drawbacks of your particular plot. For instance, you should decide which part gets most sun and also consider what particular eyesore would be best concealed. Your ideas can be committed to paper, but before you start work, mark out with stakes where you will be putting the more important items such as flower beds and trees.

You will no doubt want some paving at the back of the house, if only to provide a dry surface to walk on as far as the clothes line. In future too you might want a greenhouse. So before you commit some of your ideas to the planning stage, think where that greenhouse could be positioned. The ideal site is with the ridge running east to west and with the greenhouse sufficiently close to the house that you can get a ready supply of water, electricity

and natural gas, although you would be amazed at the wide variety of plants which can be grown in a small greenhouse without any heat at all.

Another important feature in a small garden is a pool. If you have a young family you may not want to have a pool immediately, but do earmark a section of lawn, for example, which gets sunshine for part of the day for a pool with water lilies and colourful fish in the future. Ideally the pool too should be close to the house so that you can use the mains electricity supply to power the fountain.

The mention of sunshine in these plans would give the impression that if a garden is mainly in the shade there is little that can be done. Nothing could be further from the truth. There is grass seed suited to shady conditions, and most seedsmen offer their own particular mixture. Certainly a lawn is best made by sowing seed rather than by laying turf of doubtful origin. And sowing is much easier in any case than the back-breaking job of turf laying. If your lawn will get a lot of use, do consider a grass seed mixture with dwarf rye grass, which provides a hardwearing evergreen lawn. Rye grass was once disliked because its tough stalks in summer defied the

efforts of cylinder mowers to cut them. However with a rotary mower such problems cease to exist. In fact, even an electric cylinder mower will make short work of rye grass and give a beautiful, banded lawn finish which is so much admired. Certainly avoiding work should be your aim as much as possible, and a good mower is a sound investment. There are small electric machines which require no more effort than that of vacuum cleaning a carpet. For larger gardens there are excellent petrol-driven rotary and conventional cylinder cutting machines. A rotary is the best bet in areas where the grass frequently has to be cut in summer when it is wet.

You will also save work in the garden if you get the right tools for the job. The basics are a spade, a fork, a hoe, a rake, a pair of secateurs for cutting jobs, a pair of grass edging shears, a trowel, a small hand fork, a garden line, a pressure sprayer, a watering can with fine rose and a bucket for carrying things. If your garden is large enough, you may want a hose and a barrow.

When planting a garden, there is no need nowadays to wait until autumn or early winter. Garden centres always have a good stock of container grown plants and shrubs, so that additions can be made to the garden at any time of the year when the weather is favourable for planting. However trees and roses are best planted at the conventional time.

Choosing a tree can prove a problem particularly if you have a small garden and you do not wish the tree to grow to gigantic proportions. There are many trees suitable even for tiny gardens. Depending on your soil, you could have a dwarf Japanese maple or perhaps Young's weeping birch with its graceful head of light feathery branches. There is the Japanese crab apple which in spring has a mass of flowers which look like pink candy floss. And when one thinks of pink blossom, the Japanese flowering cherries come to mind. The most suitable for gardens are Pink Perfection, a small tree outstandingly free flowering and with rose pink blossom, and Pendula Rosea, a small tree with branches which sweep down to the ground and which in April are clothed in pink blossom. If you must have a weeping willow, do not plant the golden kind which soon swamps even the largest gardens. Your best choice is the American weeping willow, Salix purpurea Pendula, which produces a graceful umbrella an eventual 15 ft. high. There is also a certain magic about having a mountain ash, rowan or whitebeam tree, as all of these have attractive foliage and berries in autumn. Of course, if you have the space and you want beautiful leaves, there are a number of trees worth investigating. The Indian bean tree, Catalpa bignonioides, has huge fresh green leaves and seed pods like brown "runner" beans in autumn; the Honey Locust tree, Gleditschia triacanthos Sunburst, has magnificent golden foliage; and the False Acacia, Robinia pseudo-acacia Frisia, starts off in spring with a head of yellow leaves which by autumn have developed coppery tints to complement beautifully the tree's red thorns.

The second most popular addition to most gardens is a rose. We are extremely lucky in the number of beautiful roses available to us from the usual single-headed and multi-headed kinds and related climbers to the many shrub roses with their exquisite perfumes. If you have a small garden, you can find roses which grow to around 1½ ft. to 2 ft. and which will provide you with flowers from June to December. Be bold in your choice of colour. Roses look best when several of one variety are planted together. Be generous to your roses: feed them three times a year, spray them to protect them from pests and diseases and prune them hard annually in early March. Your bushes will reward you with a display of colour and scent which cannot be matched by any other shrub in the garden. Roses too look good on walls, where the perfume is often more readily appreciated.

Walls too can be clothed with all sorts of other climbers to give even a house in the middle of a city the air of being a country cottage. After the rose the clematis is deservedly the most popular, but consider too some jasmine and honeysuckle. You could also have a firethorn (pyracantha), or a passion-flower if you have a warm wall in a climatically favourable part of the country. Also on your list should be the wistaria, the grape vine and the cotoneaster.

The cotoneaster comes from a large family of shrubs — and shrubs will also figure high on your list of priorities in furnishing your garden. A valuable tip is to ensure that you have twice as many evergreen shrubs as deciduous ones. The latter tend to flower more freely, but that is little consolation on a January day when the garden is full of bare skeletons. Among the many shrubs do not overlook the dwarf conifers, especially the low growing, spreading kind which are marvellous for covering man-hole covers and other unsightly objects.

Heathers too can be used extensively to provide year-round colour. However your choice of shrubs will be largely dictated by their intended position in the garden and the local soil and climate. Do not despair about shade. Shrubs such as azaleas, camellias, choisya,

5

daphne, hydrangea, mahonia, ribes, skimmia, spiraea, viburnum and vinca, to mention just a few, are happy in sunless positions.

The same applies to your choice of perennial plants. Most will thrive in sunshine, but an area is almost perpetual shade worries some people. It is no problem. You can choose shade lovers such as acanthus, astilbe, bergenia, Christmas roses, hosta, lily-of-the-valley and saxifraga. In a small garden you can use many of the so-called rock plants to edge flower beds or to plant in troughs and tubs. You would be amazed at just how many of these little plants there are, and some such as the dianthus are gloriously scented.

Gaps in your flowering scheme can be filled in with annuals and biennials raised from seed on the kitchen window sill until you get that greenhouse. You could also save yourself some money by sowing the seeds of perennial plants such as lupins, delphiniums, columbines, foxgloves and hollyhocks. In a new garden it is often a good idea to use plants like these until such time as you have definitely decided on the shape you want your garden to take.

Bulbs are also a marvellous investment for the garden since many of them provide colour at a stage in the year when there are few flowers around. You can start the year with yellow aconites, crocuses and chionodoxa and move on to the daffodils and tulips. It is worth getting the more expensive dwarf tulips and daffodils as they are more in keeping with smaller gardens as well as providing many more flowers. Do not overlook too the hyacinths, the snowdrops, the irises, the scillas and the wide assortment of lesser known bulbs, which all have the great advantage that, once planted, they come up year after year with little attention.

Even in a small garden many people like to be able to grow their own vegetables. My tip, where space is short, is to concentrate on the salad vegetables such as lettuces, the beetroots, spring onions and radishes. You could also grow the more expensive vegetables such as courgettes and French beans.

On a patio, in a backyard or on a balcony you can use growing bags to raise everything from tomatoes to cantaloupe melons. The new gardener will wish to make use of these modern aids even when the same plants might be grown in soil. For there is no doubt that the money spent on growing bags produces superb crops of top quality.

In a small greenhouse you can use growing bags for aubergines, peppers, cucumbers and tomatoes, and once these crops have been harvested, the bags can be used for winter lettuce. Heating in the greenhouse is not vital. It is best to raise difficult seeds in the warmth of your home and to move them into the greenhouse once they are at the stage of having been transplanted.

An unheated greenhouse can be used in winter to give frost protection to pelargoniums and fuchsias, although in the coldest areas it will be necessary to use a small heater to keep the temperature just above freezing point. Without heat you can grow freesias, ixias and beautiful blue brodiaea flowers from bulbs in pots. You can also start a collection of cacti and succulents.

But it is in spring that a greenhouse comes into its own, particularly if the weather is wet. You can start off broad beans, cauliflowers and cabbages. You can raise lettuce, leek and onion seedlings. You can "force" some strawberry plants to give you a crop as early as May.

As I said there has never been a more exciting time for the gardener. In this book virtually all the problems that you are likely to come up against are dealt with; you will also find numerous ideas and the best way of tackling the various tasks.

But above all, enjoy yourself. Happy gardening.

JANUARY
CULTIVATING NEW GROUND

Preparing new ground for cultivation is a job which many gardeners have to tackle. Such work can be proceeded with through the winter provided the conditions are right, i.e. the soil isn't frozen or waterlogged, etc. If in any doubt or if the ground consists of really heavy clayey soil it's best to leave the job until the spring when the soil starts to dry out.

The first step is to expose the surface of the soil that is to be cultivated. If you are converting a lawn into a garden bed, you must first remove the turf as shown in Inset A. You can use this turf to make good fibrous loam by stacking it upside down in a heap for about a year, or put it face down at the foot of the trenches you will be digging during cultivation. A site consisting of weeds, long grass, small bushes, etc. should have the top growth cut down and cleared prior to being dug over; one covered in builder's rubble must have all the broken bricks, sand and gravel removed.

Whichever type of site you're dealing with, once the soil has been exposed you have two main tasks ahead. The first is to turn the compacted ground into much looser soil into which roots can easily penetrate. The second is to remove as many roots as you possibly can; concentrating on those of pernicious perennial weeds such as nettles, bindweed, couch grass, docks, ground elder, etc. This is a fiddly job as it entails picking over each and every spadeful of soil, but in the long run is well worth all the trouble as it is far easier to eliminate these weeds when the ground is vacant than when crops are growing in it.

Turning back to the first task I mentioned, that of getting the soil into a state suitable for cultivation: gardeners who either own or can hire a cultivator will have no problems. Those who have to tackle it by digging will find it hard but rewarding work.

The first thing to do is to take out a trench about a foot wide and a spade's depth and to move the soil from this trench to the farther end of the plot. The soil at the foot of this trench will most likely be very hard and compacted. Loosen and break it up with a fork or even with a pickaxe if necessary; the loosening being done to the fork's depth and over the whole width of the trench. If you have any well-rotted manure or compost spread it on top of this loosened soil at the foot of the trench as this will greatly benefit subsequent crops.

The next step is to make another trench parallel and adjacent to the first one. Earth from this second trench is used to fill in the first one. Soil loosening, manure adding, etc., are repeated and the same process continues over the new plot until at the end the soil which was excavated from the first trench will be there waiting in the right position to fill in the last trench. Inset B shows the sequence which should be followed.

JANUARY
WINTER SPRAYING

Although most of the pests of fruit trees and bushes can be controlled by a spring and summer spraying programme, it is also possible to prevent some of the troubles developing by killing off the insects at the egg stage. Some winter washes which do this, such as tar-oil, will also help to destroy lichens and mosses.

One of the great virtues of these winter washes is their wideness of application. Thus tar-oil, although it may have to be applied at different concentrations, may be used on the tree fruits (apples, pears, plums, cherries, etc.), the bush fruits (gooseberries, currants), the canes, such as raspberries, and even on rose bushes; in fact, wherever there is a known risk of trouble with aphids, apple suckers, scale insects or mealy bugs.

Aphids, which suck the sap out of plants thus weakening them, may have been present without you even realising it — thus if last year you had leaf curl on currants (Inset A), they were probably aphid-infested; or if your raspberries had the characteristic mottled effect associated with virus disease (Inset B), you would be well-advised to spray with tar-oil, as the virus diseases are often spread by aphids.

Tar-oil must be sprayed when the plants concerned are totally dormant, but for a spray applied slightly later (up to bud-burst), a product containing bromophos in oil may be used. This has a very similar range of pest control but is less messy to handle, avoids the risk of scorching other plants and is useful when bad weather in the early part of the year makes tar-oil spraying impractical.

Spraying should always be done on a windless day when the tree or bush is dry and there is no danger of the spray freezing on contact with the bark. Grass may be scorched by a tar-oil spray but will soon recover: any other green vegetation may be covered by newspapers or sacking. When applying the spray, keep the pressure up in the sprayer, as you want the wash to penetrate into all the cracks on the tree where eggs may have been laid. Remember the buds and tips of shoots are the most likely places for aphid-infestation.

Tar-oil washes in particular are unpleasant chemicals to deal with, and they should be used with the utmost caution. Wear old clothes, even goggles if you have them, and rubber-gloves. Don't breathe in any of the spray and be quick to wash off any of the concentrate that gets on to your skin. In short, always follow the manufacturer's instructions, and don't forget to give the sprayer itself a thorough clean-out after use.

Some tar-oils may additionally be used for killing off mossy and algal growths on surfaces such as concrete paths, brick walls, wooden fences, etc. They can also be used as sterilising agents in the greenhouse, effective on both structure and soil, although all plants must be removed prior to use.

JANUARY
APPLE PRUNING

Pruning fruit trees is a subject that causes some apprehension to first-timers but they should take heart because heavy pruning is only necessary on young trees which are being formed into shape. For older, well-established trees, pruning amounts to no more than controlling growth and removing dead or diseased wood.

A cautionary word is needed about apples' varying fruit-bearing habits. Some produce fruit all the way along or at the tips of young shoots (the tip-bearers), and some produce fruit on short spurs (the spur-bearers). It is vital to know which type of tree you are dealing with, because otherwise you could unwittingly remove most of the fruit buds while pruning. If in any doubt, leave the pruning until next year, when you'll have had a chance to see the tree in actual growth and to see where the fruits are produced. Inset C should help to distinguish which buds are which — the fat bud at the tip is a fruit bud, the smaller, more pointed bud on the side of the shoot is a growth bud.

The object of pruning is to produce a tree with a well balanced shape, no tangling of branches and a controlled number of fruit buds. Hard pruning induces vigorous growth and this is most likely to produce lush foliage at the expense of apples. The right way of making a pruning cut is shown in inset B: note the slope of the cut away from the growth bud, the fact that the cut is immediately above the bud, and remember that growth from outward-pointing buds will be spreading in shape; from inward-pointing ones it will be more upright. Always use a sharp instrument, whether it's a pruning knife or a pair of secateurs, so that the cut is a clean one.

The next stage is to differentiate between the types of shoot. In inset A the main shoot (marked 1) is the leader, while those lengthy shoots (marked 2) growing off it are laterals. The much shorter shoots on which the fruit buds are generally found are called spurs.

Whilst establishing an apple tree, i.e., in its first four or five years, the system of pruning requires leaders to be shortened by about half and laterals to be cut back to three or four buds from the leader, as is also shown in inset A. As the tree grows the need for pruning diminishes, until with an established tree it's only necessary to tip the leaders (i.e. to remove their tips) and to cut back the more vigorously growing laterals to encourage the development of fruiting spurs. After a while the spurs themselves may need thinning out — this is done by removing the older spurs altogether, cutting back the longer ones and reducing the numbers of fruit buds on spurs where a large cluster of buds has developed.

With tip-bearing trees, whose apples are produced on the laterals, the need is to leave some of the laterals (preferably the outward growing ones) intact while cutting the others back to one bud.

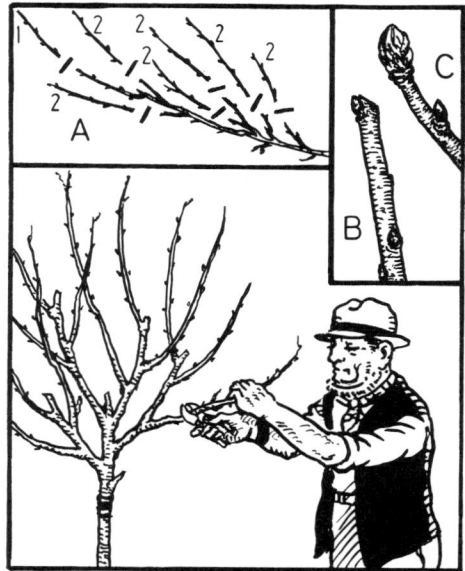

JANUARY
BIRD DAMAGE

There's no doubt that birds are one of the gardener's great allies in the war against insect pests and hence highly desirable visitors to our gardens at any time of the year. But there are one or two species which can do a great deal of damage to plants in a very short space of time, and some ideas about how to protect the plants concerned may prove useful.

Woodpigeons normally have a very varied diet including all sorts of wild seeds and fruits, but during the winter months when supplies of food are limited their attention often turns to brassicas, both as farm and garden crops. Particularly at risk, because of their young and tender foliage, are spring cabbage seedlings, which can often be reduced to a row of leafless stalks overnight.

Bullfinches have achieved an even greater notoriety than woodpigeons through their ability to do quite spectacular damage to buds of fruit bushes and trees, and ornamental shrubs as well. Characteristic bullfinch damage consists of the bird working its way along a branch from the tip inwards removing each bud as it comes to it. The outer part of the bud is discarded, the inner part eaten. One bullfinch can remove thirty buds a minute, but

it's worth noting that it prefers operating close to the cover provided by hedgerows and that gardeners suffering bullfinch damage might reduce it by planting fruit bushes, etc. in more open sites.

House sparrows also attack fruit buds, although they can't remove them as neatly as bullfinches can; they often make a terrible mess of primrose and polyanthus flowers by tearing the petals off, besides taking off the leaves of young carnations, chrysanthemums, etc.

Anything small, such as polyanthus flowers, can be protected by winding black cotton around sticks to form an effective but inconspicuous web of threads over and around the flowers (Inset A). Really small brassica seedlings could be protected by pea guards, but for larger plants plastic netting is more useful. To keep the netting off the ground, try putting jam jars over the top of the sticks and secure the sides with skewers or even large stones (Inset B).

Protecting fruit bushes or trees is rather more of a problem because of their greater size. Netting of course affords the best protection but if it's put up in the form of a fruit cage great care should be taken to prevent any weight of snow building up on top of the cage during severe weather. Bushes can also be covered fairly easily with netting using a minimal structure of canes for supports.

A possible alternative to netting is a product called Scaraweb consisting of a mass of rayon fibres which can be pulled out and wound round and over branches. The material gradually disintegrates so that most of it has gone by the time the fruit crop is ready to pick.

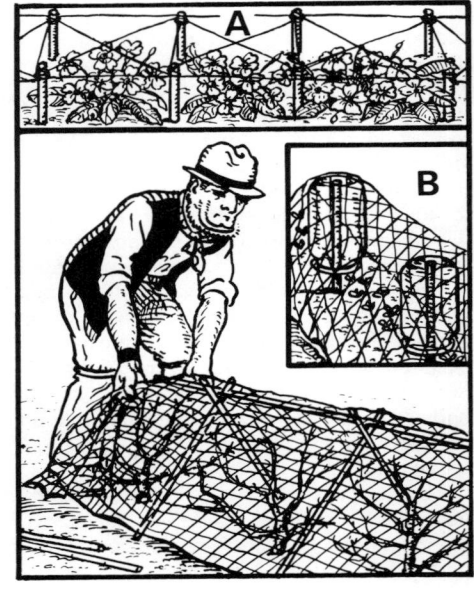

JANUARY
SEED AND POTTING COMPOSTS

As we approach the seed-sowing season which will probably necessitate the purchase of seed and potting compost, it seems a good moment to say what goes into these composts, and how you can make up your own to exactly the same formula as that which you'd otherwise be buying.

Seed and potting composts may be either peat or loam based. Those with loam, known as John Innes composts, may be mixed up at home to the same formula as bought compost. These John Innes composts were developed to meet the needs of as wide a range of plants as possible, always using the same ingredients mixed in the same ratio. The three ingredients are loam, peat and sand.

Loam is obtained from stacking turves upside down in a heap (Inset B) for about twelve months and letting them decay. The end result is a mixture of soil and fibrous matter that is ideal for potting composts. Loam should be sieved before use and also partially sterilised to eliminate soil pests and diseases and kill off weed seeds. If you must use ordinary soil or unsterilised loam, stick to potting rather than seed composts to avoid some of the problems of weed seed germination.

The peat should be one of coarse texture and may be replaced by sifted leaf-mould if that is available; the sand likewise should be coarse and of "sharp" texture.

For all potting composts (JI Nos. 1, 2 and 3) the loam, peat and sand are mixed in the same ratio: 7 parts loam, 3 parts peat, 2 parts sand. All these parts are measured by *bulk* rather than weight. One of the easiest ways of measuring the parts out is simply to use a flowerpot as a measure.

To this mixture must be added a fertiliser known as John Innes Base fertiliser. This consists of 2 parts superphosphate, 2 parts hoof and horn, 1 part sulphate of potash. All these parts are by *weight*, and to them should be added 3/4 oz. of ground limestone or chalk (except where the compost is for use with azaleas, rhododendrons, etc.) per 4 oz. of base fertiliser. This 4 oz. quantity is sufficient for one bushel (eight gallons) of loam, peat and sand mixture. All the ingredients must be mixed thoroughly, either by hand (Inset A) or by spade if larger quantities are involved.

This mixture is JI No.1; JI No. 2 has 8 ozs. of base fertiliser, 1½ oz. chalk; JI No. 3 has 12 oz. base fertiliser, 2¼ oz. chalk — both per bushel of mixture.

The JI seed compost formula is 2 parts loam, 1 part peat, 1 part sand, the ingredients to be sieved to give a finer texture than potting compost. To each bushel add 1½ oz. super-phosphate and 3/4 oz. ground limestone or chalk, and again mix thoroughly.

Finally, as a rough guide to usage, use JI No. 1 for all plants when first potted, JI No 2 for when they require pots larger than 4½ inches, and JI No. 3 for all pots of 8 inches or more in diameter.

JANUARY
GREENHOUSE SOIL PROBLEMS

To avoid the build-up of pests and diseases which could occur through continually growing the same vegetable on the same site it's a standard practice to adopt some form of crop rotation in the vegetable garden. Greenhouses, though, are expected to produce the same crops year after year, and if the crop happens to be one like the tomato, which is particularly susceptible to diseases, the quality and quantity of fruit produced is sure to deteriorate unless remedial action is taken.

There are a number of alternatives, the first two of which neatly sidestep the problem by not using the greenhouse soil at all. Growing bags (Inset A) of specially prepared, sterilised compost are becoming increasingly popular, while the ring culture method shown in Inset B still has plenty of adherents.

This latter entails growing tomatoes in bottomless pots on a layer of moisture-retaining material into which the moisture-absorbing roots of the plant grow, while the feeding roots remain in the pots of compost. By marking out the area required with a line of bricks, covering the bricks and the space within them with heavy-duty polythene and then putting the moisture-retaining material

(usually a fine gravel or peat) on top of the polythene to a depth of 4-6 inches, the greenhouse soil is effectively isolated.

Fine crops can be obtained with both growing bags and ring culture, but these methods do have their disadvantages, particularly with regard to watering which needs to be done both plentifully and often on hot summer days and can present quite a problem at holiday times.

It's easier to look after the water requirements of plants growing in a greenhouse soil bed, but to make this soil a worthwhile growing medium it's necessary to be sure that, firstly, it's well supplied with humus and nutrients and, secondly, it's not harbouring the pests and diseases which might have built up through several seasons of growing the same crop, as I've already mentioned.

Regarding the supply of humus and nutrients, this is achieved by preparing in the same way as one would an outdoor plot, i.e. incorporating generous amounts of well-rotted compost, manure or peat to satisfy the humus requirements and giving a dressing of a balanced fertiliser like Growmore to supply the plants with their initial feed.

To tackle the soil health problem, it's advisable to change the greenhouse soil every year, if at all possible, replacing it with soil taken from a part of the garden where neither potatoes nor tomatoes were growing last year.

Whilst putting in the new soil or whilst digging over the bed if you're not replacing the soil, always sterilise with Jeyes Fluid or a similar product. By soaking first the trench and then all the soil as it's put in you should end up with a good healthy medium for growing the plants. Instructions about the amount of Jeyes Fluid to use are printed on the tin.

JANUARY
SEED STORAGE AND VIABILITY

One of the questions raised as the sowing season approaches concerns the advisability of using seeds from packets bought in previous years. The short answer is that most seeds should germinate satisfactorily in their second year after purchase and in some cases for several years afterwards. They must, however, be properly stored to make this possible.

A seed that's five years old may look the same as one that's just been harvested but will in fact have been deteriorating over the years. Seed firms with specialised equipment can keep seed in fine condition for long periods, but gardeners have to provide the best they can, with dry conditions and low temperatures the most important requirements.

Even then, different species have vastly different seed 'lives'. The period of viability, which is while the seed is capable of germinating and growing into a healthy, adult plant, ranges from a matter of days or weeks in the case of some trees such as willows, to the Indian lotus whose seeds germinated perfectly after having been immersed in a Manchurian peat bog for 1,000 years! Nearly all the seeds of our commonly-grown vegetables and flowers come rather in between these two extremes and may be expected to remain viable for, say, 2-10 years if kept under optimum conditions.

Such conditions mean constant low temperatures (down to freezing point and below) but also accurately controlled low humidity. Most gardeners may have access to places that are cold like cellars or even fridges but they are almost invariably both cold and moist, and this moisture immediately cancels out the benefit of the low temperature. Obviously some sort of compromise has to be made, and my method would be to look for the coolest room in the house where the atmosphere always remains *dry* and then to store all seeds there at all times (i.e. never to leave opened packets out in the shed or greenhouse where they are likely to be subjected to both unfavourable temperature and humidity levels).

If seeds are kept too long, more than two or three years, say, not only will their germination rate fall but there will also be a likelihood of those seedlings which have germinated successfully being less vigorous than similar seedlings from a fresh batch of seed. The only exceptions to this would be those seeds which have been bought in moisture-resistant, sealed, foil packets which are extremely good at keeping seed fresh as long as the packet remains *unopened*. On opening such seed will begin its ageing process like any other.

Although it can't be more than a rough guide, the inset shows the periods you should be able to keep some of our most common vegetable seeds; namely, parsnip and onion — 1 year; beetroot, beans, peas, carrot and lettuce — 3 years; cabbage, swede, turnip and radish — 5 years.

13

JANUARY
SOWING SEEDS UNDER GLASS

Many seeds can be sown either under glass from January to March, or in the open during April and May. Each method has something to be said for it, but I find that the controlled conditions of the under-glass method very often give better results, especially when dry or cold spring weather makes for poor germination and slow growth outdoors.

You don't have to be a greenhouse owner to raise seeds under glass — a frame, conservatory or even a window sill can be used. Don't worry too much about temperatures: once the seeds have germinated most seedlings will be quite happy with a temperature that stays above 40°F at night. For seeds that require a high temperature for germination, you could always try using the airing cupboard, but remember to take the seedlings out of the cupboard immediately they show through.

There's plenty of choice for containers these days — flowerpots, peat pots, seed boxes and seed-trays. Flowerpots are useful where only a small number of seedlings are required; peat pots where it's advantageous to put the young plant out without any root disturbance. Boxes or plastic seed-trays are best where larger numbers of seedlings are required. Seed-trays are easy to keep clean, which is a vital factor in raising healthy seedlings: there is no point in using sterilised seed compost if it's going to be put into a container which isn't itself free of possible sources of plant disease.

If you use a seed-tray, put a thin layer of peat on the bottom and then cover this with seed compost to within ¼ inch of the top. Firm the compost down (the base of a flowerpot will do this effectively (Inset A); do the corners with your fingers), water it with a fine rose on the can (Inset B) and leave it to drain. If the seeds are large enough, space them out individually; if not, sow them *thinly* and then cover them lightly with a little more compost passed through a sieve. They only need to be lightly covered (very small seeds can even be left uncovered on the surface of the compost): covering them too deeply is a frequent cause of poor germination.

The next step is to cover the trays, each with a piece of glass over which is spread newspaper (Inset C). Once a day remove the glass and wipe off any condensation on the underside. Do this until the seedlings emerge, when the glass and paper should be removed altogether. If the compost shows sign of drying out at any stage after the seeds are sown, water it with a mist spray.

When the seedlings are big enough to handle (usually at the first "true" as opposed to seed leaf stage) prick them out into further trays, boxes or pots filled with John Innes No. 1, again placed over a thin layer of peat. Pricking out should always be done as soon as possible to avoid any unnecessary root disturbance and should be done by holding on to a leaf rather than the stem of the seedling.

JANUARY
BEGONIAS

As a genus containing literally hundreds of species begonias are potentially a very big subject, but here I shall be limiting the discussion to those that are suitable for growing outdoors as bedding plants (although these can be grown as pot-plants as well).

For simplicity's sake these outdoor types can be divided into two categories, the tuberous-rooted and the fibrous-rooted. The former have large, very often double, flowers and intermediate sized leaves as is shown in Inset A, while the latter, often listed as Begonia semperflorens, have much smaller, glossy leaves and an abundance of small flowers in various shades of red, pink and white (Inset B).

The tuberous-rooted kinds can be grown, naturally enough, from their tubers or from seed while the fibrous-rooted are always raised from seed. The degree of heat required makes this an indoor or heated propagator job rather than an unheated greenhouse one.

If you have bought some tubers or saved some from plants grown last year they may be started into growth any time between now and March. The usual method is to put them in boxes of moist peat so that the peat comes up to the top of the tuber (Inset C). If a temperature of 60°F can be maintained they should show signs of life fairly soon and can then, before there's very much shoot and root growth, be potted up individually in John Innes No. 1 or its equivalent. Water should be given rather sparingly until the plants are well-established.

Raising begonias from seed is not the easiest of jobs because of the smallness of the seed (Begonia semperflorens weigh in at 1,000,000 per ounce) and the necessity of maintaining a high temperature for germination. The seedlings, too, are on the small side and are rather fiddly to prick out. But, that said, the cost of buying the plants will reflect the cost of the heat that someone else has had to provide for them and I find there's something particularly satisfying about seeing one's own sowing of such minute seeds grow into sizable plants all within the space of a few months.

Making sure the surface of the seed compost is fine, level and moist, sow the seeds as thinly as possible but do not cover them with further compost. If a propagator is available, that will be ideal for providing the warmth and humidity which will be needed for germination. Otherwise it's a question of covering the seeds with a sheet of glass and a piece of paper in the normal way and finding somewhere with a temperature of 65°-70°F and a night minimum of 60°F.

After germination the seedlings should be pricked out into trays as soon as they are big enough to handle and grown on in light conditions at a temperature continuing at the 60°F mark or as near to that as possible, gradually hardening the plants off in May until they are ready for planting out at the end of that month or the beginning of June.

JANUARY
POTATOES

It may be a couple of months before planting time, but it's not too early to buy seed potatoes which can then be "sprouted" before planting, a process which ensures the tubers get off to the best possible start.

When buying the seed potatoes, it's advisable to look for certified seed, the certification indicating that the tubers come up to certain standards of freedom from disease. The sacks in which the potatoes are usually seen standing in the shops have to be marked with the grade they've achieved — this is most likely to be FS or AAI, and of these two FS (foundation seed) is the higher standard.

That said, it's also worthwhile having a good look at the particular potatoes you're thinking of buying to make sure that they haven't started sprouting prematurely (with long whitish shoots indicating they've been kept in too high a temperature) and that they're otherwise sound (no scab, shrivelling, etc.).

The other possibility is that you might want to grow potatoes from seed saved from your own crop last year. This is probably all right if your last year's crop was grown from certified seed but if you carry on doing this from year to year the potatoes will most likely gradually diminish in quality and yield as the plants become more and more infected with the virus diseases that certified seed must be free from. If you are planting home-grown tubers, remember that large-sized ones are more likely to come from non-infected plants and will thus prove more reliable.

Whichever potatoes you are using, the aim must be to produce tubers with short, sturdy sprouts that are green or dark purple in colour. The two vital requirements for this are plenty of light and cool but frost free conditions. To make sure each tuber gets its fair share of light it's common practice to stand them upright in shallow boxes.

Place the tuber with the rose end upwards. This is the end which has the greatest number of eyes, which should by now just have the very beginnings of the young shoots starting to appear in them. If kept cool (40°F is all that's necessary) and light, the potatoes should eventually come to look like that shown in Inset A by the time they're ready for planting in late March or April. If they begin to develop like the one shown in Inset B the conditions are very likely too dark for them and probably too warm as well.

One further advantage of sprouting the seed is that it enables you to pick out the useless tubers before planting: i.e. if any tuber fails to develop any young shoots, throw it on the bonfire along with any other tubers showing obvious signs of disease. It would be quite pointless to plant them.

Wherever you choose to put your boxes of potatoes make sure they cannot be affected by frost. As the days grow warmer, there is an increasing risk of aphid infestation of the developing shoots on the tubers. Watch out for these and spray if necessary.

JANUARY
GERANIUMS FROM SEED

Growing geraniums from seed used not to be very rewarding because the plants often seemed very reluctant to bloom and did not always turn out true to type. But the introduction of the F1 hybrids has changed all that — they can be depended on to give a good show of flower in their first year, are quite uniform in type, do not need to be stopped to produce bushy plants and are quite straightforward to raise from seed.

The one drawback concerns the price of the seeds which is very high compared with most other flowers, but the seed is always scarified (i.e. the hard outer coating is broken up by machine treatment) so that germination should be virtually 100%. Also, of course, the plants are perennials and stocks can be further increased by taking cuttings in the normal way.

To get plants flowering early in the season from seed, early sowing is essential. January is certainly not too early although it's not always easy to meet the temperature requirements of the seed at this time of year. Ideally germination should take place at 65-70°F, which makes it more of an indoor window-sill job than a greenhouse one. Growing on also requires a relatively warm temperature (60-65°F) if quick growth is to be made.

Plenty of light is vital too, and that can be more of a problem with seedlings growing indoors early in the year. Try to find a bright spot for them or else the young plants will become drawn and lose the bushiness which makes them so attractive.

Because the seeds are so expensive, sow them individually and well spaced out in the seed trays so that in the event of irregular germination the first seedlings may be potted up (into 3 inch pots — Inset A) without disturbing the seeds yet to germinate. This potting up is done when the seedlings are about an inch high.

F1 hybrids are more vigorous in growth than the ordinary varieties and to get the best results from them they should be encouraged to grow with all the vigour they possess. This means potting them on regularly and not allowing them to become potbound which would slow up their progress to mature flowering plants.

A quick glance through the seed catalogues will show you the wide range of varieties available. Just singling out a few for special mention, the *Carefree* mixture are strong-growing bushy plants up to 2ft high in a good range of colours. Slightly less tall but with an equally attractive colour range is the *Sprinter* mixture (Inset B), which is, as its name suggests, very early to bloom. Finally, a dwarf mixture called *Playboy* (Inset C) which only grows to about 10 inches, but has very attractive leaf markings and makes a good winter house plant if lifted in September, trimmed back and potted up in, say, John Innes No. 2 when it should develop a fresh head of blossom for Christmas.

HEATHERS — THE EASY WAY TO BEAT THAT WINTER GLOOM

Take a close look at your garden this morning. How much colour is it providing to delight the eye?

Are there large areas of bare earth with little to relieve the general winter gloom?

For a few pounds spent now, I could transform all that for you.

For instance, you could have a shrub bed which flowers all year round, and which would required little if any pruning, feeding or weeding.

The solution is so very simple; plant a selection of heathers.

The heathers which can be obtained nowadays for garden planting vary as much from the wild kind of moorland and heath as a delphinium differs from a daisy.

For a start, many of these excellent heathers originated in Southern Europe and they are absolutely smothered in flowers for up to four months of the darkest and most unfavourable time of the year.

Compared with most shrubs, they are not expensive.

Heathers are superb plants in beds by themselves, as an edging to a shrub border and in window boxes and tubs.

You can grow them either in full sun or partial shade. There are also heathers for virtually all soils and conditions from Cornwall to Caithness.

In fact, there can hardly be a garden anywhere that could not be improved considerably by the addition of a few heathers.

Ericas

Heathers fall into two main categories. The types that flower in winter and spring and the ones that flower in summer and autumn.

The first group are commonly called ericas, and despite the fact that they originated in exotic spots in Southern Europe and along the Mediterranean, they are tough enough to survive the worst that winter in this country can offer. The beauty of this group too is that they can grow in all soils, including those containing lime.

The second group of heathers (summer and autumn flowering) are the more familiar lings or heaths, which are common to all the countries of the British Isles. Our native heathers have the botanical name calluna to distinguish them from the erica types, which if you look closely enough, have a different form of flower.

The lings like an acid kind of soil. This can be provided in all but the most chalky soils by the addition of plenty of moss peat.

The choice of heathers is vast. Most of the flowers are pink or white, but an increasing number of new plants have extremely beautiful foliage in various shades of green, grey, gold, yellow and orange.

This means that even if your soil limits you to growing only winter-flowering heathers, for example, you can still have a very attractive carpet of colour in your garden in the summer months.

Another point about heathers; unlike expensive spring and summer bedding plants, they never need to be replaced.

You should aim to plant not less than three, and preferably five, of any one variety. Irregular groups look more effective than, say, rows of heathers strung along a path.

Varieties

Within three years most heathers will grow to a weed-suppressing mat 18 in. or more across. In order to get the plants to knit quickly together and to provide the best possible show, I have planted my own heathers 12 in. to 15 in. apart.

What should you choose? Of the winter

flowering Erica carnea varieties I recommend: Ann Sparkes (February/March) with purple-red flowers and orange-yellow foliage: King George (November/March) with rosy pink flowers, and Myretoun Ruby (February/April) with dark green foliage and ruby red flowers. All of these will grow to about 1 ft. high.

Should you want something shorter, you will not find better heathers than Springwood White and Springwood Pink, which form a dense 6 in. thick mat covered in flowers from January to March.

Any of these heathers can also be used to make a cheerful and permanent display in tubs and window boxes.

By crossing a couple of Southern European species a group of new winter flowering hybrids were produced which share the general name Erica darleyensis. Under this heading you can find many other worthwhile additions to your garden.

For example, Arthur Johnston (Dec./April) with light green foliage and sprays of magenta flowers which are useful for cutting, and Silver Beads (Nov./April), the best white heather of all with sweetly-scented, silvery white flowers which are sheer magic in the garden in winter. Most of these particular hybrid heathers are 2 ft. high.

When it comes to choosing a selection of summer and autumn-flowering heathers, there are so many beauties to tempt you. You can select from the numerous Cornish, Scottish, Irish, Mediterranean and Bell (native to such countries as diverse as Norway and Madeira) heathers.

Just to give you a helping hand, I recommend H. E. Beale (Sept./Nov., 2 ft.), with exquisitely beautiful, silvery pink flower spikes ideal for cutting; 6 in. high Multicolour with foliage which turns orange, yellow, bronze and red with the changing seasons; and J. H. Hamilton (Aug./Sept., 10 in.) with bright pink flowers.

Soil

If you want to fill in the flowering gaps between the winter and summer flowering kinds to give yourself a year of glorious colour, you could also have the 10 in. high Bell heather Pink Ice (June/Sept.), and the 2 ft. tall Mediterranean heather Irish Salmon (April/June) with grey foliage and salmon flower buds which open to a clear pink. Mediterranean heathers will also tolerate soil containing lime.

Heathers for window boxes and tubs can be planted in either John Innes No. 3 compost or a special ericaceous compost.

In the garden the heathers should be planted in weed-free soil enriched with moss peat. You should also incorporate a good handful of damp peat around the roots of the individual plants, which should be set slightly deeper in the soil than they were at the nursery and firmed carefully with your fingers.

Annually in April the soil between the heathers should be top-dressed with more peat until the heathers have completely knitted together. If the heathers are slow in growing, you can also feed them in April with a general granular fertiliser.

The only other job that needs to be done is to keep the young heathers free from wind-blown leaves in autumn. If you wish, the dead flower heads of the summer-flowering heathers, ornamental in winter with their russets and yellows, can be trimmed away with hedging shears in spring. Winter flowering varieties can be snipped over lightly after flowering to keep them neat and to encourage them to knit together more rapidly.

But that is the counsel of perfection.

The real joy of having heathers in the garden is the magnificent return they give for so little outlay in cash and attention.

FEBRUARY
CLOCHE WORK

It's around this time of year when cloches are of greatest value to the gardener, enabling seeds of quite a few crops to be sown several weeks earlier than would otherwise be possible in the open ground and of course affording the seedlings invaluable protection during their first few weeks of life.

Glass and rigid plastic cloches have become very expensive to buy, but polythene cloches or the polythene tunnel cloche are just about cheap enough to bear some relation to the actual value of the crops they'll help to produce, even if they won't give quite as much protection as their more expensive counterparts.

In February and early March the main use of cloches is to help warm the soil *before* any seeds are sown. Sowing seeds in wet, cold soil and then covering them with cloches would just be a waste of time as the low soil temperatures would prevent germination and the seeds would rot in the ground; but if the soil is fully covered by a row of cloches, sealed properly at the end (Inset A) to prevent the wind-tunnel effect, then, given some sunshine and reasonable daytime temperature levels, the soil will begin to dry out and then warm up, after, say, a fortnight's cover.

It's at this stage that the seeds may be sown, i.e., when the soil has become friable enough to produce the fine tilth that's required. Replace the cloches after sowing, leaving them until the weather conditions allow their total removal, although before this it will probably have been necessary to introduce ventilation of some sort on warm sunny days.

Provided that the soil was moist enough for successful germination, watering need not be a problem as water from rainfall will tend to move downwards and sideways through the soil to the area where the roots of the cloche plants are.

Choosing a site where the soil has been enriched with manure or compost during the winter will also help with better moisture retention; the other obvious points about the site are that it must receive maximum sunshine in order to warm the soil as quickly as possible and that if it has some protection from strong, cold winds the heat loss from that quarter will be minimised.

Suitable crops for cloche cultivation include lettuce (quick-maturing varieties like Fortune or Tom Thumb), carrots (Amsterdam Forcing or Early Nantes–Inset B), beet (Boltardy), any early varieties of pea (but watch out for mice taking the seeds), radishes, turnips (Milan White, Inset C) and even, perhaps, a patch of mint. When these early crops are safely under way, the cloches can be redeployed for such vegetables as dwarf beans, courgettes, sweet corn, ridge cucumbers and bush tomatoes. These all need relatively high soil temperatures for quick germination and the use of cloches can give several weeks' advantage over unprotected sowings.

FEBRUARY
CHRYSANTHEMUM CUTTINGS

Chrysanthemums being perennials, one might well think that the question of how to propagate them was of only minor importance. But just as the border types are divided with only the new outermost sections being replanted in order to retain the vigour of the plants, so the showy varieties flowering under glass from late autumn to winter are usually propagated from cuttings to ensure strong-growing plants capable of producing the best blooms.

The cuttings are always taken from new shoots arising at the base of the plants, and to encourage these new shoots to develop, the old growth is cut down after flowering has finished. At the same time label each plant. Plants growing in the greenhouse border should send up new shoots readily enough — if any are reluctant to do so, or to save space with plants in pots, take out the stools, shake off the old soil and put them in boxes of John Innes No. 1 where they should soon start into growth.

The time to take cuttings depends on the variety involved. Some exhibition chrysanthemums may have them taken in December or January, but in general February or March are good months because of the increased light and the higher temperatures to be expected in the greenhouse or frame.

Also, by February or March, the new shoots should be about the right length to obtain the 2-3 inch cuttings from them. Take out the shoots with a sharp knife, trim off the lower leaves (Inset A), and make a clean cut through the stem just below the lowest leaf joint (Inset B). After dipping their bases in hormone rooting powder the cuttings are inserted firmly about an inch deep into pots. Arranging them round the edge of the pot (Inset C) generally leads to more successful rooting.

The compost used could either be a special cuttings compost or one made by adding small amounts of peat and potting grit to John Innes Seed or No. 1. Peat and grit mixtures by themselves are fine for root development, but because of their lack of nutrient materials, the newly rooted cuttings would need potting on much sooner than they would do otherwise. To prevent moisture loss the pots of cuttings can be enclosed in the usual way in polythene bags until the cuttings can be seen to have rooted, i.e., when they begin to start growing. This should be in four to five weeks if a temperature of 45-50°F is maintained and the pots are kept in a partly shaded spot in the greenhouse to prevent wilting in strong sunlight.

After successful rooting the new plants want plenty of light and air to produce strong, non-spindly stems. This is best achieved by potting them individually into, initially, 3 inch pots and gradually hardening them off out of doors, all the while keeping a look out for leaf miner and aphids which are both fairly common early in the season.

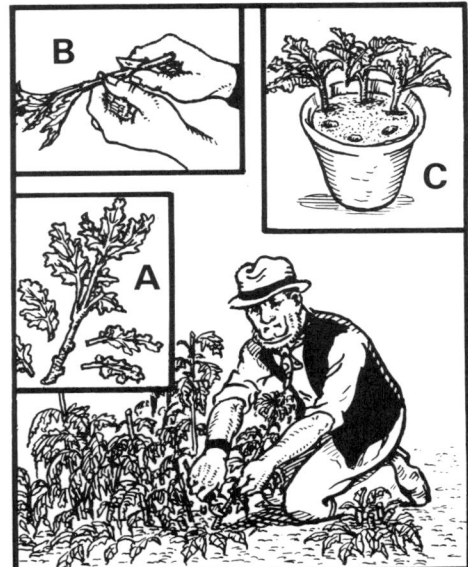

FEBRUARY
JERUSALEM ARTICHOKES

The Jerusalem artichoke is not one of the most logically named plants — it comes originally from Canada rather than Jerusalem and in no way resembles the more commonly known globe artichoke. Its botanical name is Helianthus tuberosus which means it is, in fact, a member of the sunflower family but one that very rarely blooms in this country and is grown solely for its edible tubers.

The flavour of these tubers is not to everyone's liking and indeed their sometimes knobbly shape can make them rather more of a nuisance to prepare for the kitchen than, say, potatoes. But for those who do appreciate the taste or for those who want an effective summer screen for a compost heap or shed (Inset B) or indeed for anyone looking for a really easy, undemanding vegetable to cultivate, the Jerusalem artichoke is ideal.

Their ability to provide a screen is because the plants grow very rapidly to a height of 6-8 ft; and if grown in a not too exposed site they do not need any form of support. I should also add that, having bought one lot of tubers, you will never need to buy any again as a few tubers from one year's crop can be selected for replanting the following year and so on.

These artichokes are remarkably unfussy about the conditions they'll grow in, but they will show their appreciation of a good fertile soil by providing rather more and better quality tubers than they would do if relegated to poor soil in some out-of-the-way corner of the garden. If you know your soil is short of nutrients, give the plants a liquid feed every fortnight from June to August.

Planting may be done in February if the soil conditions permit it, but may have to be left until March or April on heavy, wet land. The tubers are set 4-5 inches deep in drills about 2ft.6ins-3ft. apart, leaving fifteen inches between each tuber (Inset A).

Apart from an occasional hoeing to keep the weeds down, you can sit back and watch the plants grow until late autumn or early winter when the foliage will die down and the long stems may be cut down to near ground level, just leaving sufficient showing to remind you of where each plant is.

The tubers can be left in the ground and dug as required until February when any remaining ones should be lifted before they start into growth again. You'd be well advised to make sure you find and remove every single tuber as any "volunteers" will certainly interfere with any subsequent crop on the same piece of land.

Do not worry about tubers getting damaged by frost when in the soil. They are completely hardy and, in fact, are far more likely to come to harm if dug up and put into storage. Unless great care is taken, stored tubers tend to become dry and soft, whereas the soil provides a naturally moist environment in which the artichokes keep perfectly.

FEBRUARY
AUTUMN FRUITING RASPBERRIES

February may seem an unusual month to be discussing autumn-fruiting raspberries, but it is in fact the time for pruning such varieties and is also suitable for planting them. These autumn fruiters have never been quite as well-known as their summer counterparts but are certainly worth growing. Their fruiting period extends roughly from September to early November, i.e. when most of the garden soft fruits are long past, and their more compact growth means that they will not usually need any form of support.

The fundamental difference between summer and autumn fruiting raspberries is that the former produce all their fruit on canes that grew the previous year while the latter produce theirs on canes of the current year's growth. Hence the difference in pruning times, although the actual pruning is done the same way and is simple in the extreme: i.e. cutting all the old canes down to ground level. In the case of the autumn fruiting varieties this is best done in the second half of February after which the new canes will soon begin to develop.

If you are thinking of planting some of these autumn fruiting raspberries two commonly available, high-quality varieties are Zeva and Heritage. Good croppers though they are, they won't yield quite as heavily as the summer fruiting canes and therefore I think they should only be considered as complementary to these summer fruiters rather than substitutes for them.

The planting details are the same for all types of raspberry. The ground should be well prepared, deeply dug and any well-rotted manure, compost or peat incorporated into the soil will prove very beneficial. Planting is usually done by taking out a trench sufficiently deep to allow the canes to have three inches of soil on top of the roots. Space the canes at eighteen inch intervals, filling in the trench to make each cane secure as you go along (Inset A). Planting may be done up to and including March but the soil must be nicely friable and not too sodden to do the job properly. Heeling the canes in and waiting for the soil to become workable is far preferable to planting them in ground that's wet, sticky, cold and lumpy.

After planting cut back each cane to about twelve inches (Inset B). Allow plenty of room on either side of the row because the new canes will not necessarily spring up in the immediate vicinity of the original one. Encourage growth with a spring dressing of a general fertilizer like Growmore, and mulches or watering if the weather demands it during the course of the summer. The canes of the autumn fruiting raspberries do not usually grow more than four feet high and they should be sufficiently sturdy to stand up through the season without the system of posts and wires that summer raspberries require.

FEBRUARY
ONIONS FROM SEED

Onions can either be grown from seed or from sets. This article deals with seed-grown plants. Onion sets are dealt with in the March section.

It's never worth trying to grow onions on unprepared ground. The best site to select will be one where any compost or manure was incorporated into the soil early in the winter and one that receives maximum sunshine, which will help to ripen the bulbs for winter storage.

If the soil has been ridged in the winter, break down the ridges as soon as this can be done and then rake over the bed to make it level. It's then advisable, and this also applies to beds which haven't been ridged, to firm the soil by treading and follow this with another raking to produce a very fine tilth. The timing of this operation will vary from area to area — the best rule to observe is wait until the soil is dry enough so as not to stick to one's boots.

The seeds are sown in drills ½ inch deep in rows from 12-15 inches apart, and the seedlings are thinned out at two stages: the first being when they're about two inches high, and the seedlings are left spaced an inch apart (Inset A). The second thinning should be done when the plants are just big enough for the thinnings to be used as spring onions and should leave the plants spaced at six inch intervals. Remove any weeds which appear in the rows and hoe lightly between the rows to prevent any weeds growing there.

For seed sown last autumn, the seedlings of the traditional varieties should be transplanted in March, being set out 6-8 inches apart in rows 12-15 inches apart (Inset B). Be careful not to set the plants too deeply in the ground or else the bulbs will grow partially covered by soil which will hamper their proper development. The more recently introduced Japanese varieties are not transplanted, merely thinned out in situ to give a crop that will mature in June and July.

The most common pest of onions is the onion fly, whose eggs are laid on the neck of the young onion and whose maggots then enter the bulb. This can be controlled by dusting along the rows of seedlings when they're at the "loop" stage with calomel dust. This dusting should be repeated each time the onions are thinned out and none of the thinnings should be left lying on the ground. Any affected onions should be removed immediately and burnt.

A final word about fertilisers for onions — a general fertiliser applied before seed sowing will be useful if you have any doubts about the fertility of the soil; otherwise remember the onion has a higher potash and phosphate requirement than a nitrogen one, and that one of the easy ways of feeding is with a liquid feed applied occasionally while the plant is in active growth.

FEBRUARY
GLOXINIAS

For a plant so exotically attractive, the gloxinia is surprisingly easy to cultivate. Grown either from tubers or seed, their velvety foliage and brilliantly colourful trumpet-shaped flowers produced from August until autumn make them well worth a try for any gardener.

If you decide to buy tubers, plunge them into a layer of moist peat (Inset A) where they will form roots and develop shoots fairly quickly provided you maintain a temperature of about 60°F. When the shoots are an inch long transfer the tubers to five inch pots filled with, say, JI No. 2 on top of a good layer of peat. Position the tubers so that their tops are level with the soil surface and water carefully while growth is still slow. Try to maintain a temperature of 60° all the while.

Not quite so easy as growing gloxinias from tubers, but a rewarding challenge for the more adventurous gardener, is growing them from seed. This can be quite a money-saver as all the plants you raise will of course form tubers for you to grow on in subsequent years.

The difficulties of this method are all in the early stages: the seeds are very small (750,000 per ounce) and must be sown thinly on the surface of the seed compost which should have been moistened beforehand. Press the seeds into the compost surface and cover with a sheet of glass. Germination requires a temperature of 70°F and the seeds germinate better when exposed to light.

As with the tubers, aim for a temperature of at least 60° after germination and prick the seedlings out 1½ inches apart as soon as they are big enough to handle, remembering to hold them by the leaves *not* the stem. The seedlings are very small and can seem reluctant to grow at this stage, but it's advisable to get them pricked out early to avoid the risk of damping off. Use trays with a layer of peat at the bottom topped off with JI No. 1 (Inset B). Later transfer the seedlings to 3 inch pots and ultimately to 5 inch ones where you should end up with a specimen as shown in Inset C.

The conditions gloxinias like, whether grown from tubers or seed, are warmth, high humidity and shade from direct sunlight especially in the summer months. Although the amount of water required in the early stages will be small because growth is slow, later on growth becomes very rapid and the water requirement very high, and they continue to need plenty of water through the flowering period. Keep water off the leaves though and if possible stand the pots on trays of gravel or peat which can be kept moist and hence create the humid atmosphere gloxinias appreciate so much.

Like African violets, to which in fact they're related, gloxinias have foliage which can be spoilt by strong sunlight so that shading will be needed if they're to be greenhouse grown. A windowsill other than a south-facing one would be better during the summer for those in the house.

FEBRUARY
FERTILISERS FOR FRUIT

Although many fruit trees and bushes receive a good deal of attention at planting time which will help them through their first years of life, it will be beneficial to introduce an annual feeding programme to enable the plants to go on producing good crops of fruit in subsequent years.

The traditional method of feeding is the annual application of a mulch of rotted manure in the spring. Farmyard manure usually contains a balance of all the requisite nutrients for the garden and when applied as a thickly-spread mulch will help to conserve soil moisture and prevent the growth of weeds. Don't be in too much of a hurry to apply it — wait until March or April when the soil begins to warm up, and then only put it on when the soil is moist and free of weeds.

Those gardeners to whom manure is not available can supply all the nutrient requirements of their plants with one or other of the so-called "artificial" fertilisers — sulphate of potash, sulphate of ammonia or nitro-chalk, and superphosphate. The potash feed, the most important overall in the fruit garden, should be of sulphate of potash applied at from ½-1 oz. per square yard. A nitrogenous fertiliser, nitro-chalk or sulphate of ammonia (which will promote leafy growth at the expense of fruit if excessively applied) is put on at 1 oz. per square yard; while the phosphate requirement, which is not so important for most fruits, can generally be satisfied with superphosphate at 3 oz. per square yard every three years. Remember when applying any fertilisers that the feeding roots may be well away from the base of the cane, tree or bush and that feeding should be over an area at least corresponding to the spread of the plant concerned.

Taking a look at fruits individually, apples very definitely require potash but their nitrogen requirements depend on whether they are being grown in grass (in which case extra nitrogen is useful) or whether they are making poor growth, which also indicates a possible lack of nitrogen. Pears are similar to apples but with a more definite need of nitrogen, and the same is true of plums.

Turning to the bush fruits, gooseberries and red and white currants are very intolerant of a potash deficiency and one remedy for this is the application of generous amounts of woodash (Inset A), provided it has been stored in the dry. Blackcurrants, however, need to be encouraged to make as much new growth as possible for the following year's fruit and thus a nitrogenous fertiliser is more important (Inset B).

For raspberries, potash is, once more, vital, and if you can manage a surface mulch of some sort (even lawn mowings are quite satisfactory), you are sure to be rewarded by the results. Finally, strawberries, which should always be grown on land thoroughly manured *before* planting, will benefit from a light dressing of potash early in the spring.

FEBRUARY
PARSNIPS

Parsnips are one of those vegetables that gardeners are often urged to sow very early in the season. In principle, this is fair enough advice as parsnips do benefit from a long growing season, but it would probably be even better to advise sowing them as soon as the soil can be broken down into a fine tilth. This may be in the first half of March on light soils in a good year but it can equally well entail delaying until April on heavier ground. Even May sowings in the South of England can still produce quite acceptable results.

Parsnips are one of the most obviously deep-rooted of vegetable crops and this is reflected in the depth to which the soil needs to be cultivated. They should not be grown on land that has been freshly manured but the length of the roots does make it essential to dig the ground deeply before sowing. After digging, the soil should be given several weeks to settle before putting the seeds in. The purpose of the digging is to break up any large clods of earth, so that the roots can penetrate the soil easily. On soils which are shallow or stony it is sensible to concentrate on growing short to medium rooted varieties. Long types grown on badly prepared ground will develop into roots with many different growing points that will be totally useless for the kitchen.

Before sowing, give the ground a dressing of general fertiliser such as Growmore: 3 oz. per sq. yd. is about the right amount, and it should be hoed in. When the soil is right for sowing make a shallow drill, in which the seed will just be covered but no deeper, and, sow the seed fairly generously along the row. The seed is big enough to be handled easily and I like to leave one seed per inch in the drill.

Parsnip seed is just about the least reliable of all vegetables and it is not one that can be used after several years in storage. It is best to buy a new packet each year. It is because the seed can be erratic in germination that I have advised rather thicker than normal sowing. The seed is also notoriously slow in coming up. This is partly because it is among the earliest of vegetables to be sown, but in any case do be prepared for a wait of at least six weeks before expecting to see any seedlings from early sowings. Eventually the seedlings are thinned out to six inches apart.

If you wish to produce exhibition-quality roots you can use the method shown in the insets. Make deep holes by wiggling a dibber around in the soil (A), each hole large enough to accommodate a full-sized parsnip. Fill each hole almost to the top with good quality sifted soil or potting compost, sow a group of four or five seeds (B), cover the seeds with another layer of sifted soil (C) and then thin out the seedlings, leaving the strongest only.

FEBRUARY
ROSE PRUNING

If roses are to continue giving fine displays of bloom year after year, they should be subjected to a regular annual feeding, spraying and pruning programme. At this particular time of year our thoughts should be turning towards the pruning that will help to control the shape of the bushes, stimulate new growth for flowering and give you an opportunity to remove any old or diseased wood.

When to prune will vary from year to year and from one part of the country to another, but the ideal moment is immediately before the bushes break into growth. The danger to avoid is that of pruning the bush too early, only for the tender new growth that the pruning stimulates to be damaged by a late frost. In practice, this means that pruning can begin in late February in the milder SW districts of the country, be left until mid-March for most other areas, but should be delayed until the start of April in hilly and exposed areas.

When pruning, make a point of cutting out all weak, spindly shoots and dead or diseased wood first of all. Then look for shoots touching or crossing and remove the offenders, bearing in mind that the ideal shape for the bush is one with a relatively open centre and a series of branches radiating out from it.

The way the shape of the bush is controlled is also affected by where the pruning cut is made — in order to ensure outward growth the cut should always be above an outward pointing bud. The correct method of making the cut is shown in Inset C. Note the slope of the cut away from the bud to prevent moisture settling on the wound and the distance from the cut to the bud: it should be about ¼ inch.

After the preliminaries of removing diseased wood, crossing shoots, etc. have been attended to, the real pruning can begin. The question which has to be answered is how far to cut back. As with most shrubs and trees, roses will respond most vigorously to a really hard pruning, and so the general principle should be light pruning for vigorous growers, ranging to severe pruning for weak bushes or old plants that need rejuvenating.

The post-pruning shape of a vigorous grower is shown in Inset B, while a moderate pruning, such as is suitable for most hybrid tea bushes, is shown in Inset A. Notice that most of the stems for this method have been cut back by about half their length, while the weaker stems have been cut back proportionally more.

Such treatment is ideal for hybrid teas; floribundas need similar attention except that pruning is less severe. By cutting back old wood fairly hard but leaving two-thirds of the stem of growth made last year, it should be

possible to maintain flowering over a long period. With standards the pruning is similar to that of hybrid teas, but slightly less hard in order to avoid stimulating too much growth and making the plant unshapely. This trouble will also be avoided by making sure that all the stems are cut back to the same length.

FEBRUARY
EARLY STRAWBERRIES

One effective use for cloches, polythene tunnels, etc. is to bring forward the ripening time of strawberries. Glass cloches can advance this ripening by three or four weeks but are considerably more expensive than the polythene tunnels which should be able to give you strawberries about ten to fourteen days earlier.

If you have plants of the variety Redgauntlet the securing of an early crop can be especially advantageous because of this variety's ability to flower and fruit again in the autumn. Normally this second crop either fails to ripen at all or at best produces only a few ripe berries, but when the summer crop has been brought forward the autumn crop will be produced that much earlier when conditions are much more likely to favour its ripening.

Around the middle of February is a good time to get the strawberries covered but first of all tidy up the plants by removing any dead foliage and weeds growing in or around them. Strawberries do not require a lot of feeding and what is given is often applied when the beds are being cleaned up after cropping, but if this has not been done some sulphate of potash (1/2-1 oz. per sq. yd.) or a light dressing of general purpose fertiliser can be gently hoed in around the plants.

Owners of glass or rigid PVC cloches will of course have an easy time covering their plants. A much cheaper alternative is the polythene tunnel, even if it does involve more work fixing it into position. Such tunnels can be bought, in which case the larger size giving a 24 inch width and a height of about 15 inches is most suitable for strawberries. They can also be satisfactorily constructed at home, which can be especially useful when only a short row has to be covered.

The principles are the same — namely, having a series of wire hoops over which a long, 4ft. wide polythene sheet is stretched and either tied to wooden stakes at both ends of the row or buried in the soil (Inset A). To keep the polythene really taut it can be tied down over the top where each hoop is placed. This can be done by putting a twist (Inset B) in each leg of the hoop (wind the wire round a circular object) to which the string can be tied.

Keeping the polythene taut and well down to ground level will help keep out draughts and avoid wind damage. Keeping out draughts will of course help raise the temperature inside the tunnel, which is just what is needed in late winter and early spring. When flowering starts and the heat from the sun is much stronger some sort of ventilation is needed to prevent excessive temperature levels and to ensure adequate pollination. Ventilation with cloches is effected merely by spacing them further apart; the polythene tunnels can have the polythene pushed up on either or both sides of the row.

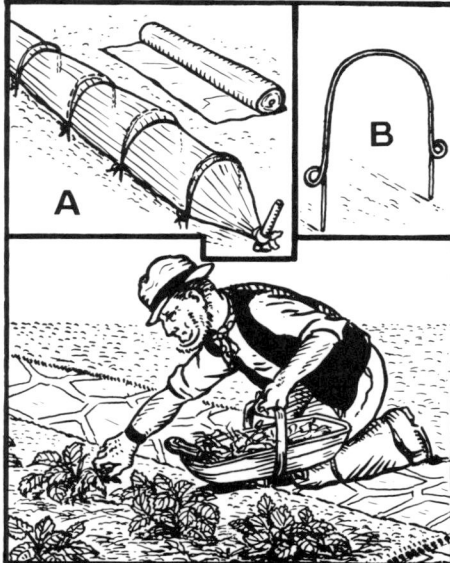

FEBRUARY
SOLANUMS

The solanum genus includes those very popular houseplants that may be seen laden with bright red (but definitely inedible) fruits through the winter months. Both the winter and the very similar Christmas cherries, known botanically as Solanum capsicastrum and Solanum pseudocapsicum, can be propagated quite easily from seed or cuttings.

If the plants are to be retained from year to year give them a short rest after the berries have fallen by cutting down on the watering. Just before starting them into active growth again, cut back the shoots so as to keep the plants in nice bushy shape and encourage plenty of fresh young growth. When the new shoots begin to form the plant can be repotted into John Innes No. 2, or its equivalent.

New side shoots about two inches long are ideal for cuttings and will root quite readily in a cuttings compost or peat/grit mixture if kept in a warm place. Taking cuttings may be found preferable to growing on the old plants, which have a tendency to become over-woody and more sparsely foliated.

If plants are to be raised from seed a temperature of 60-70°F should be maintained for germination but after this stage the seedlings will tolerate slightly lower temperatures (55-60°F). These seedlings are usually first potted into 2½ inch pots, followed by an intermediate stage in 3½ inch ones and 5 inch ones for final development.

To create a shapely plant it will be necessary to pinch out the tips of the growing shoots. This is best done after the plants have been potted for the first time as soon as they reach a height of three of four inches (Inset A). That way the branches should all break from near soil level. Giving the seedlings as much light as possible will also help to make them short-jointed and hence free of the leggy look that can spoil solanums. Subsequent stopping (the pinching back of the shoots) may well be needed but will vary according to the strain being grown and the amount of light it has.

If the foliage of solanums looks yellowish and unhealthy or the leaves actually begin to drop off, the usual cause will be found to be a magnesium deficiency, sometimes coupled with overwatering. The easiest way to remedy this is to add Epsom salts (magnesium sulphate) to the water used for watering the plants. The proportion is very small (¼-½ oz. per gallon of water) and the plants can be given a dose and then retreated every three weeks or so to prevent the deficiency reoccurring.

During the summer months, from early June to late September, the plants may be stood outside and it is during this period that flowering will take place. Provided that the plants are in a not too exposed position insects will assist with pollination and the fruit should set satisfactorily. Giving flowers a daily spraying with a fine mist of water (Inset B) will also help if the insects don't seem to be doing their job properly.

PRIMROSES HAVE ALL THE MAGIC OF SPRINGTIME

What a joy it is to see the first primroses. Even with a few false starts we can be sure that spring has arrived.

For most people the mention of the word primrose brings to mind a particularly lovely hedgerow flower with yellow petals and distinctive green wrinkled leaves.

Yet beautiful as the wild primrose undoubtedly is, it is just one of a very large family of plants which can do wonders for your garden in springtime.

Primroses are extremely versatile plants. They will thrive in sun or shade. They put up with prolonged heavy rain and the indignity of being covered with snow. They are happy under the spread of trees or alongside a path. Primroses too are superb for tubs and window boxes.

Colours

When it comes to producing a display of colour combined with glorious scent, you simply cannot do better than grow primroses. A vast number of these plants can be obtained right now to enhance various parts of the garden.

There are, for instance, the so-called drumstick primroses with 2 in. to 3 in. wide globular heads on 12 in. high stems. These plants, which are best-suited to damp soil and shady positions, flower from March to May. The colours are usually in the range of rose pink to deep carmine or pale lilac to deep purple.

Drumstick primroses are natives of China and the Himalayas. By making use of these exotic primroses, flower breeders have come up with some new and startlingly lovely plants.

For example, I strongly recommend you to look out for some of the new candelabra hybrids, which, as you might expect, have a cluster of flowers on top of the stems. In this case the stems are generally 2 ft. high and the flowers are produced in May and June.

The range of colours is magnificent. There are rich reds, deep blues as well as orange, yellow, pink, salmon and white. Plants such as these can do wonders for a previously dull and uninteresting part of the garden.

Scent

You may not have realised it, but the common cowslip is also a form of primrose. The special attraction of these flowers lies in their delicious scent. There are numerous garden forms of the cowslip from 9 in. to 3 ft. high. They flower in May and June and you can get them in the common pale yellow as well as in various red shades from orange to ruby. Cowslips are happiest in a shady spot where the soil can be kept moist.

Yet it is primroses proper that most people will want to get for their tubs and window boxes.

Many of the ones on sale at garden centres are the splendid Colour Magic variety. They are about 6 in. high and have large 2 in. wide flowers which come in colours such as navy blue, rose pink, dark red and sulphur yellow.

Compost

In my own garden I find that this variety blooms from March to June and again from September to December. If ever a plant deserved to be called magic it is this one.

If you prefer your primroses to be the cluster-headed type called polyanthus, then you will have a larger choice of varieties. The Pacific strain offers colours such as crimson, pale blue, gold, pink, orange, yellow and white. If you want to have a tub or window box full of a single shade, then I recommend Pacific Giants. Blue shades with large, scented flowers in varying shades of blue and violet.

The soil for primroses should be prepared by forking it over and incorporating some well-rotted compost or moist peat. A good handful of moist peat should also be worked in around the roots of each plant when setting it into the soil. If your soil is poor, you may have to add a general fertiliser at the rate of 4 oz. to a square yard before planting.

Whether in tubs, window boxes or simply outdoors in the soil, the primroses should be spaced at least 9 in. apart. For these modern varieties are fairly vigorous.

The compost for window boxes and tubs should be John Innes No. 2, which seems to suit primroses best.

Minis

Most of the primroses which you buy from a nursery will cost you anything from 50p to 70p each. Certainly the plants are perennials and they can be divided in autumn to produce three or four new plants from the original.

Buy why not consider raising a few of your own from seed sown now or over the next month or two?

An advantage too of raising your own plants from seed is that you will be able to get some of the better varieties which may not yet be available at your local nursery.

Ideal for a window box, or tubs on a patio, for example, are the new mini primroses

called Juliet and Juliana. They grow to a mere 3 in. high and are completely "weather proof." There are colours such as apricot, blue, rose, pink and gold which sparkle like gems against the neat, dark green foliage.

You could grow the Jumbo mixture of polyanthus, a brilliant range of fragrant plants in a whole host of colours and magnificent in any spring or autumn bedding scheme. For the same amount you might spend on one plant from a nursery, you could raise 20 beauties such as these from seed.

Moisture

The seed should be sown now in a small seed tray, containing moist peat-based compost. Try to space the tiny seeds as evenly as you can. Since they are so small, there is no need to cover them. But do cover the seed tray with a clear polythene bag to maintain moisture and place the tray out of direct sunlight where the temperature is about 60°F.

Alternatively, if you have a greenhouse or garden frame, you could delay sowing until April or May and raise your plants under glass without the need for any additional heat.

The germination of primrose seeds tends to be slow and erratic. One trick I pass on to help you is to rinse the seeds thoroughly with cold water before sowing. It is also essential that the compost is always kept adequately moist and

that the plants are never exposed to direct sunshine before they are planted out in their final positions.

Once the seedlings can be handled easily, move them, using a matchstick or similar implement to help you, to a seed tray containing peat-based compost, and space them 2 in. to 3 in. apart. At this stage the plants will be quite happy to stand outdoors in a shady spot.

The plants will be ready to be set in their final positions when they look large enough, which could be in June or July. Plants raised from seed sown in March will give you your first flowers in September.

Should you wish to try sowing some of the more exotic primroses, such as the drumstick or the giant cowslip, they are raised in exactly the same way. But you will need patience; the seed takes anything from 24 to 42 days to germinate.

MARCH
BROAD BEANS

While those gardeners who made a November sowing of broad beans should have some growing plants to show for their efforts, another sowing from now to mid-April of maincrop beans should extend the picking season considerably.

Most of the beans available from the seed companies are suitable for sowing at this time of year, the main exception being Aquadulce which should be reserved for autumn use. If there is any confusion about different varieties, it's worth remembering that basically only three categories are involved — the dwarfs (the Sutton and the Midget), the Longpods and the Windsors.

The dwarf varieties only grow 12-15 inches high and are useful where space is very restricted. Both Longpods and Windsors are considerably taller and may have green or white seeds in the pods, although the colour of the seed does not affect the flavour of the bean. Longpods are generally recommended for earliness and weight of crop; Windsors are acknowledged to have the edge in flavour.

Planting distances of beans sown now are the same as for the November sowing: namely a double row arrangement with nine inches between the rows and two feet between the pairs of rows. Sow the beans eight to nine inches apart in drills two inches deep and, as with peas, if you have a mouse problem in the garden, be sure to set traps or try the old remedy of arranging branches of gorse over the area where the seeds have been sown. If the soil has not been enriched with manure or compost in the winter, a dressing of general fertiliser at 2-3 ozs. per sq. yard will benefit the crop.

Weed and hoe around the seedlings when they emerge and prepare to stake all but the dwarf varieties when they are about eighteen inches tall. The easiest method is to position canes down each side of the double row, surrounding this double row with pieces of string, arranged at various heights as the crop grows. Tying the beans in this way will also make it easier to get between the rows of beans to pick the pods when the time comes to harvest the crop.

No-one will need telling that the main trouble to affect broad beans is blackfly, and it is to discourage them that the tips of each shoot are pinched out (Inset A) when the plants are in full flower. Removing the tips in this way also encourages better development of the pods, but it may not entirely eliminate blackfly.

If they do appear, spray with any suitable insecticide (Inset B); or anticipate the problem by using one of the systemic insecticides lightly sprayed every three weeks until a fortnight or so before the crop is ready to start being picked. But read the instructions carefully to check the recommended interval between spraying and picking.

MARCH
SYSTEMIC FUNGICIDES

Systemic fungicides are among the most useful of all the products available for disease protection and control in the garden. What's more, they have the virtue of being pleasant and safe to use (i.e. crops can be picked and eaten on the same day as spraying with many products), and they have a wide range of application (i.e. one mixture of spray will be suitable for treating not only the currant and berry fruits but also apples and pears and in some cases roses and other ornamentals too).

The difference between systemic fungicides and non-systemic ones is that the former are absorbed through the leaves and are transported upwards through the sap-stream of plants that are in active growth, whereas the latter will only kill fungal spores where the spray is deposited on the leaves. From this several points emerge about how to use systemic fungicides to get the greatest benefit.

Firstly, the plants must not be dormant or else there would be no green leaf material to absorb the spray. Secondly, spring and early summer being the times of greatest plant activity are the most effective for movement of the fungicide within the plant. Thirdly, by spraying on a calm day and using as fine a spray as possible, the greatest possible leaf coverage will be achieved.

Fungicides of this type, being absorbed by the leaves, won't be rendered ineffective by subsequent rain, but they will require a series of applications to maintain the necessary plant protection throughout the growing season. Fortnightly intervals are the usual recommendation.

For general use in the fruit garden products based on benomyl and thiophanate-methyl are particularly effective. The types of disease they control include mildew (Inset A) on apples, pears, currants, grapes, gooseberries and strawberries; grey mould (botrytis) (Inset B) on currants, gooseberries, strawberries, raspberries, grapes; leaf spot on currants and gooseberries; cane spot (Inset C) and spur blight on raspberries and blackberries, and apple scab. The same concentration of spray is used for treatment of *all* the diseases just mentioned which makes the mixing and application a straightforward procedure.

These fungicides should be thought of as plant protectors just as much as eradicators of disease. In other words, it's much more sensible to spray a plant that you think might be liable to disease attack before the symptoms appear, rather than wait to treat the disease itself, which might be one such as leaf spot or botrytis not necessarily in evidence at the beginning of the season.

Certain vegetable diseases, black spot and mildew of roses, botrytis and mildew of pot plants and a variety of lawn diseases and bulb rots can all also be treated successfully with systemic fungicides although not necessarily at the same strengths as for the fruit diseases mentioned. Full instructions are issued by the manufacturer.

MARCH
ONION SETS

There are many people in the colder and wetter parts of the country who find it impossible to produce a good crop of onions from seed in a normal season. Onion sets are the answer to their problem, and they'll also do very nicely for anyone else looking for one of the easiest vegetable crops to grow.

The advantages that onion sets have over seed-grown onions are that they are quick to mature and don't often suffer from attacks of either the onion fly or mildew. The sets are, in fact, just immature bulbs, grown the previous season, whose growth is arrested when lifted in the autumn, but which will quickly begin to grow again when planted out in the spring.

The site to select for onion sets is one in full sunlight, but not one that has been freshly manured. A site that has been manured for a previous crop where the soil is still in good heart should be suitable, and can be improved still further by raking in a dressing of a general fertiliser such as Growmore at 3 oz. per square yard. Preparation prior to planting is the same as for seed sowing, i.e., raking the surface until a fine tilth is obtained.

If you obtain your sets before your're ready to plant them, they should be taken out of the packet and spread out in a cool spot where they receive plenty of light (Inset A) — this should prevent early sprouting. The right time to plant is when the soil is just beginning to warm up, which will range from March to early April, depending on local climatic conditions.

The sets are planted in shallow drills at four to six inch intervals, the drills themselves being a foot apart. The drills need to be only of sufficient depth to leave the neck of the bulb showing when the earth has been firmed back around the planted sets.

Having planted them, it is probably worthwhile devising some means of protecting them from the birds which seem to delight in pulling them out of the ground. One method I've found satisfactory is with pieces of wire netting, as shown in Inset B. These only need to be left in position until signs of growth are seen when the sets will be putting down roots. The pieces of wire netting will then make excellent seed guards.

Cultivation of onion sets is the same as for seed-sown onions and demands nothing more than the light hoeing of the bed to prevent the growth of weeds.

Two final points — a ½lb packet will contain about 100 sets, and of the two types most commonly available, Sturon and Stuttgarter Giant, Sturon, although usually slightly more expensive, has a reputation for being less likely to run to seed.

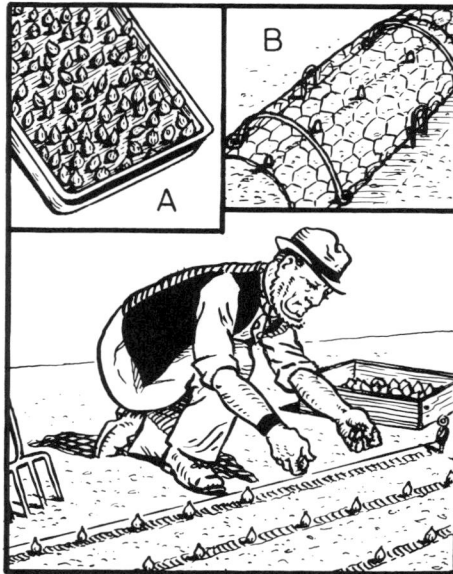

MARCH
DAHLIAS

March is the month to start the propagation of dahlias. There are three choices: seed, for raising new plants; tuber separation or cuttings for increasing one's stock from existing plants.

Dahlias are very easily raised from seed and such plants will of course form tubers to grow on in subsequent years. The seeds are sown during March in a temperature of 55°-65°F and should germinate within a fortnight. To encourage quick, strong growth prick them out singly into small pots rather than seed trays and then pot on to prevent the seedlings becoming potbound. The seedlings should then be nicely developed when planted out after hardening off at the end of May or whenever there's no further risk of frost.

For the small garden two recommended varieties are Rigoletto, with compact growth and double flowers in a good range of colours, and Redskin, whose bronze foliage is attractive in itself and which also has flowers in all sorts of unusual colours for dahlias.

A point to note about raising dahlias from existing tubers is that, unlike potatoes, new shoots only develop from the tops of the tubers near to where they join what remains of the old stem (Inset A). This fact is relevant to both methods of increasing stock from tubers.

The simpler of the two methods is by separation of the tubers which is done in early May when it's safe to plant them out. By this time buds should be visible in the area around the base of the old stem. Make sure that each tuber or group of tubers separated has at least one bud to it. In fact, separation of the tubers is a good method of rejuvenating old plants which otherwise accumulate large numbers of tubers, producing too many competing shoots for the plant's own good.

Dahlia cuttings are produced by standing the old tubers in boxes of moist peat so that the tubers are half-covered, and then waiting for young shoots to grow. This will happen much quicker if the tubers are given some warmth. When the shoots are 2½-3 inches long, cut them off cleanly (Inset B), preferably with a small piece of the old tuber attached, and set them firmly in a cuttings compost either round the edge of a medium-sized pot or individually in very small pots.

Kept humid in a polythene bag (Inset C) and shaded from very strong sunshine, the cuttings should root fairly readily. You can tell that they've rooted by looking for signs of new growth in the growing tip of the cutting. When this happens, pot them on, just like the seedlings, into a nutrient-containing compost such as JI No. 1 and from then on treat them in the same way as the seedlings.

Finally, although the dwarf bedding dahlias and those grown from old plants with several tubers will become bushy naturally, seedlings and cutting-grown plants of the larger varieties will benefit from stopping. When they're planted out and well-established pinch out the top after six pairs of leaves have developed.

MARCH
SWEET PEPPERS

In recent years more and more gardeners seem to have been growing sweet peppers (capsicums), and this upsurge in popularity is not hard to explain: the plants are easily raised from seed, the conditions they like are very similar to those required by tomatoes growing under glass (hence if you can grow one, you can most certainly grow the other), the plants don't grow to any great size and lastly, for the average household, three or four plants should provide an ample supply.

Peppers need a fairly long growing season and it would be advisable to get the seeds in (Inset A) as soon as possible from now onwards. 65°F is the temperature to be aimed at for germination. If the temperature is lower germination will be slower but should eventually take place. I've known seeds take six weeks to germinate, so be patient and don't give up in disgust at apparent failure.

To encourage rapid growth prick the seedlings out into individual 3 inch pots of JI No. 2 and before these become potbound pot them on either straight into 7 or 8 inch pots of JI No. 3 or through an intermediate size pot before the final potting. Growing bags also give good results with peppers.

The JI No. 3 will contain sufficient nutrients to keep the plants growing well for some while but they will eventually need feeding to get the best results. A balanced fertiliser with an equal nitrogen/potash content should be satisfactory, but if there are signs of a lot of leafy growth and a reluctance to flower and set fruit, then use a tomato-type fertiliser with an extra high potash content.

The peppers will grow to some two feet in height (Inset B) and a cane inserted in the pot at the time of the final potting can be used to provide support. As I mentioned earlier, the growing conditions they require are very similar to those of greenhouse tomatoes. This means not putting them out too soon into a cold greenhouse, and, later on, making sure they are watered regularly. During the summer months it's as well to make regular checks for aphids or caterpillars, the two most likely forms of pest attack.

Trying to grow peppers out of doors is at best a chancy business and even in the South of England only likely to be a success in a fine summer. I would not think it worth trying unless you have sufficient space so that you could use ground which would otherwise be unoccupied anyway.

When it comes to picking the peppers, I should perhaps point out that "green" peppers are the fruits as they first appear; they will eventually ripen further to become "red" peppers if left on the plant long enough.

However, picking the fruit at the green stage will ultimately lead to greater yields as the plants will be able to devote their energies to further fruit production rather than merely ripening existing fruit.

MARCH
FLUID SOWING

One method of obtaining quicker germination of seeds in a cold spring is by using a technique known as fluid sowing. This involves germinating the seeds in controlled warmth indoors, transferring them into a semi-fluid medium and squeezing a strip of this medium into the drills outdoors.

The advantages of using this method are that when the seeds are put out they are known to have germinated and there is no delay such as would occur were soil temperatures too low to permit speedy germination of conventionally sown seeds. The disadvantages obviously include the amount of extra work involved, but this is still a useful way of ensuring quick emergence of spring-sown vegetable crops.

Although it is possible to buy fluid sowing kits there is no reason why you should not achieve equally good results using ordinary household materials you probably already possess.

The first requirement is a container such as a plastic sandwich box or margarine container with lid. Line the bottom with several thicknesses of absorbent paper; make the paper thoroughly moist but pour off any excess water. Place the seeds on the moist paper,

spreading them out well so that the seeds are not touching one another. Replace the lid on the container and make sure it fits tightly enough to maintain the high humidity inside. The box must be placed in a temperature of around 70°F and close watch kept on the seeds to see when they germinate.

Inspect the seeds at least once a day — you should find that most vegetable seeds germinate within a week and it is very important that the roots should not be allowed to grow too long (more than $\frac{1}{5}$ inch) before moving on to the next stage of the process. This involves transferring the seedlings into a gel in which they will be sown outdoors.

The gel can be made up of ordinary wallpaper paste provided that it does not contain a fungicide. Mix it up at half the normal strength and divide what you have mixed into two equal parts. Next you must remove the seedlings from their box but without touching them. This is best done by washing them very gently under a tap into a fine-meshed plastic sieve (A). The seedlings are put on to half of the gel, the other half is added and the whole is gently stirred with a wooden spoon until the seedlings are evenly distributed (B). If they sink to the bottom, the gel is not thick enough.

The mixture is now ready for sowing — either fill a wide-nozzled cake icing syringe or use a polythene bag with its top tied and one corner cut off to squeeze the mixture out. The seed drill is prepared in exactly the same way as for a normal sowing but for fluid sowing it is especially important that the soil is moist. Squeeze the mixture out evenly along the row (C) and cover with soil in the normal way.

MARCH
PRUNING BUDDLEIAS AND HYDRANGEAS

As a rule, those shrubs which flower in the latter part of the summer or during autumn do so on wood of the current season's growth and therefore any pruning of shrubs in this group is usually done early in the year. This gives the new shoots the maximum amount of time to develop before the flowers are produced.

The amount of pruning required, if any, will vary according to the growth being made, the shape of the bush, the site, etc. but certain species are often given rather drastic treatment each year in order to produce particular effects. Thus the Buddleia which produces the long spikes of, usually, mauve flowers in late summer and which is known as Buddleia davidii or the butterfly bush is cut back hard each year in order to keep the bush within manageable proportions and to make certain of good-sized flowers on a limited number of strong-growing shoots.

Inset A shows one method that's often adopted for Buddleias — having a basic framework of older wood which is left from year to year and from which the flowering shoots (the new wood) develop each spring and summer. The flowering shoots of the previous year are cut back almost to their points of origin to encourage this new growth.

Similarly severe treatment is given to those species of Cornus (dogwood) which are grown for the beauty of their red stems during the winter months: Cornus alba is probably the commonest grown of these. Because the brightest winter colour comes with new young growths the old stems are cut back every spring to within an inch or two of the ground in order to produce a new flush of growth to provide the following winter's colour.

Hydrangeas, on the other hand, do not require anything like such drastic action to keep them flowering well. Hydrangea macrophylla, which is the commonly grown one with the large globular heads in blues, whites and pinks, usually has the old flower heads left on it through the winter to provide some protection for the plant. Those flower heads obviously have to be removed: when this is done, cut back to strong buds as Inset B shows. These buds, usually arranged in pairs, will be found in varying degrees of plumpness; the plumper ones will be the source of the flower heads for this coming season, so don't cut too many of them out.

You've probably noticed how hydrangeas of this type readily produce new growth from ground level. With older bushes it often pays to carry out a continuous rejuvenation programme by each year cutting out altogether some of the very oldest wood: this will in turn stimulate the production of the new growths to replace it. This job too can be done at the time of the removal of the flower heads.

MARCH
SEQUESTERED IRON

A frequent problem encountered when growing camellias, rhododendrons, azaleas, heathers and other calcifuge (lime-hating) plants occurs when the leaves take on a yellowish aspect, growth is very restricted and the whole plant looks decidedly unhealthy. This condition is known as lime-induced chlorosis and it can occur on neutral soils as well as the chalk and limestone ones where it would be most expected.

It is caused by a lack of available iron in the soil. Iron is normally thought of as being one of the minor or trace elements in plant nutrition but some iron is essential for the making of the chlorophyll which gives all plant leaves their greenness. When insufficient iron is being taken up by the roots, the leaves become chlorotic (yellowish) and are unable to play their proper part in making the plant grow.

I mentioned 'available' iron in the soil, and that brings us to the main difficulty when trying to correct an obvious deficiency in a particular plant. This is that the iron which is actually present in the problem soils is there in an insoluble form which cannot be taken up by the roots of calcifuge plants. What's more, the chemical composition of such soils is such that if iron is added to them in the form of, say, sulphate of iron, this iron too will quickly become unavailable because of its chemical reaction with the lime element in the soil.

Therefore to create the right conditions to combat lime-induced chlorosis the iron that's applied to the soil must be in a particularly stable form which will remain available to the plant even in the most adverse conditions. The iron which does fulfil these conditions is known as sequestered iron and it contains iron in what is known as 'chelated' form that will both remain in the soil and remain available to the roots as required.

Sequestered iron does not reduce the pH value of the soil and it will need to be applied at least once a year every year in the late winter-early spring period to any chlorosis-affected plants. It is rather expensive, but should produce a quick and noticeable effect when used, provided the plant concerned has a healthy enough root system to absorb the iron quickly.

Application is by dissolving the sequestered iron in water and applying this water over the area covered by the plant's branch spread (Inset). Incidentally, rainwater is often preferable to tap water for watering calcifuge plants as tap water, especially if 'hard', can contain harmful amounts of lime. At this time of year there should be sufficient rain to carry the iron down to the roots of the plants but, if there is a dry period after the iron has been watered on, a further watering may be needed to take it to the root area.

MARCH
TOMATOES FROM SEED

Tomatoes, both for greenhouse and outdoor use, are easy plants to raise from seed. Provided proper seed composts are used and the seeds are not sown too early, there is no reason why home-grown plants shouldn't be just as good as any nursery-bought ones.

The time of sowing is important because, although tomatoes are easy enough to germinate, they turn to poor-looking, long-jointed specimens if sown too early and grown in conditions of insufficient light and warmth. The end of the first week in April is a good time to sow outdoor varieties while for greenhouse crops mid to late March is quite early enough.

Because tomatoes are susceptible to many different diseases it pays to use properly sterilised seed and potting composts (i.e., bought ones) rather then home-mixed ones or garden soil. For sowing, take a small pot or seed-tray, fill it near the top with seed compost, water the compost and then sow the seeds on top, covering them with another very thin layer of compost. The seeds are quite big enough to handle easily so that you can space them out individually. Don't sow too many — they germinate very readily so that if you want, say, four plants, sowing half a dozen seeds should be quite adequate.

Cover the pot or tray with a piece of glass and a sheet of newspaper and keep it in a warm position or, alternatively, just put the pot straight into a propagator if you have one. At 70° the seeds should germinate within four or five days. The glass must then be removed and the seedlings kept in moderate warmth (60°F). Growth is quite rapid and the seedlings can be pricked out when the seed leaves have developed.

Put them into 3½ inch pots containing either a peat-based compost or John Innes No. 2. Handle the plants by their seed leaves (A) and *not* by the stems (this principle also applies to any handling of seedlings). It is at this stage that the need for good light becomes critical. The overhead light of a greenhouse is much better than windowsill conditions, but in an unheated greenhouse the temperature overnight can drop dramatically: hence the need for relatively late sowing so that by the time the seedlings are out in their pots on the greenhouse staging they are less at risk from really cold conditions.

If you can maintain a minimum temperature of around 50°F, the seedlings should rapidly develop akin to those shown in Inset B, having both short joints and rich, dark foliage. Any that look at all abnormal should be discarded. Stake any that grow tall enough to warrant it and remove any side shoots that start developing by pinching them out as Inset C shows.

Plants for greenhouse use should be ready for planting in their permanent positions by the start of May; those for outdoors will need to be hardened off gradually until they may be safely planted out at the end of May or beginning of June.

MARCH
SUMMER FLOWERING BULBS

As there are so many familiar spring flowering bulbs it's easy to overlook some of their less well-known summer-flowering counterparts.

Sparaxis (A) is a member of the iris family and is rather appropriately nicknamed the harlequin flower because its blooms appear in shades of red, yellow, orange and white usually with a centre of contrasting colour. These bulbs are suitable for planting in any warm, sunny location such as a rockery or a border. They grow 8 ins tall, and the corms should be planted 2 ins deep and 2-3 ins. apart in April for flowering in June and July. Light soils suit them very well; heavier ones will benefit from having some coarse grit worked in to the immediate planting area.

Acidanthera is another member of the iris family and is a native of Ethiopia. The one you are most likely to come across is called A. bicolor murielae which has white star-shaped flowers with a maroon centre (B). The flowers are scented and are carried on stems that grow about 2ft. tall. The corms are planted 2-3 ins. deep and 4 ins. apart in mid to late May and will come into bloom from August to October. Like sparaxis, give them a warm, sunny, sheltered spot and if possible incorporate peat or leaf mould into the soil they are to be grown in. It is advisable to lift the corms of both sparaxis and acidanthera in the autumn after the foliage has withered and keep them in dry, moderately warm conditions over the winter.

Montbretia (C) must be one of the easiest of all bulbs to grow — indeed it spreads so rapidly that some gardeners look on it as a nuisance but it has attractive flowers, it doesn't need to be dug up for the winter and it flourishes in all sorts of conditions. It is a hybrid developed from species of crocosmia (another fine summer bulb in its own right) and it is possible to buy mixtures containing colours such as yellow and red as well as the familiar orange shades. The corms are planted 2 ins. deep in April, leaving three inches between them. They flower in August and September, will even tolerate semi-shade and will need to be dug up and divided just as new growth begins in the spring every three years.

Eucomis (D), another South African plant, of the lily family, has a basal rosette of broad green leaves. It is the flower spikes that arouse comment and give rise to the name of pineapple-flower. E. pole-evansii can reach 4-5ft. with its flower stems; E. bicolor is smaller at 1½-2ft. but they both have fleshy stems leading up to small starlike flowers clustered on the flower spike which is itself capped by leafy bracts looking like the top of a pineapple. These bulbs will do especially well at the foot of a south-facing wall — they should be planted in April 6 inches deep and 1ft. apart to flower in July and August. In light soils they may be left in the ground in the winter if covered with a mulch of peat, but in heavier ground they should be lifted and stored in dry sand after the first frosts of the autumn.

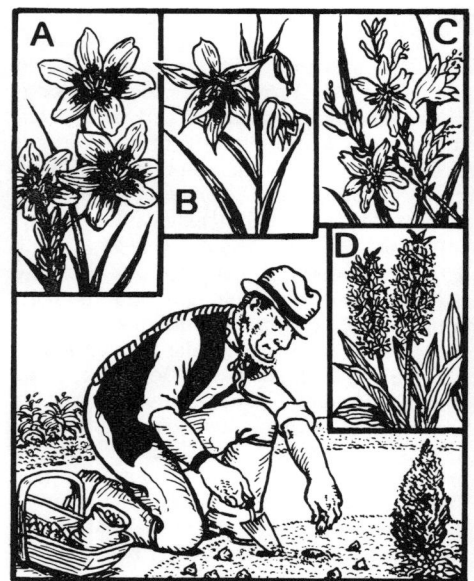

MARCH
ZINNIAS

For a long-lasting, colourful display of flowers through the summer Zinnias are certainly worth considering. Coming in sizes which make them suitable for both edging and border flowers and having a range of colours almost as wide as Dahlias and Chrysanthemums, they can be easily raised at home from seed either by sowing under glass or by outdoor sowing in May.

The secret of producing really successful Zinnias is to be able to grow them on without any checks to their growth. This of course can be done easily enough with outdoor sowings, but by the time the soil is sufficiently warmed up for such sowings to be made, we're usually into May or June and there will inevitably be some delay in these plants flowering when compared with those that have been raised from seed sown under glass.

Even when sowing under glass it's advisable to delay sowing until the latter half of March or the beginning of April so that the plants do not become ready for planting outdoors before the weather is suitable for them. This is likely to be middle to late May in the South of England ranging to early June in the colder parts of the country. In this respect Zinnias are treated much as one would treat Dahlias, which is not surprising as both have their origins in the same part of the world, Mexico.

Zinnias have relatively large seeds, which makes them easy enough to handle. Sow them in a pot or box in seed compost, just covering the seeds with a thin layer of compost, place a piece of glass and a sheet of newspaper over the pot and keep in a temperature of about 60°F. At that temperature the seeds will probably germinate in 7-10 days; at slightly lower temperatures expect them to take a little longer.

When large enough to handle, the seedlings should be pricked out into individual pots, preferably 3 inch ones containing a compost like John Innes No. 2 or its equivalent. This individual treatment may seem extravagant but does give them plenty of scope to develop without checking their growth. Spaced out in seedtrays they seem to resent the interference to their root systems caused by separating the seedlings at the planting out stage.

There are plenty of different types of Zinnia to choose from. Of the dwarf varieties, Thumbelina (Inset A) has double or semi-double flowers in single shades while Persian Carpet has the same types of flower but in very unusual colour combinations. There are many different larger varieties, often named after their resemblance to Dahlias or Chrysanthemums (e.g. Dahlia-flowered) or sometimes just referred to as Giant Double, etc. These and the more expensive F$_1$ hybrids usually have large showy flowers but some of the smaller-flowered varieties like Chippendale Daisy (Inset B) are well worth investigating as bushy plants that are absolutely covered in flowers right through the summer.

CAN YOU GROW PERFECT MELONS?

Some fruits have colourful skins which gleam and attract the eye when they are fully ripe.

But in the case of the melon, you do not even need to see the fruit to know that it is ripe.

For the melon emits a strong fragrance when it is really ready for harvesting.

The melons in the shops have been gathered by necessity while they are still firm. Which is a pity. A melon develops most of its sweetness and flavour in the last few days before it reaches maturity — and perfection.

There is hardly a country in the world where melons of some sort are not grown. Your best bet in Britain is the cantaloupe melon, the small type which is not much bigger than a large grapefruit.

This is the melon which is produced in great numbers along the Rhône and Garonne in France. It is also the melon which has been made very popular in Britain through the import of the excellent Israeli Ogens.

The beauty of the cantaloupe is that it can be grown in a greenhouse, in a garden frame or under cloches with equal success.

And with a hybrid cantaloupe such as Sweetheart, for instance, which closely resembles an Israeli Ogen, you can grow melons under cloches even in Scotland.

Harvest

In this country to ensure absolute ripeness we usually aim to produce just four melons from one plant. With Sweetheart, for example, these melons will be about 5 ins. in diameter. So an individual melon can be served to each person at lunch or dinner.

It takes about 14 to 16 weeks from sowing the seed until you can harvest the first fruits. Sowing can be carried out at any time between the end of April and early May.

The secret I have found with melons is to sow them at a time when you can guarantee a spell of continued warmth (indoors or outdoors) over 60°F. The best fruit is produced when the plants are kept growing steadily.

You have a splendid choice of cantaloupe varieties. For cloches you can grow Sweetheart, Early Sweet, Ogen or Charantais, the French melon.

If you have a garden frame or a greenhouse, in addition to these you could have American varieties such as Minnesota Midget and Resistant Joy. All these melons have orange to salmon pink flesh which is extremely sweet and juicy.

The seed is obtainable from all the major mail-order seedsmen, who also have many retail outlets.

The seeds should be sown in individual 3 in. pots containing a moist peat-based compost. Press a seed edgeways into the compost about ¾ in. deep. Then place the pots in a dark spot where the temperature is about 65°F.

Germination will take a mere four or five days, at which point the pots containing the seedlings must be taken promptly into the light and stood on a sunny window sill in a warm room.

The plants can continue to be grown indoors until they have four or five rough-edged leaves. However, take care if your plants are on a window sill in hot sunshine that they do not run short of water.

While the plants are growing steadily, you can make preparations for them outdoors. The simplest, and best way to grow melons in a greenhouse, or in a frame, is to use a growing bag. One standard sized bag will hold two plants.

In a frame the plants are allowed to trail on the ground, but in a greenhouse they are normally grown up wires attached to the greenhouse wall nearest the sun, although you can grow them on the floor if you wish.

If you have a patio or balcony which faces south and gets a lot of hot sunshine, you could also grow melons in a growing bag, but without the need for cloches.

With cloches the normal practice is to prepare special soil pockets for the plants. I do this by taking out a block of soil the width of and depth of my spade at 2 ft. intervals and replacing the soil with an equal mixture of soil and garden compost.

If your cloches are large enough, you could also use growing bags. Their advantage is that, being above soil level, the compost warms up quickly and encourages the plants to make an extra spurt of growth.

At the beginning of June your plants can go out into the greenhouse or garden frame. But wait until the middle of the month, especially in Scotland, before putting the plants under cloches. Also under cloches it is wise to put down some slug pellets for protection.

Once the plants are 6 ins. high (if they have not already reached this height indoors), nip off the tip of each plant to encourage it to make side shoots. When these side shoots are growing strongly, retain the two most vigorous and pinch off all the others.

In the greenhouse the two main shoots are trained up the wires. Elsewhere they are placed on either side of the plant. These main shoots will in turn produce their own side shoots, which should have their tips removed once they have produced five leaves.

In a greenhouse the two main shoots can be allowed to grow to 5 ft. high, but elsewhere these shoots are normally limited to 2 ft.

While this training routine is going on, the melon plants will produce yellow flowers; small males and larger females with embryo fruits behind the petals.

Bees cannot be relied upon to do the pollinating efficiently to ensure that the fruits develop simultaneously and evenly.

So we have to do the job ourselves by stripping the petals off the male flower and pressing it against the centre of up to four females.

Allow only two fruits to develop on each main shoot. The best plan I find is to wait until a number of fruits are about walnut size. Then I select four of equal development and I remove all others.

Melons should be kept well watered at all times, but avoid soaking either the compost in the growing bag or the soil. Feeding is unnecessary until the fruits start to swell. Then you can give each plant four pints of a diluted liquid general fertiliser every ten days in place of the normal watering.

When the fruits are tennis-ball size, they should be rested on upturned flower pots to prevent them from rotting. In a greenhouse the melons can be supported at this stage in strings of plastic netting attached to the wires.

Once the melon starts to emit its delightful scent, you can stop all watering and increase the ventilation if necessary. For that is the signal that the final ripening process has begun in earnest.

The fruit is ready for harvesting when the neck of the stalk begins to crack. The melon itself will also yield to slight pressure from the thumb at the opposite end from the stalk. Simply cut the stalks with scissors about 2 in. away from the fruits.

Then you will have melons at the absolute peak of perfection, melons which are fragrant and which have meltingly soft, sweet and juicy flesh.

Growing perfect melons, even in Britain, is really quite easy. It is all just a matter of following your nose.

APRIL
POTATOES

It's a great temptation, if there's a warm spell in March, to rush out into the garden and plant one's first early potatoes; indeed, there's nothing wrong with that, but it will probably mean having to protect the haulm from late frost damage. By leaving the planting of first earlies to the first week of April and the maincrop varieties to the middle of the month onwards, the risk of frost damage is reduced, and the means of coping with the problem made that much easier.

Potatoes respond well to being grown in ground that has been well dug and supplied with well-rotted compost or manure in the winter. In fact this organic material reduces the likelihood of scab and generally produces cleaner tubers. Potatoes make a good crop on newly broken ground, but if the site was previously grassed over, watch out for wireworm damage. Don't grow them on soil that has been limed or on ground which was used for growing potatoes last year. Some general fertiliser is advisable — 3 to 4 ozs per sq.yd. raked into the surface before planting should be sufficient.

The best seed tubers to plant are those that have been sprouted beforehand: the sprouts at planting time should be ½ to 1 inch long,

dark green or purplish in colour and reduced to two or three per tuber. Large tubers may be cut in half (Inset A) provided that two or three sprouts remain on each section planted. The cut surfaces should be allowed to heal before planting.

First early varieties should be planted 12 inches apart in rows 24 inches apart; for maincrop potatoes the distances are increased to 15 inches and 28 inches respectively. The best method of planting is to take out drills 4-6 inches deep with a draw hoe and space the tubers out at the required intervals in the drill. Afterwards rake the soil back over them so as to leave a slight mound over the drill (Inset B).

If growths from the planted tubers have appeared and frost is forecast, the most effective means of protection is to draw up earth over the plants with a draw hoe. This, in effect, is just carrying out the first step in the earthing-up programme that will be necessary to encourage the development of tubers and prevent them from going green. Two or three earthings-up to produce ultimately quite large ridges (Inset C) are recommended. Each time it's done remove any weeds and add a further light dressing of fertiliser to the soil. The ground should be hoed afterwards to loosen the trodden down soil.

Apart from giving them an occasional thorough soaking in any spells of prolonged dry weather, the plants will need little attention until July when maincrops may need spraying against blight, especially in Southern England. First earlies will probably be ready when the flowers start to wither in June or July, but if dug only as and when required the tubers may continue to put on weight.

APRIL
AIR LAYERING

Layering as a method of propagation is a very effective technique for many trees and shrubs, but is quite obviously impractical with those that grow upwards on long single stems which cannot be held down to soil level. The answer to this problem is to take the rooting medium up to the point on the plant where new roots are required, fix it there in a moisture-proof container and then wait for new roots to develop.

This technique, known as air layering, is very commonly used on house-plants, such as the rubber plant (Ficus elastica) and the dracaenas, which may lose their lower leaves, resulting in an unsightly, long, bare stem. By getting new roots to grow near the top of the old stem, the plants are effectively rejuvenated, for when potted up, these plants will consist of only fresh young growth.

Air layering is best done in spring to early summer, when new roots will form much more readily. These roots, however, would be disinclined to develop on old, hard wood so that the layering needs to be done fairly high up on the plant, on part of the stem that is green and not too "woody". This could quite easily entail having to remove a few of the existing leaves to give sufficient stem to work on.

Using a sharp knife, make a clean cut upwards into the stem of the plant, preferably starting just below a leaf joint, passing through the joint area and finishing just above it (Inset A). To avoid the risk of slicing through the whole stem, you might find it easier to carry out the first stages of the operation with the stem being tied to a cane to make it rigid. An alternative to making a cut in the stem is to remove a ring of bark about ½ inch wide just below a leaf joint (Inset B).

Whichever method you use apply some hormone rooting powder with the blade of the knife to all of the cut surfaces, and in the case of the cut-into stem, wedge a little damp moss into the cut to keep it slightly open. If you've been using a cane, remove it at this stage. Pack the rooting medium (damp sphagnum moss is ideal) tightly round the area where the roots are to form. Tying it firmly with a piece of string (Inset C) will help to keep it in position.

All that remains is to bind polythene round the moss so as to form a completely moisture-proof exterior. Being made fast at top and bottom with tape or string (Inset D) is the easiest way to do this. By using transparent polythene you will be able to see when the new roots are growing through the moss, and then the new plant can be severed from its parent just below where the roots are growing

and potted up as a nice leafy specimen.

Don't throw the parent plant away — by cutting back the stem to near ground level, one may reasonably hope to see new growth developing, thus giving one another presentable plant.

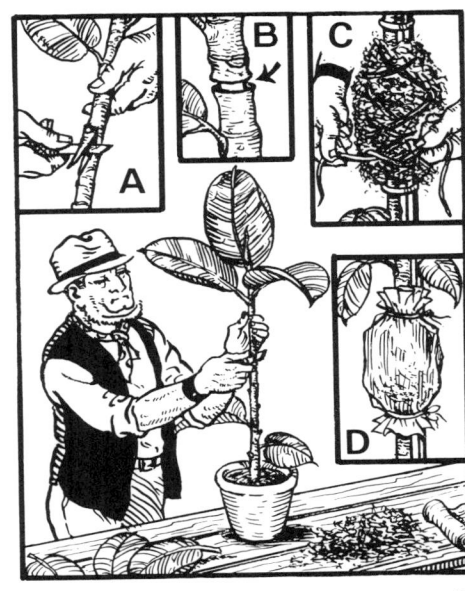

APRIL
CARROTS

Carrots are not among the easiest of vegetables to grow and many gardeners are disappointed with the yields they get. There's no method guaranteed to give a plentiful supply of well-shaped, disease-free carrots, but a few ideas about soil conditions and dealing with the carrot fly might be a help in making the best use of available resources.

The sort of soil in which carrots seem to do best is one that is deep, rich (but not freshly manured), friable (not merely friable at the surface level but deep enough to take the whole root) and not too heavy, i.e. tending towards the sandy side of loam. Two common causes of failure are having soil that has been too recently manured or composted and not properly dug. Freshly manured and lumpy or stony soils can result in "fanging", the development of the forked roots shown in Inset A.

Having said that carrots prefer deep, rich and lightish soils does not mean that those gardening on heavy, clayey land should give up their attempts. Trying to grow the long-rooted varieties might not be successful but concentrating on the shorter, stump-rooted forms of the Amsterdam Forcing, Nantes and Chantenay types should be quite practicable. And even if this has proved unsatisfactory there are always the round-shaped varieties such as Early French Frame and Kundulus (Inset B) which produce roots almost like golf balls in shape, about two inches in diameter and obviously not requiring a very deep soil.

Carrot seed is very fine and however thinly one tries to sow it some thinning out at the later stages of growth always seems necessary. Since the smell of the crushed foliage attracts the carrot fly, which causes the common sort of damage shown in Inset C, as little thinning as possible is desirable. So thin sowing is sensible — shallow sowing is equally necessary and running the rake over the seeds in the drill is quite sufficient to cover them. Poor germination is very often the result of burying the seeds too deeply.

If carrot fly is a problem, various other precautions can be taken. Grow the crop in an exposed site, away from tall plants. Do any necessary thinning in the evening or on dull days, clearing the thinnings away immediately and firming the soil round the remaining plants before giving them a watering. Chemical controls also help: dusting a soil pest killer containing bromophos, diazinon or chlorpyrifos along the drills will give some protection, as also will soil drenches of an insecticide containing trichlorphon. These should be applied in May and June for the first sowings, July and August for the maincrop.

Symptoms of carrot fly attack include a reddening of the foliage. This is also evident in parsnips attacked by carrot fly, so include them in any control measures you take. Successional sowings of carrots can be made until July and these are usually less liable to carrot fly attack than earlier ones.

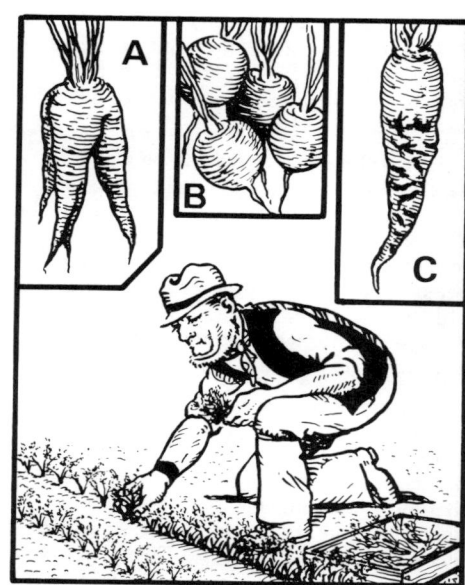

APRIL
PROPAGATING PERENNIALS

Although the traditional method of propagating herbaceous perennials by dividing them in the autumn works well enough with many species, there are some which actively resent having their roots disturbed and yet others which can tolerate the root disturbance but only if it is done when the plants are starting into growth in the spring. These include some of our most popular border flowers such as delphiniums, lupins and red-hot pokers, and March and April are the months to set about propagating them.

Delphiniums and lupins both come into the first category — those which take such a long time to settle down again after they have been lifted and divided that it is better to leave the parent plants in position and take cuttings from them. Both these plants can also be grown from seed but that will mean waiting until the seedlings' second year to see what colours they are, whereas taking cuttings from plants of known colours will ensure perpetuation of that particular colour.

The method of taking cuttings is to wait until the new growths springing up from soil level have grown to a height of three or four inches and then to sever those required for cuttings from as low down as possible on the plant, using a sharp knife. Scrape away a little of the soil from around the shoots concerned if that facilitates the making of the basal cut. If there are any leaves low down on the cuttings, trim these off and then insert the cuttings round the edge of pots (Inset A).

A suitable rooting medium for the cuttings would be a mixture consisting of equal parts of peat and coarse potting grit or you could use one of the specially formulated cuttings composts that are available. Keep them out of direct sunlight but in a close, moist atmosphere such as a propagating frame or even polythene bag provides. When the shoots have begun to grow will be an indication of when roots have formed — a sharp tap on the pot they're in and the cuttings should come out with their rootball as in Inset B. They are then separated and either potted up in individual 3½ inch pots (Inset C) or hardened off and grown on in nursery beds until ready for planting out next spring.

Plants which can be divided at this time of year include red-hot pokers, border chrysanthemums, catmint, the perennial scabious, monardas, gaillardias and coreopsis. Some of these can be tricky to divide because they don't have the mass of fibrous roots that make Michaelmas daisies, for instance, so easy to split up. Wait until each of the plants concerned has just started into growth and then lift it by inserting the fork well under it so as to get as much root out as possible. You should be sure of a reasonable degree of success by following the obvious principle of ensuring that each divided section has both root and leaf growth on it and replanting it as soon as possible after lifting.

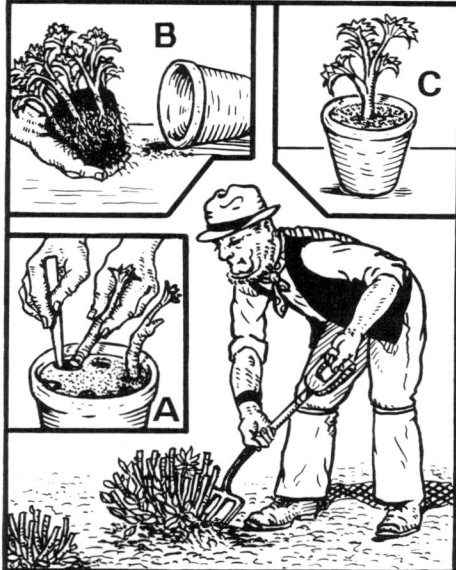

APRIL
SELF-BLANCHING CELERY

Any gardener deterred from growing celery by the work involved in digging trenches and earthing up, should give a thought to the self-blanching varieties. These are grown on the flat and need no earthing-up whatsoever; they are similar in flavour to the trench-grown varieties, but they mature earlier and need to be used before the first sharp frosts of the winter.

They can make life much easier for anyone gardening on really heavy ground where digging trenches is particularly hard work and the soil tends to become waterlogged in the winter. Ordinary varieties may suffer both from the stems rotting and from slugs in such conditions.

Two reliable self-blanching varieties, whose names are self-explanatory as to colour, are Golden Self-Blanching and American Green types. Despite their colour differences, both golden and green varieties require exactly the same treatment.

Seeds should be sown in March or April in pots or trays of seed compost under glass. Celery seeds need light for germination, so sow them on the surface of the compost and do not try to germinate them in a dark place.

Keep them at around 55-60°F and they should germinate within three weeks.

Prick the seedlings out into a good quality potting compost as soon as they are large enough to handle. Grow them on under glass until they are ready for hardening off in May.

In early June, when there is no further likelihood of night frost, the seedlings should be set out on a bed preferably enriched with either compost or manure and given a dressing of Growmore at 3 ozs per sq.yd. The most successful method of planting the self-blanching varieties is to arrange them in a block (Inset A) with the seedlings nine inches apart each way. A closer spacing of six inches apart each way gives a high yield but of much smaller sticks. By planting the seedlings in shallow drills, three to four inches deep, the task of watering them will be made that much easier.

This mention of watering leads to one of the most important points concerning the cultivation of the plants — because the crop is required as early in the season as possible to avoid autumn frost damage, the plants must be kept growing steadily at all stages of their development. They will benefit from liberal amounts of watering and must never be allowed to dry out. Once the seedlings have become established, once-weekly liquid feeds will help to hurry them along until eventually you should have a block of celery plants like those shown in Inset B.

A final word of warning: the moist conditions around the plants frequently attract slugs, so keep an eye open for them and put down slug pellets at the first signs of any damage.

APRIL
SPRING LAWN CARE

Judicious lawn treatment in April can go a long way towards ensuring good-looking, healthy grass throughout the summer.

Just as spring is the season of most active growth in lawns, it's also the time when the most obviously beneficial effects can be seen from an application of fertiliser. Although nitrogen-based fertilisers will produce an immediate growth of lush grass, the first spring fertilising should be done with a compound fertiliser, i.e., one containing both phosphates and potash as well as nitrogen. There are several proprietary brands available which you'll find very satisfactory for the job.

Most people apply their fertiliser by hand, but if you use a fertiliser spreader (Inset A), you'll find it much easier to get an even distribution and consequently an even growth of grass afterwards. The best time to apply fertilisers is always before rain, so that granules will be dissolved and the fertiliser washed into the soil soon after application.

Give a second application of fertiliser, either a compound one again or a nitrogenous one, sometime in June and you'll be surprised how good the results are. But be especially careful to make sure this second application coincides with some wet weather.

From now through May and into June, when both grass and weeds are growing vigorously, is also the best time to apply hormone weedkillers. These kill the weeds by over-stimulating growth in them and, when applied in liquid form, may be used with sprayers or watering cans with spray bars (Inset B), to ensure accurate and even coverage of the turf. It is best to keep a separate can or sprayer for this job. Another useful tool for removing individual weeds such as daisies and dandelions is the daisy grubber (Inset C) which takes out weed plus root without marring the appearance of the lawn.

The other obvious topic concerning lawn care is mowing. Here the best policy is always "little but often" — namely cutting frequently with the blades set fairly high. To leave the grass to get too long and then cutting it right back is a sure way to spoil the turf, because the grass plants are weakened and weeds will quickly begin to grow. In active growth, cutting once a week is essential, twice a week preferable.

Should you put the box on the mower or not? Briefly, returning the cuttings to the lawn is certainly useful in dry weather and at all times lessens the rate at which the soil fertility is reduced. But just as cuttings left on the lawn act as a mulch, the same cuttings, if removed, can be used as a mulch elsewhere or will contribute to compost-making.

Patches of coarse grass can be taken out and the ground reseeded at this time of year, but this problem can also be overcome to some extent by altering the angle at which the lawns is cut, i.e., following a North-South cut with an East-West one.

APRIL
BEETROOT

Mention the word 'beetroot' and most gardeners immediately think of the familiar red beet in its common globe form, but not only are there certain varieties which have tapering cylindrical roots but also other round-shaped ones that are golden and white in colour. There's not much difference in flavour between any of these various sorts but some of the less usual kinds are worth trying to see how they compare and perhaps to add a different colour to the dinner table.

The tapering-rooted varieties are considered to be extra suitable for cutting into slices, but because of the shape of their roots they do need to be grown on well-cultivated deep soils to avoid the risk of the roots becoming forked. Cheltenham Greentop is a recommended beet of this particular type and is shown in Inset A.

To introduce some variation in colour you could try either Burpee's Golden or one with a pure white flesh now called Albina, but which was sold as Snowhite for some years. The foliage of both these varieties serves as a vegetable in its own right — it can be cooked and eaten like spinach.

Of the more conventionally coloured beet in globe shape, a good one for April sowing is called Boltardy: it is very resistant to running to seed. For the main crop and for successional sowings made from May to early July, Globe and Detroit are both good, reliable varieties.

Beetroots are not difficult vegetables to grow — a well-dug but not freshly manured site will give good results especially if a light dressing of general fertiliser (about 2 oz. per sq.yd.) is raked into the soil surface about a fortnight before sowing. Rows should be twelve inches apart with the seed sown thinly along the drills and then just lightly covered with soil.

Beetroot seed is quite large enough to be handled easily and it will save work in the end if seeds are placed individually in the drills at, say, two inch intervals instead of being sown more thickly. This is because each 'seed' is in fact a cluster of seeds from which several seedlings may grow. These will have to be thinned out to leave just one plant every 5-6 inches (Inset B) and a lot of unnecessary thinning will have to be done if seeds are sown thickly. Another possibility is to reduce the need for thinning by growing plants of what are called 'monogerm' varieties. These produce only one seedling from each seed cluster.

As beetroot seed does not germinate well in cold soil, wait for a spell of warm weather for sowing. A soil temperature above 45°F is needed for quick germination. Cloches can be used to warm up the soil if necessary.

Weeding around the plants and hoeing between the rows are really all that will be required in the way of further cultivation as beetroots are usually remarkably free of pest and disease problems.

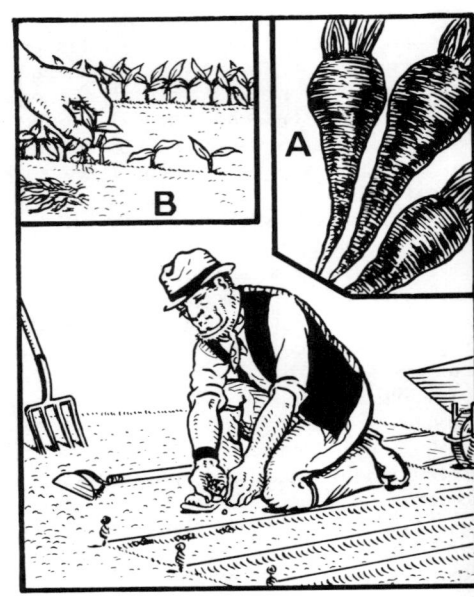

APRIL
WIREWORMS

If you have ever had the misfortune to dig a row of potatoes only to find their surfaces punctured by a number of small holes (Inset A) and their interiors riddled with eaten-away tunnels, then you have almost certainly come across evidence of wireworm activity. Other vegetable crops can also be affected but the consequences are usually more severe with potatoes, where damage can sometimes make the whole crop virtually worthless.

Wireworms are the larvae of certain species of click beetles and are rather frequently confused with various species of millipede and centipede. Inset B should help to make identification of wireworms possible. When the larvae are fully grown, which is after they have spent up to four or five years in the soil, they are golden brown in colour, up to an inch in length and have tough-skinned bodies. Other characteristic features are heads which are darker in colour than the rest of the body and three pairs of legs just behind the head.

Click beetles generally lay their eggs in grassland but where they do encroach on cultivated land it will almost certainly be where there are plenty of weeds to give some protection to the newly laid eggs. This suggests the best methods of cultural, as opposed to chemical, control: i.e. continual cultivation of the vegetable plot so that no sections of it ever become weed infested. The actual disturbance of the soil in such cultivation seems also to have some effect in controlling wireworms.

It's also useful to know that wireworms feed more at certain times of the year than others. March to May and September-October being periods of marked activity. This means that early potatoes should be much less affected than maincrops and that early maincrops or even late main crops dug early will stand much less chance of damage than those left late in the ground.

Potatoes are often grown as a clearing crop, i.e. a crop being grown in land being cultivated for the first time. This has risks in that the ground having previously been grassed down or weed infested is likely to have a higher concentration of wireworms than cultivated ground. There are various precautions one can take to minimise damage.

Either avoid growing potatoes or other root crops for one or two years after the land has been cleared, or apply one of the garden chemicals for the control of soil pests. But for potatoes and root crops in general it must *not* be one of the pesticides containing gamma HCH as this can cause an off-flavour in the crops. Any pesticide bought must contain the name of its active chemical ingredient somewhere on the container so that you can check what that ingredient is. To deal with wireworms both Bromophos and Diazinon are effective if worked into the top couple of inches of the soil at the recommended rate before sowing or planting.

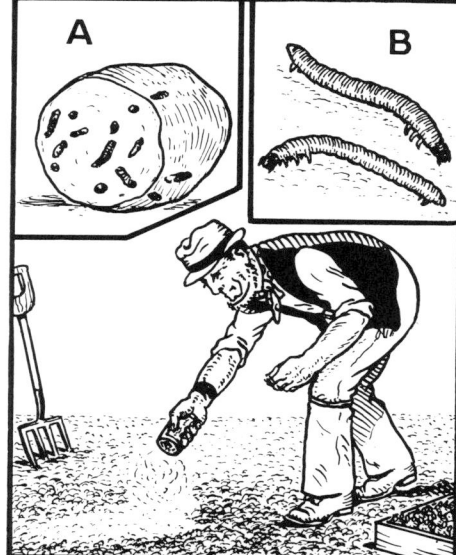

APRIL
SHRUB PRUNING

Two of our commonest early-flowering shrubs, the forsythia and the flowering currant, produce their flowers on the new growths of the previous season. This means that any pruning that is necessary is best carried out immediately after flowering, so that this year's growths (which will, of course, carry next year's flowers), have the maximum opportunity to develop and ripen.

Both forsythia and the flowering currant respond readily to pruning, having a natural tendency to throw up new shoots from ground level. As a result of this, the shrubs can be continually rejuvenated over the years, the old wood gradually being replaced by the new growths that pruning helps to stimulate.

The flowering currant, Ribes sanguineum, is pruned, and indeed cultivated as a whole, in a way very similar to that of its relation the blackcurrant. The best flowers are produced on the well-ripened wood of the previous year's growth. Such new growth is encouraged by removing each year a little of the oldest wood on a mature plant, perhaps as much as a quarter of its total growth.

As soon as the flowers are beginning to fade the old wood should be cut back cleanly to a bud as near to ground level as possible. If car-ried out regularly to mature plants, and they are also given a light dressing of a general fertiliser or a mulch of well-rotted manure, they should continue to flower well for years.

The same principles apply to the forsythia, but with this subject it's even more important to remember that the object of the exercise is to create a naturally shaped bush. There's no point in pruning for its own sake, especially on younger plants which have not reached their full size. Too much pruning leads to an excess of leafy growth and very few flowers.

A mature plant can be kept growing and flowering well by removing one or two of the oldest branches each year, cutting them down to a bud just above ground level immediately flowering has finished. This constantly rejuvenates the bush but should be done carefully to keep a balance between top and side growth — i.e. a well-shaped bush (Inset A) will have foliage extending down to ground level, not merely a collection of long, leggy shoots (Inset B), the result of overpruning.

A certain amount of upper-level pruning can be done each year to promote shapeliness; that is, cutting back just the flowering stems (last year's growths), but on the whole this is likely to upset the balance of the bush if done on a large scale: too many new shoots breaking high up in the bush would soon lead to congestion, a reduction in flowering potential and a top-heavy appearance.

Any very old or neglected forsythia can be cut back right down to ground level. Given some fertiliser and a mulch of manure or compost it will, within two or three years, develop a totally new framework of branches.

APRIL
HANGING BASKETS

If the right conditions are available, i.e. a cold greenhouse, conservatory, etc., it's often a good idea to get hanging baskets planted up fairly early, hardening off the plants gradually to have nicely established, well-filled containers to hang out at the end of May or whenever the risk of frost is past.

When preparing the basket, the objective should be to make it as moisture retentive as possible whilst making sure that no stagnant water can accumulate at the bottom of the container. The container usually used is a wire basket: standing it on top of a bucket will make it easier to fill.

Sphagnum moss makes a good outer lining; an alternative is to use thin turves with the grass side facing inwards. An inner lining of peat will reinforce the water-holding properties of the moss or turf, or you could try using a sheet of polythene (Inset A) placed on the moss with drainage holes punched through it in places.

The compost (Inset B) needed to sustain several plants growing vigorously in a relatively confined space needs to be a fairly rich one. John Innes No. 3 is certainly suitable for the job, although even this will benefit from some supplementary liquid feeding later on in the season when the basket plants are in flower.

When choosing the plants to be grown it is certainly sensible to select some with a trailing habit to grow over and hide the sides of the basket. Particularly suitable for this purpose are petunias, the trailing varieties of lobelia, impatiens, nasturtium (the gleam varieties) and verbenas which can all be grown from seed, plus such perennials as Campanula isophylla, Begonia pendula, the drooping varieties of fuchsia and the ivy-leaved pelargoniums (Inset C).

The plants just mentioned will need hardening off prior to being set in a final outdoor position. When the time arrives for putting them out try to find a place where they can be watered easily and where water dripping from the basket will not be a nuisance, where there are no cold draughts, and where there's neither full sun nor full shade. Too much sun makes the compost very liable to dry out, too much shade is likely to inhibit flowering. Although it might seem obvious, remember that a full basket with moist compost can be surprisingly heavy so that care should be taken in making sure it's securely hung.

Getting the watering right is the key to success with hanging baskets. It could involve two or three waterings a day in any very hot spells in the summer. Keeping any moss or peat moist is essential because they are difficult to saturate again if allowed to dry out. In fact, were that to happen, lowering the basket into a container of water and allowing the moisture to soak in would be the best way of restoring the right moisture level.

APRIL
BULB AFTERCARE

When bulbs have finished flowering it's a great temptation to cut down the foliage as soon as it begins to look untidy, or to dig out the bulbs to make way for summer bedding plants, and generally to think that the bulb has done its job for yet another year and, in consequence, to neglect it.

Below ground, much is going on. The period between the fading of the flowers and the final withering of the foliage is when the bulb is replenishing its food supplies and fattening itself for its long dormant period until it flowers again next spring. Inside the bulb are forming, in embryo, new leaves, flower and stem as the cross-section of a hyacinth bulb in Inset B shows. These will only grow when conditions are right, i.e., next spring when they will provide us with the next year's flowers.

For bulbs to continue to give of their best over many years, as they are quite capable of doing, they need as much care and encouragement after flowering as they do before. There are two things to remember.

Firstly, remove the flower heads as soon as they have faded to prevent the energies of the plant being channelled into seed setting. Secondly and most important of all, leave the foliage to die down naturally over the month or so that it takes to do so, making no attempt to cut it off prematurely or tie it into bundles for neatness, etc. That way the leaves get the maximum opportunity to carry out their proper function, assisting the bulb's development below ground.

If you want to give the bulbs a real stimulus you might try watering their foliage, after flowering, with a liquid fertiliser like Phostrogen. Done with a normal strength solution three or four times at ten-day intervals whilst the leaves are still green, you should get an extra fine display of bulbs next year.

Should you find it absolutely necessary to lift the bulbs before the dying down of the foliage is complete, then help them to continue that process by lifting them carefully with bulb and root intact and heeling them in a trench deep enough to accommodate them at the depth they were originally planted at (Inset A). Firm the soil around them, water if necessary and leave them to die down in their own time after which they can be lifted, dried and stored in a cool dry spot prior to replanting in the autumn.

The same principles apply to bulbs grown in bowls. Don't throw them away when they've finished flowering. Take the whole contents of the bowls, without disturbing the roots in the fibre, and plant them out in the garden as soon as flowering has finished, leaving the foliage to die down naturally.

Alternatively, let the bulbs grow in the bowls after flowering, watering and keeping them in a bright position until the foliage withers. Then after drying, they can be planted outdoors in the autumn, but they should not be forced again for indoor flowering.

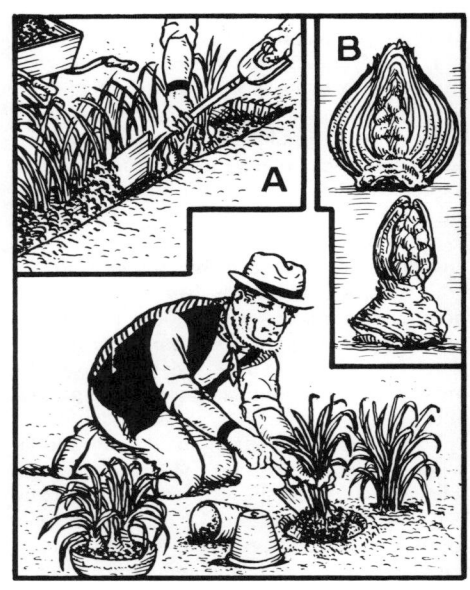

BLUEBERRIES GAVE ME A SURPRISE

It is easy to understand how Columbus must have felt when he sighted the land later to be called America.

Or Isaac Newton — even if, as legend has it, he was hit on the head by a falling apple.

One can sense too the thrill that must have made Archimedes cry "eureka".

It is always satisfying to find the solution to a problem or to make a startling discovery.

I am certainly no Columbus, Newton nor Archimedes. But for me there is a certain magic in the discovery I have made about a fruit bush which is relatively new to my garden.

It is the American highbush blueberry, and the quality of its fruit is quite magnificent.

An American highbush blueberry is a distant relative of the ground-hugging, wild bilberry of our moorlands.

But there the similarity abruptly ends. The highbush blueberry is an American fruit bush which grows 4 ft. to 6 ft. tall and yields a huge crop of sweet, juicy, bluish berries about ¾ in. in diameter in distinct contrast to the tiny, sharp-flavoured berries of the bilberry.

Sheltered

In the United States people eat this fruit for breakfast, lunch and tea. There are blueberry pies, blueberry crumbles, blueberry muffins and blueberry cheesecakes.

Yet it seems a waste to be using this sweet and juicy fruit stewed in puddings and in jam when it is absolutely marvellous eaten fresh with cream.

Blueberry bushes should be planted between November and March. They grow best in a sunny position, sheltered from north and east winds. The soil should be well-drained and free from chalk or lime.

In most gardens the ideal soil conditions can be achieved by forking a generous quantity of moss peat into the top 12 in. The peat also helps to loosen sticky soils, but if the drainage is bad, you should try to find an alternative position.

The solution can be to grow your blueberry bushes in tubs, and there are few fruit bushes which seem so ideally suited to this method of cultivation.

The tubs or pots need be no more than 12 in. wide, although a larger quantity of soil around the roots will naturally entail less frequent watering.

The tubs can be filled with either John Innes No. 3 compost or a peat and sand "ericaceous" compost. The latter, which is normally sold for container-grown azaleas and rhododendrons, is much lighter than the usual composts. This is a great advantage for tubs situated on balconies and also if you wish to be able to move the tubs around.

The highbush blueberry, apart from its demands for special soil conditions, is one of the easiest fruits you can grow. The bushes are also self-fertile and they can be grown in any part of the British Isles.

It is vital to cover the bushes with plastic netting when the fruit is ripening in August and September. Better still, you can grow your blueberries in a fruit cage.

There are around 10 different varieties which produce ripe fruit from mid July to late September. If you live in the North, you should choose a variety which ripens early in the season.

My recommendations for most areas are Bluecrop with long sprays of large, sweet, Cambridge blue berries. Herbert produces very heavy clusters of large Oxford blue berries which have the flavour of a Muscat grape. This one is my particular favourite.

Then there is Berkeley with large, sugary, pale blue berries, and finally Jersey which bears huge crops of delicious fruit and which is the most vigorous and reliable of all four.

All of these bushes will measure 4½ ft. by 4½ ft. in most gardens and they can be planted 3 ft. to 4 ft. apart. Four bushes would give most families a good supply of fruit.

The blossom, which is creamy-white and bell-shaped, has the sweet scent of cowslips, and despite its opening between March and May, it is in my experience totally resistant to frost.

Three-year-old bushes are approximately 12 in. tall. The ones I bought were that size initially and after a couple of years they had grown to 4 ft. If you want to start off with something larger, you can get 2 ft. to 3 ft. high bushes in all the varieties which I have mentioned.

Deeper

Plant the bushes when you receive them 1 in. deeper than they were planted at the nursery. You can scatter some general fertiliser around the bushes in March at the rate of 2 oz. to a square yard. In early April a thick layer of moist peat should be spread around the bushes. Then at the end of April feed each bush with just 1 oz. (two level dessertspoons) of sulphate of ammonia.

Such a programme will ensure good steady growth in even the least favoured areas for fruit growing.

Although feeding is not essential, it is a good idea to surround each bush with the thick moisture-retaining and weed-suppressing layer of moist peat or compost in spring.

If your blueberries are in tubs, feed with a liquid general fertiliser in April, and, whenever possible, use rainwater in preference to water from the tap.

Pruning is not required until at least the third year after planting. Then some pruning may be beneficial if a particular bush has not made the right sort of growth or is not producing as much fruit as you had expected.

Blueberries have two spells of growth. Small side shoots form in spring once the flowers at the tips of the previous season's growth have turned into berries. Strong renewal growth *should* push up from the base of the bush in July. If it does not, the crop will be light in the following years and action is called for.

Unique

In winter cut away one or two older branches as close to the ground as possible to encourage the production of new fruit-bearing stems.

Bluecrop, incidentally, is unlikely to need this treatment as it produces so many renewal branches that they may need to be thinned out.

Of all the fruit bushes which can be grown in the garden, the blueberry is unique in not requiring spraying against pests and diseases.

The foliage in spring is a handsome light to mid green, depending on the variety, and every blueberry, with the exception of Jersey, produces spectacular orange scarlet autumnal tints before the leaves fall.

A highbush blueberry planted now will yield fruit for 50 years or more. So you can look forward to a lifetime of desserts from the same bush.

Our American cousins often boast that things are much bigger and better in the United States. In the case of the highbush blueberry you do not have to be a genius to discover that it is true.

MAY
LETTUCE

Even the smallest vegetable plots can usually be made to accommodate a row of lettuce, and yet it's a crop that all too often is not grown in a very sensible way — it's made to fill in gaps between other rows of vegetables so that the plants suffer in competition for limited resources, or such large sowings are made that too many plants mature at once with a consequent wastage of the crop.

A resolve to set aside a suitable part of the plot and then to sow "little but often" will be amply rewarded in the course of the summer.

If you have some ground available that was manured for a previous crop, then you have an ideal site; otherwise choose an area that was given some manure or compost early in the winter. Freshly manured ground can result in soft growth and lettuces that show a reluctance to form hearts. A humus-rich soil is important because of its moisture-retaining properties — the best lettuces are always those that come quickly to maturity without any check in their growth, such as may be caused by a prolonged spell of dry weather.

A suitable plan to be adopted for lettuces is one that entails sowing a small number of seeds every fortnight from March until the end of July and thinning the seedlings out rather than attempting to transplant them. Lettuces can be transplanted, but the extra effort involved never seems worth it for a plant that, in the summer at least, will most likely not be the equal of one left to grow in situ.

The seeds should, as always, be sown thinly to avoid both waste and the need to spend a long time removing dozens of unwanted seedlings. Water the drills thoroughly beforehand in dry weather to assist quick germination, and give the seeds just a light covering of soil in their ¼-½ inch drills.

When the seedlings have emerged, thin them out to two or three inches apart as soon as they are large enough to handle, and later thin them again to their final distances of nine to twelve inches. If more than one row is grown, allow 1ft between each row.

There's a very large choice of lettuce varieties available in the seed catalogues, but they subdivide into cabbage lettuces (Inset A) (both butterhead and crisp-hearted types), cos lettuces (Inset B) and loose-leaf lettuces (Inset C). It is certainly worth experimenting with different varities to see how they suit your soil. Of the butterheads, try Fortune or Hilde for an early crop, Avondefiance for sowing from June onwards; good crisp types include Webb's Wonderful, Minetto or Windermere. Trustworthy cos varieties are Lobjoit's Green, Paris White and Little Gem, which is especially suited to small gardens due to its compact habit. The loose-leaf lettuces are interesting because the leaves are picked as and when required, rather than cutting the whole plant at once — Salad Bowl is the one you are most likely to find.

MAY
MULCHING

Fruit bushes and trees, dahlias and outdoor tomatoes are just a few of the plants that will benefit from a mulch applied during the spring. Mulching consists of covering the soil surface with a layer of organic material such as strawy manure, straw, peat, leafmould, compost, lawn mowings (but not after weed-killers have been applied) or even non-organic materials such as black polythene, paving stones, fine gravel and chippings.

A mulch has two very important functions — it helps to conserve soil moisture and inhibits the germination of weed seedlings. But, for it to be effective, the soil must be in a fit state before the mulch is applied. Briefly, this means that it should have a good supply of moisture, be free of weeds, should not be too cold and should have a well-cultivated surface with no large clods of earth or compaction. Mulches applied to poorly-prepared ground can be counter-productive. For example, they delay the warming up of cold soil just as much as they conserve soil warmth that's already there. Similarly, they help to retain existing soil moisture but can act as a barrier to some extent against penetration by water from above. Manures will also make weed seedlings

already growing develop with even greater vigour.

The effectiveness of mulches is dependent on the depth to which they're applied. Manures and compost need a layer of 2-3 inches to be really effective and they should cover an area similar to that of the plant's roots.

Newly-planted trees and shrubs that are particularly vulnerable to moisture deficiency should be high up on the list of plants to be protected. In the fruit garden blackcurrants and raspberries, whose current year's growth will be providing next year's fruit, will benefit especially from mulching, as will apples and pears that are making poor growth. Using a manure or compost mulch on them will have the added benefit of feeding the plants, as the nutrients from the manure will gradually be washed into the soil and the decomposition of the organic matter will increase the humus content of that soil.

With strawberries and outdoor bush tomatoes the mulch used is usually one of straw, the straw serving the additional function of keeping the fruits off the ground and preventing their being splashed with mud in wet weather. Black polythene can be used with similar effect.

Rhododendrons and azaleas which appreciate cool moist conditions for their roots will both benefit from a mulch of leafmould or

peat (Inset A). On the rockery the use of pea gravel or stone chippings as a mulch (Inset B) serves not only to keep the soil underneath relatively moist but also to simulate the scree conditions that so many alpine plants like.

MAY
CLIMBING FRENCH BEANS

To most gardeners French beans are short and bushy, yet there are some lesser-known varieties that are climbers.

Comparing them with runner beans would probably reveal that pound for pound they do not produce the same weight of beans overall simply because French beans are so much smaller. What they do offer is the characteristic flavour and high culinary quality of any French bean, plus the ability to set pods considerably more freely than runners are apt to, not to mention their starting to crop earlier in the season.

To get a good pod set on runner beans requires the cooperation of pollinating insects so avoid growing them in an exposed, windy site. French beans, both bush and climbing, have a much greater self-pollinating ability and there are rarely any difficulties in achieving a full complement of pods.

Compared with the dwarf French types, the climbers have one immediate drawback in that they obviously have to be given supports to grow up. In their favour though, the yields should be greater per square yard simply because beans are being produced all the way up the plant and there's none of that bending

down and rummaging among the foliage that's always necessary when picking dwarf French beans.

All French beans are very sensitive to cold, wet conditions when germinating. Early May is a good time to start if the soil is sufficiently warm but a couple of weeks' wait will do no harm on cold, clayey soils if they are still very wet. Alternatively cloches may be used to dry and warm such soils prior to sowing.

Spacing for climbing French beans is very similar to that of runners — growing them in double rows a foot apart with about nine inches between each plant in the row. The seeds may either be sown at these nine inch intervals with some extra seeds sown elsewhere to be used for filling up gaps in the rows, or else they may be sown at, say, 4½ inch intervals and subsequently thinned out.

Because they don't climb quite as readily as runners, it's customary to support these beans with tall (5 ft.) bushy peasticks as shown in Inset A. However, if these are not available, a runner-bean type structure but draped with pea/bean netting will prove quite adequate, as will the familiar 'wigwam'.

Of the different varieties available the purple-podded one always arouses considerable interest (although the pods do turn green when cooked), but first choice for a good all-round performer would be Blue Lake, previously named Earliest of All. It starts

producing early but continues for a long time if kept well picked and bears a very good crop of round, fleshy, stringless beans (Inset B) of very good flavour. Another good cropper is Garrafal Oro, whose broad, flat stringless pods look rather like reduced-length runners, but are superior to them in terms of flavour.

MAY
POLYANTHUS

No gardeners will need to be persuaded about the special merits of the polyanthus as a spring bedding and edging plant, but I wonder how many are aware of how easy it is to increase one's stock by division of the crowns of existing plants or even to raise new plants from seed, instead of having to buy an expensive box of plants from the nurseryman.

You've probably noticed that, when left undisturbed in the garden over a couple of years, a polyanthus plant will develop into a fair-sized clump. Such a clump can often be divided into a dozen or more new plants, which will not only help you to increase your supply but also benefit the plant by reducing the overcrowding and giving each individual offset proper scope for development.

The best time for this job is after the polyanthus has finished flowering. Lift the clumps to be divided, making sure you get as much of the root up as possible and then separate the plantlets by hand as shown in Inset A, gradually working them apart so as to cause the minimum amount of root damage.

These offsets are usually planted out in a reserve bed for the summer months and transferred to their final quarters in the autumn. To get the best results the reserve bed should be in a moist semi-shaded spot with plenty of humus in the soil for the polyanthus thrives with a cool, rich root-run. If such a spot is not available then you can at least compensate by watering whenever necessary and incorporating plenty of peat or leafmould into the top spit of the soil.

Even if you are not dividing the plants, transfer those that have been used for spring bedding to a similar moist, shady spot for the summer months instead of discarding the plants after flowering.

Many people are deterred from growing polyanthus from seed by the fact that germination is often slow and erratic; but apart from that there is little to make them especially difficult to grow this way. It is essential to start off with fresh seed, as seeds of the primula family in general do not retain their viability for long. The seed is on the small side so don't sow it any more than just below the surface of the compost.

At this time of year the seedlings are usually raised in a greenhouse or frame and it is essential to make sure that the compost is kept moist until germination. This is best done by letting the water soak up from underneath rather than by applying it from on top. In any case the compost should be moistened prior to sowing and covered with glass and a sheet of newspaper until germination takes place. After that, prick out the seedlings when large enough to handle (Inset B) and grow them on through the summer months in as cool and moist conditions as you can manage, setting them out in the autumn into their final flowering positions.

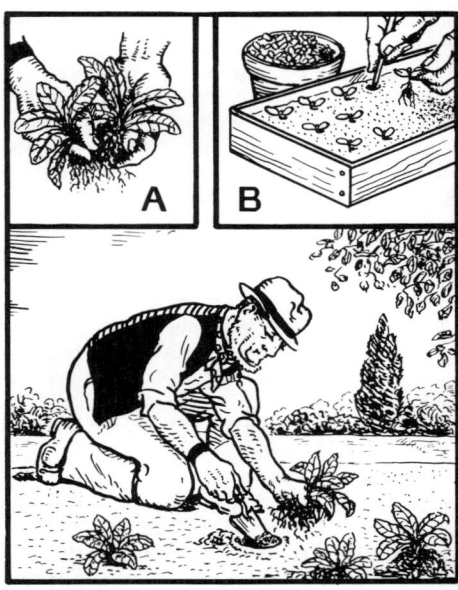

MAY
WINTER CABBAGE

May is the month for sowing cabbages that will provide us with fresh vegetables during the following winter, from November right through until March. Winter cabbages are among the easiest to grow and may well succeed on soils where summer brassicas do not.

The hardiest members of the cabbage family are the savoys with their characteristic wrinkled leaves, but there are several intermediate varieties which have some of the savoy characteristics in appearance and are the source of some of our most popular winter cabbages such as January King, Christmas Drumhead, Celtic and Aquarius(C). This is a fairly recent F_1 Hybrid introduction which promises to be a valuable addition to the winter cabbage range because of its neat habit which allows close planting, thus making it ideal for the smaller garden.

Alternatively, there are the ball-headed varieties which are susceptible to damage in the worst of the winter weather and so are grown to be cut in November or December and stored in a cool shed or garage. If given adequate spacing, at least 2ft. each way, they form very large heads (4-5lbs. each is common); reliable cultivars include Holland Late Winter and Hidena.

The normal method of raising brassica seedlings is recommended — i.e., growing them in a seed bed and transplanting to their final quarters when 4-5 inches tall. It not only saves space but also enables one to give the final planting holes and the roots of the seedlings a sprinkling of calomel dust as a way of controlling both club root and cabbage root fly.

When planting the seedlings out, give the bed a dressing of general fertilizer (2-3 ozs. per sq.yd.) and make 3-4 inches deep drills to accommodate the seedlings (Inset A). These drills will make watering the plants much easier — it's not uncommon for the plants to need water to keep them growing steadily through dry spells in the summer. The seedlings should be watered in well and the plants made very firm in the ground. Spacings, as mentioned, should be about 2ft. apart each way, although it's worth mentioning that closer spacings will give smaller heads which might be an advantage to some gardeners.

It's an unfortunate fact, but no discussion on growing cabbages would be complete without mentioning the various insect pests which are likely to attack them. Cabbage root fly has already been mentioned; cabbage aphids and cabbage whitefly can be tackled with insecticides (Inset B) based on malathion or one of the systemic types; the all too familiar caterpillars of the cabbage moth and various white butterflies can either be removed by hand or sprayed with insecticides containing permethrin or trichlorphon. Any of these pests can do a great deal of damage in a short space of time, so get into the habit of making a regularly weekly inspection to look for the offenders of the tell-tale signs of their presence.

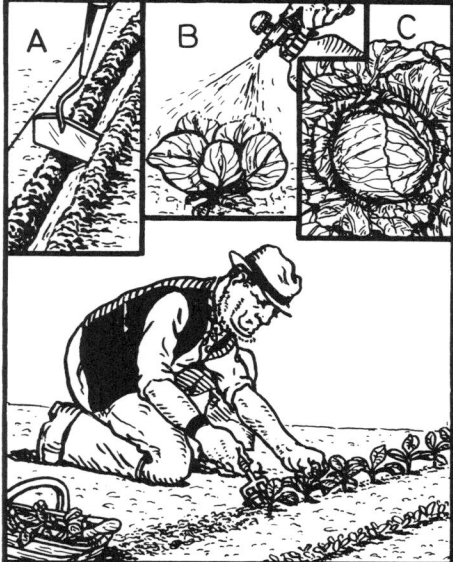

MAY
AZALEAS IN POTS

Some of the most attractive pot plants on sale during the winter are the Indian and Japanese azaleas. These are perennial plants and will go on providing winter flowers for years to come.

Of the two kinds the Indian azalea (Inset) is the most commonly seen. These are the plants that are almost entirely covered in blossom on a good specimen. The Japanese azalea, one of the Kurume hybrids, does not have such large flowers as the Indian but it is not such a tender subject. This means that it is possible to grow it on permanently outdoors when it has finished its career as a pot plant.

Both types of azalea need to spend the summer months in the light and air of an outdoors position and it is a good idea to start hardening them off in May so that they can be put out at the end of the month, when there is no more danger of frost. Hardening them off is best done by keeping them in an unheated conservatory, porch, cold frame or the like.

May is also the time to repot the plants if necessary. By inverting the pot and tapping it so that the plant comes out with its rootball intact you can see whether the roots are occupying the whole of the pot. If they are, transfer the plant to a pot one size larger.

Azaleas require a lime-free compost — such composts are known as ericaceous if you find yourself having to buy one. Similarly, watering azaleas is best done with rainwater, especially in areas where the tap water originates from chalky sources.

When standing the plants out for the summer try to find a semi-shaded position for them so that they are not baked by the sun. As their roots have only the compost in the pot to draw water from they will need frequent watering. The best way to ensure the compost is thoroughly moistened is to immerse the whole pot in a bucket of rainwater. Any surplus moisture will soon drain away when the pot is taken out of the bucket.

Alternatively, you can plunge the pots in the garden soil right up to their rims, again in a semi-shaded position. If the soil contains lime, use some lime-free material, such as sand, for the plunging. Plunged plants, too, need regular watering.

It is also a good idea to give the plants liquid feeds during the spring and summer while they are building up their flower buds for next winter. This should be done every fortnight during May and June, every 3-4 weeks in July and August. If the growth shows signs of becoming straggly pinch out the tips of the shoots to retain the compact, bushy shape.

Bring the plants back into the house in September/October before the first frosts and keep them in a cool room. Do not try to force them because the blooms will last much longer in cool, moist conditions than in the hot, dry atmosphere of a centrally-heated room.

MAY
GOOSEBERRY PESTS AND DISEASES

Many gardeners may produce good crops of gooseberries year after year without encountering any troubles but American gooseberry mildew, leaf spot, etc. can cause severe problems if and when they occur.

However, in May one of the most common gooseberry troubles is caused by a pest rather than a disease. The gooseberry sawfly caterpillar (A) can, in large numbers, defoliate a bush completely. The caterpillars emerge from eggs and move through the bush eating the leaves as they go. They are greenish but are quite easy to spot and can be removed by hand if not present in very large numbers. You may well notice leaves on which eggs have been laid — remove these as well and you will save yourself a lot of work in the future.

The caterpillars do not affect the berries but, obviously, the bush will be considerably weakened if it loses a lot of its foliage early in the season. To control the caterpillars by chemical means choose a product which allows the crop to be picked and eaten soon after spraying has taken place. Those containing permethrin come into this category.

The other common gooseberry pest is the aphid. They are most likely to be seen infesting the leaves at the tips of the shoots. Malathion, or one of the systemic insecticides containing dimethoate, should soon help to reduce their numbers.

American gooseberry mildew produces easily recognisable symptoms on affected bushes — leaves, especially young ones, shoots and fruit become coated with a white, powdery growth (B) which later turns to brown. Keeping the bushes open by pruning helps control the disease as does the cutting out and destroying of any affected shoots at the end of the growing season.

Leaf spot (C) is first noted in May as a series of dark spots on the gooseberry foliage. Gradually these spots become more numerous until eventually the whole leaf goes brown and falls off prematurely. The fruits are not affected but the bush is inevitably weakened by the premature defoliation. The disease remains dormant on affected fallen leaves so it pays to collect up as many of these as possible and burn them.

The best way to eradicate both mildew and leaf spot is through fungicide treatment. This is always more effective when the spraying is started at the beginning of the season before the first symptoms of the disease appear.

With gooseberries the first spray should be at the time of the flowers opening followed by further sprayings at 10-14 day intervals, in accordance with the manufacturer's instructions. Nimrod-T is an effective product against both diseases but it cannot be used during the picking season. Alternatives with much shorter intervals between spraying and picking are products based on benomyl and thiophanate-methyl.

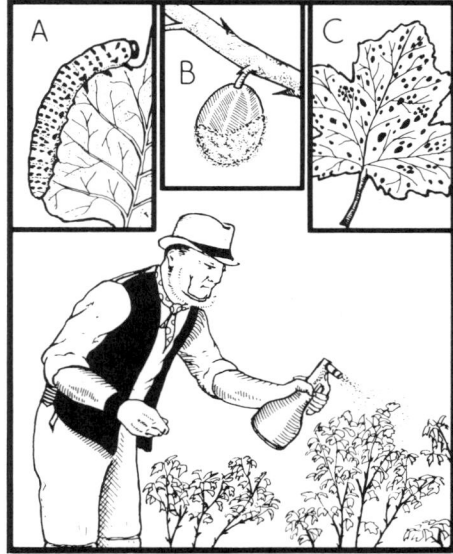

MAY
BULB PROPAGATION

One of the virtues of many species of bulb is that they multiply freely over the years forming larger and larger clumps of flowers. There comes a time, however, when the bulbs become congested and the quality of the blooms starts to deteriorate — this is the moment to lift the bulbs, replanting the largest of them and use the remainder to increase one's stock elsewhere. There's no specific interval at which this job needs to be done; it will vary according to the type of bulb, the type of soil, etc., but it often needs doing after four years of undisturbed growth.

The best time for this operation is immediately after the foliage of the plants has died down. This will be later than the end of the flowering period but it is important not to disturb the plants while the foliage is still green for it is in this period that the bulbs that will provide next year's flowers are developing underground.

Bulbs such as daffodils are 'perennials' in the sense that one parent bulb will grow on from year to year all the time producing offsets. If you lift a clump to divide it you may well see a group of bulbs like that shown in Inset A: a large bulb surrounded by offsets of various sizes. The groups of bulbs are easily split up and the larger, round-shaped ones will certainly flower next year, while the smaller may need another season to grow into flowering-sized bulbs (Inset B). Whatever size they are they can be replanted immediately, setting the bulbs 3-4 inches deep, 6 inches apart and incorporating some peat or leaf-mould to encourage vigorous root systems.

Tulips, and bulbous irises, grow in a slightly different way to daffodils in that the old bulb disintegrates after flowering to be replaced by a cluster of new bulbs. The treatment though when it is desired to propagate such bulbs is similar to daffodils — wait until the foliage has died right down, lift the bulb, separate the offsets, replant these in a nursery bed (where they may require two or three seasons to reach flowering size) and then replant the main bulb. In wetter and cooler parts of the country where tulips are often lifted and stored dry during the summer months, the replanting can be left until the autumn.

Hyacinths unfortunately are much more reluctant to produce offsets and are therefore more difficult to propagate. The following method may interest more ambitious gardeners who are prepared to wait the three years until flowers are produced. The bulbs, which must be large, mature ones, are lifted after the foliage has died down and three deep cross-cuts are made across the base of the bulb (Inset C). These cuts should penetrate into the interior of the bulbs which should be left in a warm dry spot to callus over with the cut side down. The bulbs are replanted 4 ins. deep and next spring should produce a series of bulblets which are in turn separated from the mother bulb and grown on in nursery beds.

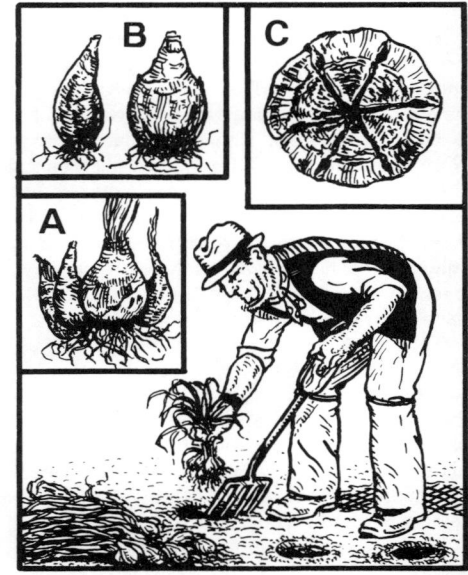

MAY
APHIDS

One of the most common but least welcome visitors to our gardens in the spring and summer is the aphis, an insect capable of breeding at an incredibly rapid rate: hence the infestations which seem to appear almost overnight on broad beans, roses, etc.

Aphids feed by sucking the sap from plants, and as they can begin to reproduce themselves soon after birth, a single plant can suddenly find itself host to a huge number of these insects. Many different plants are liable to be attacked by aphids and, similarly, there are many different types of aphid to attack them. They include the blackfly, which is an ever-constant threat to broad beans (Inset B), but which can also attack a wide range of plants from French and runner beans to dahlias, nasturtiums, etc; the greenfly whose main victims include roses, apples, plums, etc., and various other aphids which are more selective in their attacks, but which may occur on cabbages, lettuces and raspberries among many others.

Aphids multiply so rapidly that the good gardener wants to be able to spot them and take action before they have caused any lasting damage. Besides weakening plants by feeding on the sap, aphids are also notorious as carriers of virus diseases from plant to plant.

A policy of looking for the tell-tale signs of aphis infestation some two or three times a week is certainly worthwhile. On broad beans aphids always go first for the tender young leaves and shoots; on other plants the aphids themselves may not be so easy to spot, but the evidence of their presence is. The aphids usually congregate on the underside of the leaves, the leaves consequently curling (Inset A) to conceal them. This may happen on cabbages, currants, gooseberries, boxes of seedlings — in fact a huge range of plants.

Having spotted the infestation, what action can be taken? Fortunately aphids can be killed fairly easily. Natural predators may come to our assistance — ladybirds, hover-flies and lacewing flies all help to keep aphids in check. If they're not around to help, many very effective insecticides are. These can be divided into *contact* insecticides and *systemic* ones.

Among the contact insecticides are derris, pyrethrum, malathion and pirimicarb. Far more effective and long-lasting in their effect are the systemic insecticides which enter the sap stream of the plant after absorption through its leaves and then poison the aphids which suck the sap. Systemic insecticides have a more persistent effect and careful note should be taken of the interval to be left between spraying the plant and eating food crops from it.

Spraying is best done in the evening when any wind has died down and when no rain is forecast. The appropriate action with contact insecticides is obvious; with systemics the whole plant must be sprayed, not just the area where aphids are present. Try to keep the spray as fine as possible or it will merely run off the leaves.

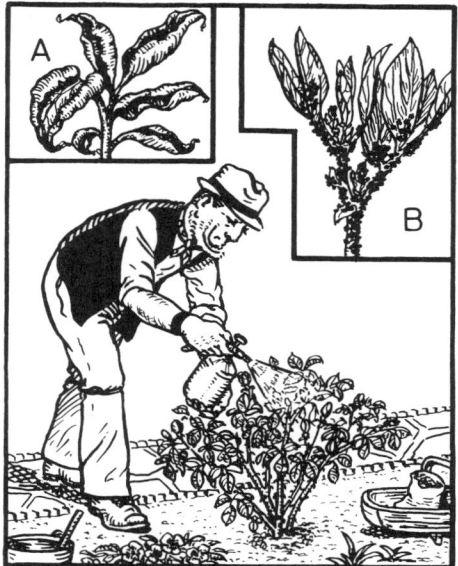

MAY
BUTTERFLIES IN THE GARDEN

One of the incidental pleasures of gardening is the sight of butterflies that the buddleias and stonecrops, for example, can attract. Although there are no longer butterflies about in such numbers as there used to be, it is still possible to entice a fair selection of visitors with a few well-chosen plants.

Spring is not the best time of year for seeing butterflies but the favourites of the early-flying peacocks, brimstones and small tortoiseshells seem to be the aubrietas; yellow alyssum they also find quite attractive.

Moving on to early summer and there's a group of the cottage-garden flowers which are not grown so much these days but which are much more popular with butterflies than most of our half-hardy bedding plants. Sweet rocket, honesty and valerian come into this category. Valerian (Inset A) with its pinky-red blooms is the flower so often seen growing on walls in the West Country and like the sweetly-scented sweet rocket and the familiar honesty is very easily grown.

The buddleia (B.davidii) is often known very aptly as the butterfly bush and is a shrub that is tolerant of a wide range of conditions. What is not always realised about this buddleia is that it can be raised from seed (flowering within 7-8 months of sowing) and that it can be found in several different shades, thus avoiding any sort of monotony. The colours range from deep reddish purple to shades of bluish purple and also white.

The buddleias are soon joined in flower by the stonecrops or sedums, to give them their Latin name. The one which is virtually guaranteed to attract butterflies is called Sedum spectabile and it is a hardy perennial whose flowers are in various shades of pink and red (Inset B). While the sedums are still in flower they in turn will be joined by the michaelmas daisies and the two of them should make any small tortoiseshells, red admirals and small coppers in the neighbourhood visit your garden.

The plants mentioned so far all attract mature butterflies to the garden. However there are one or two ways that gardens can encourage their breeding by providing patches of the plant that their caterpillars feed on. These are naturally mostly wild plants (although any brassica grower will confirm that there are exceptions!), thistles, docks and nettles being three good examples.

If, for instance, you have a small corner of the garden which you don't use and which is filled with nettles, you would be doing the caterpillars of the small tortoiseshell, red admirals, peacock and comma a great service by leaving them, for they all feed on this one plant. Indeed, by cutting back sections of the nettle bed at various times during the summer to encourage fresh young growth you will be doing the butterflies an even greater service because naturally enough the caterpillars prefer the soft new leaves.

MAY
LAWN HORMONE WEEDKILLERS

In spring, both lawns and the weeds in them are growing vigorously. This is a positive advantage with the modern types of "hormone" weedkiller used to eliminate lawn weeds. The chemicals they contain are rapidly absorbed by the roots and shoots of the weed population causing the characteristic accelerated but contorted growth followed by the death of the weed.

This method of killing weeds is ideal for ridding lawns of them, because the chemicals concerned do not affect grasses and their killing is done from inside the weed, with only a few drops of the weedkiller spray being needed to obtain the desired effect.

But this same effectiveness requires that they be applied very carefully, for if any spray were to drift on to flower beds quite a few of the flowers would go the same way as the weeds. Even more important though is getting the timing of the application right for, as mentioned above, the weedkillers work by stimulating abnormal growth and therefore must be applied when the weeds are growing strongly in the first place.

May and early June are often suitable times for this as they usually combine the right conditions of adequate soil moisture and sufficiently warm weather that quick growth requires. Even so, they can also produce cold spells or dry conditions when these hormone weedkillers should most certainly not be applied.

It is advisable that separate equipment (watering cans with sprinkle bars, sprayers, etc.) should be used for weedkillers and that the weedkillers themselves be sealed tightly and stored away from growing plants (certainly not in the greenhouse) after use.

The earliest hormone weedkillers, which were discovered in the 1940s, were called 2,4-D and MCPA. These are now usually sold in products that combine them with a later series of chemicals which include dicamba and some whose names end in "-prop", mecoprop, fenoprop and dichlorprop. It is these products which combine 2,4-D or MCPA with dicamba or one of the "-prop" series which provide the greatest range of weed-killing ability. All weedkillers will have their chemical constituents marked on the bottle or packet and it will not be difficult to find a product having such a combination of ingredients.

Some weeds, being more resistant than others, may need one or more further applications to be brought under control. Yarrow (Inset A) and field woodrush (Inset B) come into this category, while speedwell (Inset C) will need treatment with a weedkiller containing another chemical called ioxynil. Secondary applications should be after a 5-6 week interval. Grass clippings from treated lawns should be put on the compost heap and left at least six months, *not* used for mulching purposes.

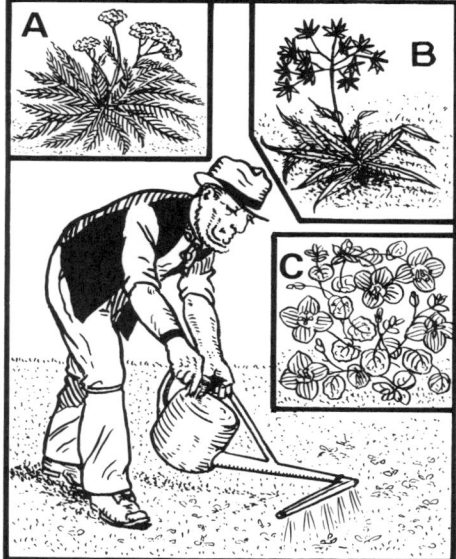

WHAT A DIFFERENCE A POOL MAKES

As summer comes and the weather is hot, how soothing the sight and sound of water in the garden.

There are the sweetly scented exotic blooms of salmon pink, bright red, sulphur yellow and brilliant coppery orange water lilies to delight the eye and the sense of smell.

There is the gentle rustle and ripple of moving water and the occasional glimpse of a colourful fish to complete the scene of sight and sound that together add up to the sheer magic of a garden pool.

A pool such as this can transform even the smallest of areas and give it something of interest all summer long. And if you were to busy yourself for a couple of weekends now you could have a pool to enjoy this very summer.

The main question is of course the cost.

Once the only way to make a pool was to use concrete. Then there were the "instant" pools made from moulded plastic or glass fibre.

Both of these kinds of pools have considerable disadvantages in the cost and the effort required in their installation.

By far the simplest and cheapest method of making a pool is the modern system of digging a hole of any shape you want and simply lining the hole with a pliable material to keep it watertight. These waterproofing "liners", as they are called, are made in a variety of materials. However, for long life (as much as 50 years) and best value, butyl, which is available in black or stone colour, is the best bet.

Plants

A pool, measuring let us say 10 ft. by 5 ft. made with a butyl liner will cost you about £50. To this you have to add the cost of plants and some essential extras.

A pool of this size will have room for two lilies as well as 10 other water plants. You will also need some oxygenating plants to help keep the water fresh and water snails to assist in disposing of any debris. The cost will be about £20-£25. The plants will need special plastic baskets and pots for which you should allow about £10.

You may also wish to have a fountain in your pool. This will cost about £50 for the simplest type but you can, of course, pay considerably more if you want a variety of spray patterns up to a height of 8 ft.

The pump for a fountain comes as part of a kit with all the vital electrical equipment to enable it to be run safely off the mains supply.

And what about fish? A pool of this size will have room for 20 fish such as goldfish, shubunkins, Japanese carp and golden orfe. The price of these will depend very much on your choice of fish.

A pool can be surrounded by grass, but more often it has a paved edge. You will have to allow at least £10 for any paving when you add up your outlay.

Yet for the £100 to £150 it costs to provide a pool in the garden you will have the pleasure of years of delight and fascination at the absolute beauty of aquatic plants and fish, as well as being soothed by the sound of water as you laze in a chair on the hottest of days, sipping a cool drink …

So let's get digging.

A pool has to be situated where it will get sunlight for at least half a day if water lilies are to flower fully.

Your pool can be any size and shape you wish. That is the beauty of using a plastic "liner", which incidentally can easily be repaired in the unlikely event of its becoming punctured.

Algae

Digging out the hole is hard work, but it is unnecessary to make the pool more than 18 in. deep, except perhaps in the few really cold parts of Britain.

When you fill your pool with water from the mains, it will not be necessary to change it again, or to add water, except to make up losses through evaporation.

Once the plants are put in their special containers with ordinary garden soil and lowered into the pool, the water may turn green.

However if you leave matters alone, the algae will vanish just as quickly as they appeared. Do not be tempted to change the water in the pool, an action which will simply make things worse.

With the smallest pools, if the presence of algae is a persistent problem, you can instal a gravel or charcoal filter or use chemicals to clarify the water.

Your plants should be ordered so that they will arrive a few days after you have put in the water, and remember that you can add plants right up to early September.

Ideally the pool should be gradually filled with fish, unless of course you live too far from a fish farm to collect your stock.

Balance

In the case of all the fish being put in at once, some of the water should be replaced every few days for the first three weeks to help keep it clean until a natural balance between plants and fish has been set up in the pool.

A 125-watt pool heater can be installed in the coldest districts to keep a small area free from ice in winter and so enable toxic gases to escape and fresh oxygen to enter the water. The fish should be fed with special pelleted fish food from late spring until mid autumn.

There are excellent water garden centres in both southern and northern England, readily accessible by car.

If you live in a part of the British Isles which is not so fortunate, you can safely have your fish sent by express train to your nearest railway station.

Plants and pool equipment are delivered by the most convenient method available.

Certainly there is absolutely no one anywhere in Britain who should be deprived of the joy of seeing the first water lily open in summer, or the fun of watching a fish mouthing at the surface of the water as it comes up seeking food.

Is your garden at present lacking a certain sparkle? Then just add water. You will be amazed at the difference it will make.

JUNE
HARDY PRIMULAS

Every gardener knows the primrose and polyanthus, most know the primulas grown as greenhouse and pot plants, but far fewer seem to know or grow the many other beautiful species that are hardy outdoors.

These are usually divided into the types that are native of rock and cliff faces and those that grow naturally in wet ground and woodland. The latter can usually be grown from seed and will thrive in moist, cool conditions that many other garden plants dislike.

Primula seed germinates very freely indeed if it is sown as soon as it is ripe, so if you can collect your own seed make sure you sow it straight away. The seed that has been left for longer should still germinate, but it might be slow and erratic in doing so. Therefore be patient and prepared to wait for a month or two if you are raising primulas this way.

The bog-loving primulas make ideal plants for the side of a pond or stream where they will often spread themselves by self-seeding. Many of them will grow well in the leafmould enriched soil of open woodland provided there is plenty of moisture available. But even if your garden has neither of these features it should still be possible to create an area in which primulas will thrive, provided that the soil is not too light and sandy.

The main task is to make sure the ground will be very retentive of moisture and this is done by digging in as much humus-forming material as you can — peat, leafmould, well-rotted compost or manure, etc. At the same time you must select a site where there is some shade from the strongest sunshine: morning or afternoon rather than midday sun will be preferable, or the dappled sunshine provided by thin tree cover.

Among the many primulas suitable for either naturally damp or moisture retentive soils, some that are quite easy to find and grow include the drumstick primula (P. denticulata, A) which has pale purple or white globe-shaped flower heads about 12 inches high in spring. The Himalayan cowslip (P. florindae, B) grows on a much larger scale than our own, and in a rich soil by a pool or in a bog garden the flower stalks, capped by yellow, fragrant blooms, can reach 3ft. tall while the broad leaves will rise to about 18 inches.

Primulas japonica and pulverulenta both have flowers set in tiers growing on strong stems about 2ft. high. They both have large leaves and a thriving group by the waterside will soon smother any weeds. Primula vialii (Inset C) only grows to 1ft. high but it has a fascinating flower that is cone-shaped and consists of scarlet buds that open from the bottom upwards into blue-violet flowers. It needs a cool, shady position and flowers rather later than most primulas, in June and July.

JUNE
MARROWS AND COURGETTES

Although the fruits of marrows come in a bewildering variety of shapes and sizes, the plants themselves all require much the same sort of treatment, the only variations being related to the size of the full-grown plant and its habit (i.e. bush-shaped or trailing).

In fact, the plants are usually categorised in this way: thus the trailing varieties, which need 3-4ft. each way spacings, are very vigorous growers, and can, if small-fruited like Little Gem, be induced to grow up "wigwam" supports (Inset B) or other trellises. On the other hand, the bush varieties, probably better suited for the small garden, only need 2ft. each way between the plants and are of an altogether more compact shape.

The other distinction that sometimes causes some confusion is that between marrows and courgettes — any marrows can be picked when they are about six inches long and used as courgettes, but some bush marrow plants naturally produce large numbers of relatively small fruits. These varieties (Zucchini, Golden Zucchini and the courgette Green Bush) always have their fruits picked small and from the point of view of flavour seem to me the most worthwhile of all marrows to grow.

When choosing a site for marrows, it's important to remember that they're tender plants and that they have a lot of growth to make in a relatively short space of time — so a sheltered spot and one with plenty of sunlight is ideal (too much shade is a frequent cause of plenty of leafy growth but very few fruits). The soil needs to be rich, both to stimulate quick growth and to help in moisture retention.

Seeds may be safely sown outdoors in late May or June where the plants are to grow — the usual method is to sow two or three seeds 1 in. deep at each station, leaving only the strongest seedling to grow. Alternatively, if plants have been raised under glass they should be planted out in June with a minimum of root disturbance but using cloches (Inset A) if necessary to help harden them off.

Getting a good fruit set isn't usually a problem with courgette varieties, but it can be with other marrows. Whatever the cause (too much shade, dull and cool weather, lack of pollinating insects, etc.) the answer is hand pollination (Inset C) which is done by folding back or removing the petals from a male flower and pushing it gently into a female flower on a dry day. The easiest way to distinguish between the flowers is to remember that the female, and only the female, has a small embryonic marrow behind the bloom.

When the fruits begin to develop, a fortnightly feeding programme with a high potash content liquid feed will help the plants to be productive over a long period, as also will picking the fruits regularly when they are still fairly small. But do be careful when picking larger marrows — the best method is to cut the marrow where it lies and then to lift it out.

JUNE
CINERARIAS

For a brilliant display of bloom during the early new year few flowers can match the cineraria. Indeed, by successional sowings you can have them flowering through until May but for many gardeners their main attraction is their blooming in January and February when any flowering plants seem an especially welcome sight.

For the winter months you need to maintain a minimum temperature of 40-45°F; i.e. they don't require a lot of heat but they must be kept frost-free, for the plants can be killed overnight by even a touch of frost.

If you sow the seed of an early-flowering variety such as Spring Glory (Inset A) at the beginning of June you should have plants that will flower at the start of the new year and go on flowering right through until April if kept in a coolish position rather than a heated room in the house.

The seed is on the small side and needs only a light covering of seed compost for germination in a greenhouse, frame, windowsill, etc. at a temperature of 50-60°F. The seedlings grow quite rapidly so prick them out before they become drawn, either directly into small pots or well spaced out into seed trays (Inset B). The plants are usually potted on into 3½ inch pots and finally grown in 5 inch ones.

Growing on cinerarias during the summer months is a question of finding conditions that are, ideally, cool and shaded. A north-facing frame would be very suitable if you have one. In a normally positioned greenhouse in full sun you will find that the larger the leaves become the more inclined they are to wilt alarmingly on hot days. They usually recover perfectly overnight but there's always a tendency to overwater them in an attempt to cure the problem of the flagging foliage.

In fact, the plants do need frequent waterings in hot weather and even quite a bit of water during their flowering in the winter months when the addition of a liquid feed will help to prolong the flowering period.

Probably the most serious drawback to growing cinerarias is their liability to aphis and whitefly attack and it's always necessary to keep an eye open for the first signs of infestation to try and control the pest before it gets well established. This advice applies just as much to the winter months as the summer ones. An insecticide containing permethrin should give good control.

During the winter the plants are best kept at a temperature of around 50°F if flowering is to continue for any length of time. They need plenty of light although they should be kept out of powerful sunlight — if the light is from over-head so much the better.

The tendency towards wilting if the temperature is too high and the plant is short of water can be lessened by standing the pot on a tray of gravel kept perpetually damp, or by packing damp peat around the pot.

JUNE
WATER FOR FRUIT

When water is applied to vegetable crops, it has to produce a quick response because the crops are annuals, or at least are being grown as such, with sowing to harvesting all taking place within the one growing season. With fruit the response to watering is not so straightforward: i.e. although water will help to increase fruit weight and yields of the current year's crops, it will also act as a stimulant to the growth of the bushes and trees involved, thus providing the potential for bigger yields in years to come.

Whether or not watering is needed in the fruit garden will obviously depend on rainfall, soil type, temperature, etc., but if it is thought necessary it's always best to give a limited number of thorough waterings rather than a larger number of mere "sprinklings" whose effect is only to wet the soil surface from which the water will evaporate rather than sink in.

As a rough guide to how much to apply, a useful minimum figure for one watering is the equivalent of one inch of rain, which is 4½ gallons per square yard. It should be applied as slowly and gently as possible so that it penetrates the soil rather than forming pools on the soil surface or running off onto adjacent land and being wasted.

Taking the various fruits individually, blackcurrants will fruit next year on this year's growths so that they are obviously likely to benefit from irrigation *if* it is necessary. Such watering can stop after the beginning of August when their growth slows down.

Although raspberries, like blackcurrants, will be fruiting next year on the canes that have grown this year, only some of the canes that have grown will be retained and tied in, the remainder being pruned out. So their irrigation needs relate mainly to providing sufficient water to swell out all the fruits on the canes this year, making sure the later fruits don't shrivel up instead of ripening. Water is best applied just as the berries start to show their pink colour (Inset A).

Strawberries will show the greatest benefit from watering that is done between the flowering and picking periods although watering done after fruiting will help to encourage runner production if that is needed.

With tree fruits watering to stimulate growth may or may not be desirable — i.e. young trees you may wish to see make further growth can be watered if necessary in June and July to promote that growth; but very often gardens contain fruit trees which are, if anything, too big to manage properly and the last thing you want is to encourage them to grow bigger. Watering such trees should be limited to the period when the fruits are beginning to swell (Inset B), usually from mid-July onwards when most of the shoot growth will already have taken place.

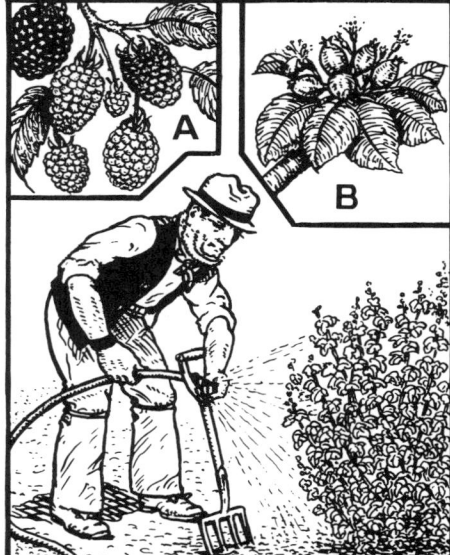

JUNE
BROOMS

Brooms are valuable shrubs for gardens of all sizes; easy to grow and generous with their flowers, their only drawback is a tendency to become long and leggy if left unpruned. However, pruning is a simple enough job, but it does need to be done yearly because brooms cannot be relied upon to break freely if cut back into old wood. These remarks apply most particularly to the common broom (Cytisus scoparius) and its many hybrids, and the Spanish broom (Spartium junceum); some of the smaller rockery brooms such as Cytisus kewensis still benefit from pruning but are basically lower-growing, spreading shrubs rather than upright types.

Prune all brooms that flower in the spring after flowering — the flowers will have been produced on wood of the previous year's growth (recognisable by its relative greenness compared with the browner, older wood) and as a general rule this one year old wood can be reduced by about two thirds. Inset A shows a typical branch. If the cut is made as shown (by knife or secateurs), the developing seedpods will be removed and the branches behind the cut will all grow out to provide the growth on which next year's flowers will form. Obviously on older bushes with many branches there

won't be time to be scrupulously exact about where to prune each one, but as long as you remember not to cut back to old wood the results should justify the time taken. Using a pair of shears will make the job quicker.

Summer-flowering brooms such as the Spanish one can be pruned after flowering but it's more common to prune them in the early spring. The same principle applies: cut back about two-thirds of the previous year's growth which will stimulate plenty of new growth to flower later in the season.

Brooms are simple plants to propagate. Seeds are the most obvious way as they are freely enough produced. If you take seed from the hybrids though (often ones with crimson or cream flowers) they will not come true to the parent plant but may well be quite acceptable in their own right. The seeds may take months to germinate and because broom seedlings are tricky to handle I would suggest sowing them where they are to grow on light soils — there will then be no need for transplanting. On heavier soils sow the seeds in pots, thin out to one seedling per pot and plant that out keeping the rootball intact.

To keep a variety of a favourite colour from the hybrid types you will have to take cuttings: 2-3 inch shoots of this year's growth put into a pot (Inset B) or even in small individual pots should root if kept in the close atmosphere of a frame or propagating case.

July-August, when the shoots are beginning to become firm, is the time to take cuttings. New plants, whether seedlings or rooted cuttings, should be regularly cut back to make bushy as opposed to leggy specimens.

JUNE
LEEKS

How many vegetables can rival the many virtues of the leek for garden cultivation? Not many have the same freedom from disease, the ability to grow well in all sorts of soils, the winter hardiness, the large cropping potential from a limited area of ground and a method of cultivation that's simplicity itself.

Leeks certainly appreciate a deep rich soil if the finest crops are to be obtained. It's a good idea, in fact, to follow a crop of early peas or broad beans with leeks, for if the soil has been enriched for the former crops it should be just right for the leeks that replace them.

The crop is usually raised by sowing seeds in March and transplanting the seedlings in June or July. The medium to late-maturing varieties such as Catalina, Musselburgh, Royal Favourite and Winter Crop can be very useful in providing a supply of fresh vegetables right through the winter months.

If you're transplanting your own seedlings, they're best moved when they're six to eight inches high — dig them out from the seed-bed by getting a fork in well underneath them so that no root is lost and then set them out in rows fifteen inches apart. The method of planting is to make six inch holes with a dibber at six to eight inch intervals in the row (Inset A)

and then merely to place a plant in each hole, watering in thoroughly afterwards (Inset B).

The watering will wash sufficient soil on to the roots to secure the plant and the depth of the hole will ensure a good length of well-blanched shank. One of the other benefits of this method of cultivation is that the planting holes make it very easy to give the plants a liquid feed. A good watering once a week if the weather necessitates it, plus a liquid feed fortnightly in the summer months will help to bring any leek up to a good size in as short a time as possible.

Apart from hoeing to keep the soil friable and the weeds down, and drawing up a little soil to the stems in October in order to lengthen the blanched part of the leek, no other attention will be necessary as leeks are completely hardy and will stand whatever the winter weather has to offer. But a useful tip to remember is that to prevent their going to seed, any leeks left in the ground next March or early April should be dug out and heeled in by a north or east-facing wall, for instance, where they're well shaded.

It's also worth mentioning one other method of cultivating leeks that some gardeners use. This involves blanching the stems by drawing up earth around them. The leeks are either transplanted on the flat or in shallow (2-3 inch) trenches and the soil is gradually drawn up around them in a way

similar to earthing up potatoes. Eventually, in late autumn, only the tops of the plants are visible and you should have a good length of blanched stem.

JUNE
LAYERING

Layering is the method of propagation in which a branch is pinned down to the ground and forms its own roots while still attached to the parent plant. Although this can be a relatively slow process (i.e. you will have to wait until next year before your new plant is ready for removal), it is also simple and quite undemanding in either time or equipment — once the layer has been made it will need no attention apart from the occasional watering in any really dry weather.

The method is usually used for shrubs, particularly those that are not easy to raise from cuttings, such as magnolias and rhododendrons. Layers may be made at any time in the growing season, spring and early summer being especially apt. Branches of young wood (one year old is ideal) will form roots far more readily than older ones.

Before preparing the branch, though, it is important to get the soil into good condition for quick root formation: forking into the ground below the branch to be layered a mixture of peat or leafmould and coarse sand will certainly help and would be strongly recommended for heavy soils.

The next stage is to decide on where exactly the branch is to be buried — about six to twelve inches back from the tip is usually about right. To get the most satisfactory rooting it's necessary to make a fairly sharp bend in the branch and bury it three to four inches deep. The tip of the branch which is protruding above the soil can be tied to a cane to keep it upright and hence accentuate the bent shape of the branch below ground. This is illustrated in Inset A.

To increase the chances of successful rooting make a cut in the branch at the point where it is to be buried. Do this with a sharp knife, making a tongue 1-2 inches long on the underside of the branch, the cut being made towards the tip of the branch and kept open by either a bit of sphagnum moss or a matchstick. If the wood proves very reluctant to bend, it is also possible to make a cut on the upper side of the branch and then twist the branch right round so that the end can easily be kept upright (Inset B).

Hormone rooting powder applied to the cut surfaces will also encourage roots to form. Making a wire pin of a hairpin shape to insert into the soil and then putting a lump of stone over the soil surface should keep the branch quite secure in its layered position. A largish stone will also help to keep the soil underneath it fairly moist.

Growth in the tip of the plant beyond the layer will indicate that some roots have been made but rather than dig the new plant up there and then, sever it from the parent (after checking that new roots have actually been put out by scraping away a little of the soil) and leave it in position until a suitable time for transplanting, usually the autumn.

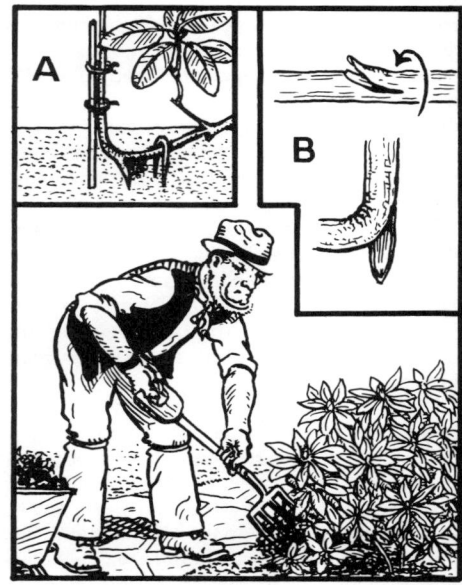

JUNE
CLUB ROOT

Two common causes of trouble in brassica crops are club root (sometimes known as finger-and-toe) and cabbage rootfly. Club root (Inset A) can attack all cruciferous plants, i.e. not only the many vegetable ones but also flowers such as wallflowers, stocks, candytuft, etc. Cabbage rootfly is most troublesome with cabbages and cauliflowers.

Club root is caused by a small soil organism which can exist in large numbers in infected areas — millions of spores to the square yard. There are several sensible ideas for gardeners to follow to stay clear of this disease.

Firstly, be strict about crop rotation, allowing a three or four season gap between brassicas if that is possible. Secondly, always raise your own seedlings. Plants are most susceptible to club root infection between germination and planting out time, although symptoms may not be so obvious then. Therefore, if you raise seedlings in pots or boxes of sterilised seed compost instead of the more normal practice of outdoor seed beds, you can be sure of starting with healthy plants.

Liming of the soil, if done well in advance of growing brassicas on it, is a useful measure although it cannot eradicate the disease. It should not be applied at more than 8-12 ozs per square yard or else other subsequent vegetable crops, notably potatoes, will suffer. Good soil drainage is also important for healthy growth of brassicas, and the practice of consigning all brassica roots to the bonfire rather than the compost heap is certainly advisable.

The main chemical control of club root is either by calomel dust or a fungicide called thiophanate-methyl. These are usually used by being mixed into a paste in which the roots of the seedling to be transplanted are dipped. This is a messy job though, and, naturally, dipping roots in any liquid tends to wash off any soil on them, making them that much more difficult to transplant. As it happens, calomel dust is also a good protectant against cabbage rootfly and if you are using it purely as a *protectant* against club root and the rootfly, it's often easier to *dust* the planting holes, the roots and the area around the base of the plant after transplanting with calomel. Keep the root dipping method for gardens where the disease is already present.

The cabbage rootfly lays eggs on cabbage stems at soil level. From the eggs emerge maggots which crawl down the stems and start eating the plant's roots. Symptoms of attack include bluish green leaves which wilt very readily (Inset B), sometimes turning yellow with the whole plant dying. Control is by calomel as mentioned, bromophos dust, diazinon granules or, non-chemically, by putting close-fitting discs (Inset C) of a flexible material (like foam underlay for carpets) around the stems so that the maggots are deterred from crawling down them.

JUNE
ROSE CARE

By June or July many gardeners will probably be looking at their roses and noticing that the foliage doesn't look quite as healthy as it did at the beginning of the season or that some of the buds may be covered with greenfly.

These days most of the common diseases like black spot and mildew can be both prevented and cured with chemical sprays just as greenfly can be eliminated by use of insecticides, but good cultivation, in itself, will help to ward off disease by producing healthy, strong-growing plants.

For instance, if you gave the roses a dressing of fertiliser in March or April a repeat dose now should produce a good effect, although it needn't be more than a light dressing round each bush at this time of year. The proprietary rose fertilisers which contain trace elements such as magnesium, calcium, iron, etc. as well as the normal nitrogen, phosphates and potash are best for this job, but the old favourite, Growmore, will do almost as well.

Hoe the fertiliser in and remove any weeds from the bed at the same time, but remember to use the hoe lightly to avoid causing the root damage that gives rise to sucker growths from the point where the root has been damaged. If these should occur don't cut them off at ground level, but remove a little of the soil, trace them down to their point of origin on the root and pull them off from there (Inset C).

As I mentioned, good cultivation should render roses less susceptible to disease but in gardens where mildew (Inset A) or black spot (Inset B) is either already beginning to show or is to be expected from previous years' evidence, action should be taken to stop it. Using one of the systemic fungicides, and there are several specially formulated for use on roses, a fortnightly spraying programme can eliminate these troubles but will prove more effective and easier to manage if started *before* the first signs of disease appear.

Similarly, with greenfly or any other aphids a systemic insecticide containing dimethoate will provide good control. With any systemic spray where the chemical is absorbed through the leaves, enters the sap-stream of the plant and provides protection from within, it is important to cover as many and as much of the leaves as possible with the spray. To do this requires a very fine spray used *sparingly* so that the liquid does not form into big droplets which then roll off the leaves onto the ground and thus get wasted.

In any very dry weather roses will certainly benefit from mulching. An easy way of obtaining mulching material is to use the clippings from the lawn, provided you have not used any hormone weedkiller on it this year. Make sure the soil around the roses is well hoed and nicely moist, and a thick layer of clippings will help to retain that moisture for weeks.

JUNE
WATERING VEGETABLE CROPS

Although the different types of vegetables have their own particular water requirements, some factors remain the same for all crops. Thus, for example, it is important to make sure seed-beds are sufficiently moist to ensure quick germination before rather than after sowing the seed. Watering the drills if the soil is dry (Inset A) might well be necessary before any sowings in the summer. With vegetables that are being planted out in their final quarters, such as leeks and brassicas, water is likely to be the critical factor in whether they're established quickly and begin to make new growth. With leeks the watering is made simple by the holes they're usually grown in — with other transplants, water them in thoroughly when planting out, give them small amounts of water daily if they show signs of wilting and shade them from hot sunshine and drying winds with newspaper or upturned flower-pots.

Seedlings and transplants might be most susceptible to damage caused by a shortage of water, but even well-established plants may well benefit from the occasional thorough soaking. Mulching has its part to play in preventing moisture evaporating from the soil, but unfortunately it cannot stop water loss through transpiration, the giving-off of water vapour into the air which is part of the plant's natural growth process.

Before watering, the soil should be prepared by hoeing, for instance, (Inset B) so that the water can easily penetrate the ground — this is especially important if the earth has been walked on. Otherwise the water will tend to form puddles on the surface and the roots will be left as dry as before. This also relates to the way in which the water is applied: a high-powered blasting from a hose will probably damage the plants, not to mention the soil structure. The aim should be to simulate natural rainfall as far as possible, which entails adjusting the nozzle on the hose to give a fine spray, applied late in the day if possible to prevent scorching of foliage and immediate evaporation in bright sunlight.

Another important point to remember is that the water you're applying is for the benefit of the plant roots which means that a watering, to be effective, must be thorough. Wetting only the surface of the soil is wasting water and may be counter-productive because it encourages the roots to grow upwards in search of moisture, which in turn will make them even more susceptible to drought damage.

As a very brief guide to what individual vegetables require, those whose foliage is eaten (cabbages, lettuces, etc.) will benefit from water applied at any stage of growth, but the "fruiting" vegetables such as peas, beans and tomatoes need water particularly at and after flowering, while root vegetables in general need less attention, water being applied merely to prevent their growth coming to a standstill.

JUNE
GREENHOUSE PRIMULAS

One good way of providing winter colour is to grow some primulas from seed. The varieties grown as pot plants flower for a long time while making modest demands in temperature; an enclosed porch, unheated conservatory or even a spare room will be sufficient to see them through the winter if they're given some protection on the coldest nights.

Primula obconica is perhaps the most widely grown of these primulas — mixed packets will provide long-lasting flowers of varying shades of reds, blues and white all held boldly above the foliage, but for a single colour try "Appleblossom" which develops to a lovely salmon-pink. Obconica, however, is the primula to which some people are allergic and which brings out a skin rash in the sufferers.

No such worries, however, with the other primulas: P. malacoides (Inset A), the fairy primula, whose flowers are much smaller and more delicate than those of the obconica types and usually in a range of reds and pinks; P. sinensis (Inset C), the Chinese primula, with fringed flowers in pink, orange, scarlet, blue and white, or P. kewensis which provides an unusual contrast with other primulas because of its fragrant yellow flowers.

One thing all these primulas have in common is very small seed, so great care needs to be taken when sowing to achieve a thin scattering. Make the surface of the compost level, water it well and merely press the seed into the surface layer. Covered with a sheet of glass to prevent moisture loss, the seed should germinate within two to three weeks if kept at a temperature of 55-60°F.

As soon as the seedlings are large enough to handle, prick them out into seed trays of John Innes No. 1. When the seedlings fill the trays, they should be potted lightly in 3 inch pots (Inset B) and then later into 5 inch ones of either John Innes No. 1 or No. 2; but the most important thing to remember about their cultivation during the summer months is to keep them cool. Always shade them from bright sunlight and try to achieve a temperature of about 50-60°F.

50°F is the sort of temperature to aim for during the winter months as well, with a minimum night value of 40-45°, so they obviously won't get on well with central heating, or respond to heat applied for forcing purposes. In fact, you'll probably find that keeping them in a sheltered spot outdoors in the summer and bringing them under glass some time in September is the best way to achieve the desired temperature.

Watering at all times is best done from underneath, i.e., by letting the water soak up through the compost from the base, but this is especially important during the autumn and winter when not much water will be needed until flowering time. Use a balanced liquid feed regularly as soon as the flower heads begin to appear from the bases of the plants.

FUCHSIAS PUT FOUR MONTHS OF COLOUR IN YOUR LIFE

What would you say was the most beautiful flower in the world? How about the hibiscus of the kind one sees in countries with a Mediterranean-type climate or the passion flower, so impressive with its saucer-shape and its centre composed of numerous thread-like filaments? The pure white gardenia too is very appealing with its ruffled petals which emit so powerful a fragrance.

Yet for sheer beauty of form, what about the fuchsia? Have you ever studied that flower closely?

The fuchsia demonstrates how nature can take colours so widely diverse as shocking strawberry pink, purple, scarlet, white, cream, cerise, magenta and carmine and produce the perfect combination every time.

Basically a fuchsia flower consists of a tube which terminates in a bell of four overlapping petals with four waxy sepals spreading out from the top of the bell.

There are hundreds of different garden varieties and hybrids all with delightful colour combinations for the "bell" and "sepals".

The fuchsia is a shrub. Yet in this country it is often treated as a pot plant, or as a suitable subject for a tub, window box, or hanging basket.

With the right sort of fuchsias you can make the most beautiful flowering hedge imaginable, or you can ensure that at least one part of the garden has ceaseless colour from July to November.

The hardiest fuchsias can be grown outdoors all year round in all parts of Britain. The tender types have to be put in pots and kept during the winter in the shelter of a cold greenhouse, garden shed or garage.

Hardy fuchsias are not expensive when one considers the years of colour they will provide.

Yet another advantage of the fuchsia is that it will grow in almost any well-drained soil from chalk to sand.

You can get hardy fuchsias which will never grow more than 2 ft. tall and others which will easily attain 6 ft.

Of the smaller kinds my favourite is Tom Thumb, just 2 ft. tall and always covered with distinctive flowers of clear violet bells and carmine sepals. This little beauty revels in sunshine and is ideal for the smallest of gardens.

The hardiest and most weather resistant of all the fuchsias is called Riccartonii after its birthplace at Riccarton in the Scottish Borders, a part of Britain not noted for ideal winter conditions for plants and shrubs.

Riccartonii has scarlet and purple flowers which are produced profusely on strong, straight stems. This variety makes an excellent hedge in coastal districts and in fact it is the most common fuchsia to be used as such.

In most gardens Riccartonii will grow to about 6 ft. with a 5 ft. spread. It is also a good choice in coastal areas for training against a house wall, where a rose might not be over successful because of black spot disease which is more prevalent by the sea.

Of the medium-sized fuchsias, generally around 4 ft. tall, I like Versicolour with silvery grey leaves edged with white and with coppery pink tints in the centres. The flowers are crimson and violet.

I like, too, the frilled flowers in carmine and purple of Margaret, the scarlet and white flowers of Madame Cornelissen and the carmine and violet flowers of Mrs Popple.

Any one of these will make a good splash of colour in a sunny or lightly shaded spot in your garden.

Living as I do inland, I cover the root area of the fuchsias in November with a 6 in. layer of dry peat to protect the roots from frost. Unlike those fuchsias grown in coastal districts, be it the South West of England or the East of Scotland, my fuchsias are virtually killed to ground level annually in winter by frost.

However, this is no real problem. For in April I simply cut back the frosted branches to near ground level, just as the new season's growth is emerging safely from the thick layer of peat.

Strange as it may seem, I do not curse a hard winter as I believe I get much better flowers on the new season's growth. So even in areas unaffected by frost it can pay to cut back your fuchsias.

The fuchsias for pots, tubs, window boxes and hanging baskets — if that were possible — are even more beautiful than those which can be grown in the ordinary garden soil. So in the heart of a city you have the chance to produce just as lovely flowers as those in Cornwall or the Isle of Man.

For the window sill or small unheated greenhouse a fuchsia can be housed in a 6 in. plastic pot.

If your fuchsias are grown in a tub, window box, hanging basket, they should be moved in November to a frost-free place for storage during the winter and allowed almost to dry out. In practice this will mean transferring the individual fuchsias to 6 in. pots, which are easier to accommodate than cumbersome tubs and window boxes.

For a hanging basket the variety Marinka looks stunning. The bell of the flower is plum purple and the sepals are cherry coloured tipped with gold. This fuchsia has the sort of trailing, arching habit which makes it ideal for a basket. It is also a good choice for a window box. You could have three such plants in the normal window box to give a massed colour effect.

Other splendid trailing fuchsias, which I strongly recommend, are Pink Galore with soft rose and deep pink flowers and Swingtime with raspberry red and white flowers.

Watering

There are also countless varieties of the normal upright tender fuchsias suitable for all purposes from tubs to window boxes. My recommendations are Ballet Girl with red and white flowers, Snowcap with ivory white bells and silvery rose sepals and Tennessee Waltz with lilac and rose pink flowers.

All tender fuchsias should be planted in containers filled with John Innes No. 3 compost. Water should be given freely so that the compost is always moist but not soaking wet. If the compost is allowed to dry out, the flower buds will fall off.

When flowering finishes in late October, gradually stop watering and after leaf-fall give no more water until growth restarts in the spring.

If you have a window box and live in a flat with no facilities for storing fuchsias indoors, my tip is to grow the tender hybrid Snowcap which has proved sufficiently hardy to spend the winter out of doors.

In April, even those fuchsias grown as pot plants should be cut back almost to soil level.

Garden fuchsias are generally free of pests and diseases, but pot-grown hybrids may be troubled with greenfly and white fly. Any number of insecticides will kill greenfly, but white fly are best sprayed with permethrin.

Few shrubs can offer four full months of non-stop colour; few shrubs are so easy to grow; few shrubs produce flowers which are so exquisitely beautiful that they immediately catch the eye …

It is my bet that if you buy a fuchsia, you will be hard pressed to think of a lovelier flower in the world.

JULY
SUMMER VEGETABLE SOWINGS

If you have some space left in the vegetable garden, there are several autumn to winter-maturing crops which are suitable for a July sowing, some of them rather unusual but well worth experimenting with. Remember that although the days are long and light now, these crops will be maturing when conditions are much less congenial: thus they will appreciate being put in a position where they will get the maximum amount of autumnal sunshine and wind protection.

All seeds need moisture to germinate — if your soil is dry at sowing time water the drills *before* sowing to ensure quick germination, and at the same time hoe in a light dressing of Growmore to make sure the germinated seedlings get off to a vigorous start in life.

Of the more common vegetables those which may be successfully sown as late as early July includes carrots (a good-keeping, vigorous grower like Autumn King), beetroot (Detroit-Little Ball is good for summer sowing), and lettuce. With lettuce the crisphead varieties are more suitable for sowing in hot weather as they germinate freely in high soil temperatures while the butterhead varieties do not. Windermere and Webb's Wonderful are both good crisphead cultivars.

Turning to some of the less common vegetables, there are now varieties of chicory which can be grown just as easily as the cos lettuce they look very much like. Variously listed in the seed catalogues as Sugar Loaf, Winter Fare, Snowflake, etc., they mature from October onwards to provide salad material at a time of the year when it's otherwise in very short supply. The plants, like the one shown in Inset A, need no forcing or winter protection and are much easier to manage than the traditional chicory plants.

Winter radishes are also rather different from their better-known summer relations. The roots are much larger (they can weigh up to a pound each) and can be left in the ground in the winter except in very severe weather. Whether you grow one of the Black Spanish varieties or China Rose (Inset B), make sure the plants are never short of water so that the flavour does not get too hot and the plants don't bolt.

Another subject which has got itself a bad reputation for bolting is the Chinese cabbage, probably because it has often been sown too early in the season. Delay sowing until July and thin the plants out in the rows rather than transplant them. Then, provided that they are given sufficient moisture to grow on without any checks, they should be hearting up in the cooler days of autumn which seem to suit them better than the higher temperatures of midsummer. Like the chicory, a mature Chinese cabbage looks very similar to a large cos lettuce, as Inset C shows.

JULY
BIENNIALS

Compared with the vast choice of annuals available to the gardener, a list of biennials will probably seem rather short, but it's a category of flowers that deserves consideration because it provides us with colour in the borders in that awkward period between the end of the spring bulbs and the start of most of the annuals and the summer flowering perennials.

Biennials are raised from seeds sown in May, June and July and transplanted to their final quarters in September or October; and although some prefer a May or June sowing, a number of others, including some of the very easiest of all garden flowers, will manage very nicely on a July sowing.

Among these are two flowers, Honesty and forget-me-nots, which seed themselves so easily that after growing them one year they are likely to be with you for evermore in the form of self-sown seedlings, which you may or may not consider a good thing. Personally, I regard it as a great labour saver for gardeners, as the unwanted seedlings can be pulled up and removed or even transplanted, leaving you with a supply of plants that have cost nothing in either money or effort.

Honesty (B) comes familiarly in purple and white-flowered versions, but there's also a variety with variegated leaves in cream and green. All have the attractive seedpods following the flowers. Honesty seeds may be sown up to August if you sow them where they are to flower and it's worth remembering it's one of those flowers that will tolerate both sunny and shady spots.

Like Honesty, the forget-me-not (A) is often thought of as a humble plant and, indeed, if you let one of the not so attractive pale blue varieties become established in your garden, you may come to regret it. However, there are a number of named varieties which come in deeper shades of blue and have the added virtue of a more compact habit: two such are Ultramarine and Blue Ball both of which form bushy plants about 6-8 inches tall.

Another easily-grown compact little plant is the double daisy, Bellis perennis, (C) whose white, pink and red flowers make it very suitable for edgings: the button-like flowers of the pomponette varieties are very attractive.

At the opposite end of the scale to the double daisy are two old favourites of the cottage garden, both of which look effective either dotted around in or at the back of borders. Verbascums (mullein) have spikes of flowers which can be obtained in a wide variety of colours and a height range of 2-6ft. The best of the foxgloves are the Excelsior hybrids, whose colour range makes them a far more attractive proposition than just allowing self-sown seedlings of the wild varieties to grow, as so often happens. Sow them in July where they are to flower, preferably in a partially shaded position.

JULY
ALSTROEMERIAS

One of the most beautiful sights in the garden during June and July is a large group of alstroemerias covered with blooms. The alstroemeria, or Peruvian lily as it is often called, is a plant of the amaryllis family with very showy lily-like flowers at this time of year.

The two which are most commonly seen in our gardens are Alstroemeria aurantiaca (Inset A) and Alstroemeria Ligtu hybrids (Inset B). Aurantiaca has orange-yellow flowers and grows to about 3ft high, while the Ligtu hybrids have flowers in shades of pink, yellow and orange, although in my experience pink is the predominant colour. The Ligtu hybrids grow to 2-3ft.

Alstroemerias are plants for the herbaceous border and although they can be slow to become established they will eventually spread to form large clumps at least three feet across and, if not restrained, rather bigger in the case of aurantiaca.

Once established, the foliage forms a mound of green as it grows each spring and provided the ground is well cleared of perennial weeds prior to planting, the alstroemerias should effectively smother any other competition from weeds. The plants are hardy, although the Ligtu hybrids are best grown in a sheltered position in well-drained soil to guarantee their survival intact through really bad winters. Anything apart from a north-facing situation will be suitable for them.

To propagate alstroemerias you must either divide existing clumps or raise new plants from seed. The plants have fleshy roots which are planted deep in the soil and do not like being disturbed. Hence you will need a large fork to dig some of the roots out for propagation purposes in either September/October or March.

To prepare a site for a new planting dig the ground deeply and incorporate plenty of decomposed manure, leafmould, etc. into the soil.- The pieces of root must be planted 6-8 inches deep and, because they spread easily, no less than a foot apart. The plants may well take two years to become properly established so do not expect a great display of flowers straight away; let the roots remain undisturbed and they will soon repay the waiting

To get very high rates of germination with alstroemerias grown from seed requires special techniques but a moderate degree of success should be achieved by sowing the seed in a normal seed compost and keeping the seeds at a temperature of about 75°F for four to five weeks. After this transfer the seeds to a place where they can be kept at about 50°F until they germinate.

JULY
TOMATO TIPS

Tomatoes under glass provide the most reliable crops but they do need more in the way of care and attention than outdoor varieties. At this time of year particular attention should be paid to ensuring a good fruit set and getting watering, ventilation and feeding right, besides such routine measures as continuing with the removal of side shoots.

Although tomatoes can and do set fruit without any human assistance, there are ways in which the gardener can get very much better results by giving them a helping hand. This is done by ensuring that the atmosphere in the greenhouse is kept humid, and by gently shaking the plants when they are in flower or by tapping the flower trusses. This helps to distribute the pollen and is best done on warm, sunny mornings when a mist-spraying of the flower trusses can also help to eliminate the condition known as "dry set" (Inset C) when fruitlets form but fail to develop owing to the atmosphere being too dry at the moment of pollination.

Closely related to problems of creating the warm, humid atmosphere that tomatoes thrive in are questions of temperature and ventilation. Basically this means the gardener responding daily to the actual weather conditions, which obviously creates problems at holiday times. Temperatures in the greenhouse rise very rapidly on hot, sunny days and although the tomato plant is an appreciator of warmth, too hot conditions can actually inhibit ripening, creating the condition known as "greenback" (Inset A) when the top of the fruit around the stem stays green and hard while the rest ripens. But, while doors and windows need to be opened judiciously in the day, they must often be shut again at night, especially if lowish temperatures are forecast, leaving an overnight temperature of about 60°F.

Watering is usually another daily requirement and is best carried out in a systematic way so that the plants receive regular waterings, rather than leaving them until they actually show symptoms of being in urgent need of moisture. This is what leads to "blossom-end rot" (Inset B) and it is quite frequently seen on fruits from plants that have been allowed to get too dry. It's as well to remember that one tomato plant in a greenhouse can require up to half a gallon of water per day in the hottest summer weather.

Because we expect our tomato plants to make a lot of growth and produce a good weight of fruit in a relatively short period of time, we should expect to have to feed them. Fortunately, there are plenty of special tomato fertilisers around (each containing a relatively high potash content in relation to nitrogen), and any of them should bring good results. But if the new growth begins to look weak, try switching to a compound fertiliser with a relatively high nitrogen content for a few feeds.

JULY
STRAWBERRY PROPAGATION

The strawberry is such a delicious fruit and is so easily propagated that it makes a lot of sense to include the crop in the vegetable garden rotation scheme, leaving the plants for no longer than two or three years before replacing them with new plants in a different section of the plot.

There are two very good reasons for this — firstly, strawberries are plants that appreciate a high humus content in the soil which must be supplied prior to planting; after three years the plants will have exhausted a lot of the available nutrients in the soil with a consequent loss of vigour. Secondly, strawberries are notoriously susceptible to virus diseases which can eventually lead to stunted plants yielding very little fruit. Hence the need for replacement of plants with either bought-in certified virus-free stock or new plants developed from runners on only the very best, most vigorous and most productive of your existing plants (i.e. the plants most likely to be virus-free).

In an ideal world, the runners would be taken from plants which had not been allowed to fruit, thus saving up their strength for runner production, but most gardeners will probably settle for a compromise of allowing the plants to fruit and taking only a limited number of runners from each parent plant: three, or at most four, would be a suitable number.

The technique for layering runners is very simple — with a trowel, make a hole (Inset A) large enough to accommodate a 3 inch pot. The hole should be far enough away from the parent plant to avoid disturbing its roots and the pot should be filled with a compost such as John Innes No. 1 and sunk in the soil almost up to its rim. The runner is pegged into the soil in the pot (Inset B) where it will develop into a small plant that can eventually be severed (Inset C) from the parent plant. This severing should be left until it has developed a good root system of its own; in fact, when it is ready to be planted out where it is to grow.

The question of timing for these operations will obviously vary from one part of the country to another, but, in principle, the earlier the plantlets from the runners are set out in their final positions the better the crop you can expect from them next year. So if you aim to start layering runners in June or July, you should be able to plant them out in the first half of August into ground well prepared with plenty of organic material.

A final word about what to do with strawberry plants after they've finished fruiting. If straw has been used as a mulching material, it should be removed together with any weeds and either burnt or composted.

Then using a pair of shears clip off all the old strawberry foliage and unwanted runners, taking care not to damage the crowns or any new growth around them. Hoe lightly around the plants to aerate the soil and give them a light dressing of general fertiliser.

JULY
VIOLAS AND PANSIES

It's quite possible to obtain summer-flowering plants of violas and pansies from seed sown in February and March but these spring-sown plants never seem quite the equal of those raised from a June or July sowing. By delaying the sowing one is in fact raising the plants as one would biennials, although, of course, both violas and pansies are perennials, the violas more reliably so than the pansy.

Their great virtue is their prolonged flowering period which extends from early spring right through the summer until well into the autumn with occasional blooms appearing during the winter months. To get the best display of bloom, as suggested above, plant out the seedlings from summer-sown seed in the autumn but don't allow them to flower then. By removing the few blooms that do appear, the plants can concentrate their energies on growth and will be that much stronger when given their head next spring.

It's not easy to characterise the differences between pansies and violas. Botanically they are all members of the viola family, but the garden pansies of today tend towards larger flowers on slightly larger plants than violas. In compensation, though, the violas like the one shown in Inset A are even more free flowering, while the cornuta varieties (Inset C) (originally "horned" violas, although this feature is no longer so apparent in their flower shape) have even smaller flowers but an exceptional number of them.

All members of the viola family thrive in cool moist conditions, making them a success in some northern and western areas where other more heat-loving flowers don't do so well. They also tolerate a little shade, another useful asset. Their moisture-loving properties would however make them unlikely to perform well on light soils in prolonged dry summer weather unless some form of humus-enriching material like peat or leaf mould is dug into the soil beforehand.

For continuity of flowering it is important to remove all the flower heads as they fade.

Raising seedlings is a very straightforward matter. They are either sown direct into the open ground in ¼ inch drills or in trays under glass. If this latter method is used, when the seedlings are pricked out they will be quite happy if the trays are left in a shaded spot outdoors until the final planting time.

Violas and pansies can also be propagated by cuttings — short non-flowering basal shoots supplying the best material. If the parent plant doesn't possess any such shoots, cutting it back should soon induce new growth of the right sort. Beware of older shoots which may have hollow stems and thus be quite unsuitable as propagating material. The cuttings should be 2-3 inches long, cut off below a leaf joint, and inserted round the edge of a pot (Inset B). Kept moist and shaded they should soon develop roots.

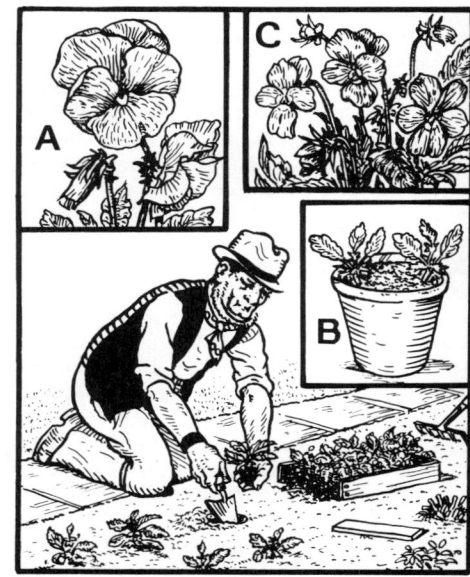

JULY
HOLIDAY CARE

Summer holidays usually raise a few problems for gardeners, mostly to do with picking and watering.

Plants growing in the soil outdoors are least at risk. Have a good tidy-up with the hoe before the holiday, removing any weeds and dead-heading any flowers. Mow the lawn and give a thorough soaking to any plants at risk if the weather is very dry. Water loss to any vulnerable plants can be further reduced by mulching with moist peat or even large flat stones.

One point about vegetables is that some of them need to be picked regularly to ensure continued production. This is particularly true of French and runner beans and courgettes. For this reason it's a good idea to invite a neighbour to pick them while you are away so that they will still be in a fit condition to supply you when you get back.

Greenhouses also benefit from neighbour cooperation, especially if growing bags are being used. These can be helped to water themselves by using a plastic growing-bag tray with capillary wicks inserted into the base of the bag, but even so are more of a problem than soil grown plants. The latter can be given a thorough watering and mulching, just as with outdoor plants. Obviously the greenhouse will have to be well ventilated while you are on holiday — a good circulation of air is vital for plant health as well as keeping temperatures down. Blinds can be effective in this respect but even more so is a coating of a shading paint such as Coolglass, which by reducing the amount of sunshine penetrating the glass will also reduce the water needs of the plants in the greenhouse.

The other big question at holiday time is what to do with pot plants, many of them accustomed to a daily watering in the summer months. The more robust specimens shouldn't come to any harm if they are put into a trench dug in a shady spot outdoors (Inset A). If the soil is brought right up to the rims of the pots and the whole lot made really wet prior to going away, they should still be all right on your return. A further refinement would be to put a layer of wet peat at the foot of the trench.

Plants being left indoors should be taken off sunny windowsills and put into a cool room. Standing them in watertight trays with damp peat packed around the pots will help keep them moist. Another possibility is to use a propagator (without the bottom heat, of course): the plastic lid will help to reduce moisture loss if the plants are stood on a layer of damp soil. The third possibility is to use capillary watering sticks: these are like wicks which are inserted into the base of uncrocked pots, the other ends going into a reservoir of water (Inset B). The pots are stood clear of the water level and, depending on the amount of liquid in the reservoir, can be supplied with water for weeks.

JULY
IRIS DIVISION

Like many of the other hardy perennials in the garden, the tall bearded irises may easily be propagated by division. These irises, like the one illustrated in Inset A, are not, however, treated quite like most of the other hardy perennials insofar as July rather than one of the autumn months is the usual time chosen to do the dividing; and, of course, their rhizomatous rootstocks require slightly different handling from, say, the roots of a Michaelmas daisy.

In fact, propagation is not the only reason for lifting and dividing the plants. After three or four years each iris in a group planting is likely to have grown to the extent that it's encroaching upon its neighbours. The competition for food supplies among such congested plants soon leads to a situation where plant vigour diminishes and flower quality deteriorates.

To divide the plants, lever them gently out of the ground with a large fork taking care to get as much root out as possible. Don't shake off any more earth than is necessary as any left will help the replanted sections of rhizome to re-establish themselves quickly. What you have dug up will consist of a parent rhizome cluster with younger "offset" rhizomes growing out from it. These young rhizomes with their healthy sprays of leaves are the ones to be replanted and they should be separated from the parent plant with a sharp knife, leaving one with a new plant something like that shown in Inset B.

These tall bearded irises always look best in large groups and when replanting you may want to keep them together in their original place or find another spot for them. Either way, go for an open sunny position and make sure the site is completely weed-free before replanting. If reusing the previous site feed the soil by incorporating some peat, leafmould or compost and give it a dressing of a slow-acting fertiliser like bonemeal.

Having firmed the soil down if it's been dug over, the irises can be replanted — set them at least a foot apart, so that the rhizomes are level with the soil surface (Inset C). The roots should have been well spread out in the planting holes and the soil around the plants should be made firm and then watered to help establish the new plants quickly. Don't be tempted to set the rhizomes any deeper — it will only delay flowering if you do so.

Propagating by division is the easy way of increasing your stock of plants if you have some to start with. Gardeners may also be interested to know that the bearded iris (I. germanica) can be grown from seed. The seedlings may not flower until their third year, so you will have a lengthy wait until discovering whether you have any interesting and unusual colours; but it would be much cheaper than buying a collection of plants.

JULY
POTATO BLIGHT

Although potato blight (Inset A) is not usually a problem with first early varieties, any spells of wet weather in July and August can result in severe problems from the disease for maincrop cultivars and tomato plants, which can also be attacked. The first you will see of the disease is the development of brown patches on the leaves. In damp conditions these spread quickly and soon the whole foliage of a plant is affected. Spraying can help to slow down the spread of the disease once it has appeared, but it's a far better policy to spray before any evidence of blight is present and hope to prevent its appearance. This is especially important in wet conditions, or even warm and humid weather, which encourages the spread of the disease.

Bordeaux mixture is a suitable spray against blight, as are products containing mancozeb. Choose a dry day for the job and apply the spray in a fine mist to as much of the foliage as possible, aiming to cover both the upper and lower sides of the leaves. To be completely effective, spraying should be repeated at fortnightly intervals.

It's also worth making sure the potatoes are well earthed up as blight spores can be washed off the leaves and on to any potatoes at or near the surface of the ridges. Tuber blight, recognisable by discoloured, slightly sunken patches on the surface of the tuber and a brown rot inside, will make the potatoes impossible to store, as the rot will continue to spread and may affect other healthy tubers as well. If you do come across any blighted tubers either when lifting the crop or in store, make sure you put them on the bonfire not the compost heap.

In August, when the potato plants are near to maturity anyway, as an alternative to spraying against blight, many gardeners cut the potato haulm down to ground level if there's any sign of the disease. If this is done, allow at least a fortnight to elapse before lifting the tubers — this allows their skins to harden, which is vital if they are to have a long storage life through the winter.

Another reason for lifting the tubers on the early side is if you know your ground to be affected by wireworms, which can turn the inside of the tubers into a maze of small tunnels (Inset C). If you discover this to be the case, it would probably be worth sticking to first early varieties in future as they are rarely badly affected by the pest.

Perhaps even more of a menace than wireworms are slugs, which create much larger holes in the tubers (Inset B) and which also start getting busier at this time of year, especially in wet weather. Putting down slug pellets should have some effect, but, again, if you know your garden to have a particular slug problem, it would probably be wisest to lift the tubers sometime in August before the problem becomes too acute.

JULY
RASPBERRY PRUNING

The pruning of raspberries is the most straightforward of the pruning jobs in the fruit garden and should be done as soon as the last of the fruit has been picked. I am, of course, referring to summer-fruiting raspberries, the autumn-fruiting ones being treated in an altogether different way. By pruning these summer-fruiting canes at the earliest possible time, the new canes get the maximum opportunity for development which is obviously a great help towards ensuring a good crop for next year.

The first thing to be done is to remove all the old canes, the ones which have borne fruit on them this year. Cut them right down to the ground with a pair of secateurs. When they are out of the way you should be left with a large selection of new growths, some tall and strong, some weak and spindly.

Basically, the objective is to retain the best of these new growths, tie them in to the wires and prune out the remainder. The number to be retained is determined by the fact that one wants them spaced at 4-5 inch intervals along the row when they are tied in. It is inadvisable to retain more than five or six canes from any one "stool" (the clump that develops from any one original planting).

The tying in may be done in two different ways, the first one being more time-consuming and therefore less practical if a large number of canes are involved. I have assumed that each row has the usual post and wire support system. The first method involves tying each cane to each wire individually (Inset A) and for this one needs to remember that the material used for the tying has got to last without breaking until this time next year. I use old nylon stockings cut into strips which are both strong and durable and yet sufficiently soft and elastic to permit tying that will prevent the canes sliding along the wires.

Method two involves continuous stringing. Taking a ball of string, tie one end to the upright at the end of the row and then unwind the ball right the way along the row as shown in Inset B, finishing off by tying it to the upright at the far end. This method will keep the canes firmly in position, but you must use string that will last the year without rotting.

Having tied in the selected new canes the other unwanted new growths can be pruned out, again cutting them down to ground level. Beyond an occasional weeding, no other attention will be needed until the beginning of next March when "tipping" should be done. Essentially, this means cutting off the top 4-5 inches of each cane (usually of soft wood that's been damaged in the winter). For some

canes this will leave the cane top near the level of the top wire, others will be much longer. In order not to waste potential fruiting material, bend these longer canes over and tie them down to the top wire (Inset C).

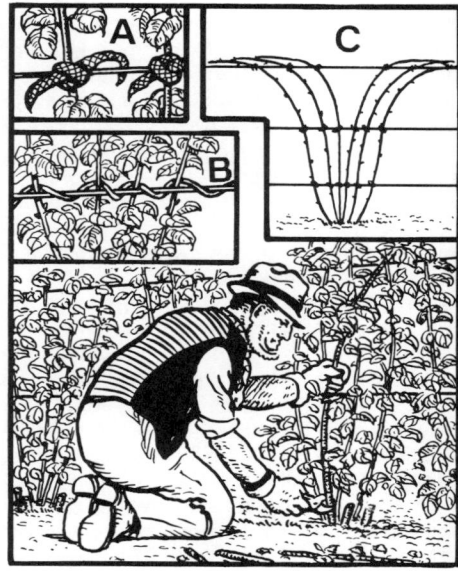

JULY
SPRING CABBAGE

Cabbages that heart up in spring are especially useful in providing fresh vegetables at a time when few others are available. Spring cabbage will grow well in most types of soil but, if you can provide good drainage for them, it will greatly reduce the risk of casualties in the winter and lead to earlier maturity in the spring.

The sowing times for these cabbages are late July in the North of England and the first half of August in the South. Sticking to these times will produce seedlings that are sufficiently well-developed to withstand the rigours of winter but not so large as would make them likely to bolt next spring. If the soil is dry at sowing time water the drills thoroughly before you sow the seed. The usual practice with brassicas, which makes the best use of the space available, is to sow seed in a seed-bed and to transplant the seedlings to their final quarters later.

With spring cabbage the seedlings should be large enough for transplanting at some stage between mid-September and mid-October. If the seed bed is dry when you wish to lift the plants give it a thorough soaking beforehand. Plant the seedlings really firmly and be prepared to firm the soil around them again after any winter frosts. These tend to loosen the soil and push the seedlings up.

The site that you select for the cabbages could well be one that has been manured for a previous crop, but it should not be one that has recently had any organic matter dug in, since this would promote soft leafy growth that would suffer in the winter. No fertiliser need be applied, either, at this stage — next spring is when it is needed. If you live in a really cold area, you might find it useful to cover the seedlings with cloches during the worst of the winter weather.

Spring cabbages can be grown for two distinct purposes and on this will depend how far apart you plant the seedlings out. The cabbages will of course produce solid hearts in due course next spring but many gardeners like to use immature plants as spring greens. If you wish to grow hearted cabbages only, they should be planted out at 15-18 inches apart each way. For a supply of spring greens and hearted cabbages, you can double the plant population (i.e. at nine inches apart each way) and remove alternate plants as spring greens, leaving the rest to heart up.

A lot of nutrients in the soil may well have been leached away, especially after a wet winter, and so an application of fertiliser in March when the plants start to grow will help to promote quick and vigorous development. Growmore at 3ozs. per square yard is a good way of doing this.

Varieties of cabbage suitable for sowing now include April (Inset A), Wheeler's Imperial and Harbinger which all produce fairly small heads and Offenham-Flower of Spring (Inset B) which produces a medium to large one.

WHEN PENNIES BUY MIRACLES AND MAGIC

When you look at the garden in summer with all the roses and other flowers in full bloom, do you wish things could always be like that?

Think what it would be like if your garden started into full bloom in February and continued to provide eye-catching colour and fragrance until the following November.

It takes just a few pence to work such a miracle in any garden.

The simple secret is to find a patch of bare soil where you can sow a few seeds right now.

At this time of year it is easy to raise, for example, those delightful spring-flowering daisies in white, reds and pinks ... forget-me-nots in many shades of blue ... Japanese and Swiss pansies ... fragrant wallflowers in a wide range of colours ... Brompton stocks in shades of white, pink, red and purple and exquisitely scented.

There are also flowers whose names may not be immediately familiar, such as the rudbeckia, sometimes called the gloriosa daisy. One variety if Marmalade, 15 in. high with golden orange, 5 in. wide daisy-like flowers which bloom from spring to late autumn.

There are also Rustic Dwarfs, a rudbeckia with a mixture of flowers in yellow, gold, bronze and dark red. These flowers soon smother the soil with a carpet of bloom and ensure that there is little room for weeds. The flowers are also excellent for cutting.

A packet of such seeds will yield dozens of plants.

Most people are familiar with wallflowers and forget-me-nots, but by raising your own plants, you will be simply amazed at what can be achieved.

Many of the wallflower plants offered for sale by garden centres in the autumn are the tall kind, which are generally unsatisfactory in the sort of small gardens that so many of us have to make do with nowadays.

Far better to have the more weather-resistant dwarf kinds which grow to no more than 9 in. This type of wallflower, pleasantly scented, is also a good choice for window boxes, tubs and the smallest of beds. You can obtain dwarf wallflowers in single shades such as yellow, crimson and deep red, or as a mixture of colours.

The way one uses these colours can be very important. I always have, for example, dwarf royal blue forget-me-nots as a carpet of colour under my orange-flowered deciduous azaleas.

Forget-me-nots thrive in sun or shade and in moist or dry positions.

The 6 in. high spring-flowering daisies called Bellis are marvellous for little beds, or for edging beds full of other flowers. They can also be used for tubs and window boxes. You can obtain varieties with a mixture of shades that includes bright red, rose and white.

By raising Japanese pansy plants in my garden this July, I am able to underplant my rose bushes so that come January and February when these are bare skeletons, the beds will be once again in full bloom. The hybrid Azure Blue is the best bet to flower from winter right through the following summer. I also recommend Golden Champion, a splendid yellow pansy, raised too in Japan.

Pansies are good plants for tubs and window boxes. If you want a real riot of colour, try some of the Swiss Roggli Giants, famous throughout the world for their size and colour.

Scent in the garden in early spring is invaluable. That is why the 18 in. tall Brompton stocks in white, pink, rose, mauve and purple should merit a place in your seed shopping list.

By sowing seed this very month there are all sorts of delights which lie in store for you next spring and summer.

You can grow outdoor carnations which are almost a match for the greenhouse kinds. This particular type, in a wide range of colours, has the advantage of needing no staking.

For window boxes, tubs and rockeries and to fill gaps in shrub and flower borders, how about growing some alpine pinks (Dianthus alpinus)? At around 8 in. high, deliciously fragrant and in a wide range of shades and combinations of white and red, it would be hard to think of a better bargain.

At this time of year outdoors I also sow the seeds of the delphinium. After all, why pay for a single plant at the garden centre when you can raise several dozen in a few weeks? The best type for most modern gardens is the hybrid Blue Fountains, 3 ft. to 4 ft. tall and almost covered in florets from ground level. Some of the blue shades are especially handsome and are among the most attractive flowers in the garden.

For shady spots among shrubs, how about some foxgloves? You can get unusual shades such as apricot. And among shrubs those awkward gaps can also be filled with dwarf lupins. Lulu is a variety just 2 ft. high, and there are colours such as pink, red, blue and purple.

The pyrethrum with its pink, red and white daisy-like flowers, so good for cutting, is easily raised from seed in July. That is the beauty of sowing now.

You do not have the hassle of sowing on the kitchen window sill, or coaxing seeds to germinate by putting them in the hot cupboard, etc. Sowing seed now is simplicity itself.

And while you are drawing up your seed list, do not forget Canterbury bells, 15 in. high and a good choice in a small garden. Bells of Holland is a variety which to my mind offers the best range of shades in blue, mauve, rose and white.

Canterbury bells are an old cottage garden flower, just like Sweet William, which also has to be sown now to produce the best possible show of flowers next year.

I have promised that I can fill your garden with flowers for nine whole months of the year. If I were to include the attractive seed pods of Honesty, which are like flat discs of silver, I could make it twelve.

Honesty, also called the satin flower and moonwort, has purple flowers, but it is those silver seed pods which are so highly prized by flower-arrangers for winter decorations. This particular plant is a good choice too for placing in the difficult positions under trees.

Once you have obtained your packets of seeds, sow the seeds in a vacant patch of soil at the depth specified on the packet. Some seeds such as dianthus will germinate in a week. Others like the foxglove, forget-me-nots, delphinium and rudbeckia may take as long as three weeks to show.

During this time the seeds have to be kept slightly watered. Once the seedlings can be easily handled, they are best lifted gently and replanted a few inches apart. When the plants look fairly sturdy in late autumn, they can be moved to their final positions.

Your surplus plants are sure to be welcomed by friends and neighbours. After all, part of the fun of gardening is being able to give things away. But don't be too hasty in discarding some of the weaker looking seedlings of the delphiniums and lupins, for example. Some of the finest shades are produced in summer by those very seedlings which the previous autumn looked the least likely to survive.

AUGUST
GREEN MANURE

One of the problems that most gardeners seem to face is that they can never produce enough compost for their vegetable plot each year. Animal manures could make up the deficiency, but they are hard to come by these days; green manuring is another possibility which is both relatively straightforward and inexpensive and worth considering.

The idea of green manuring is to sow seeds of a quick-growing crop on a section of the garden that you want composted. The crop is allowed to grow until just before it reaches maturity, then dug or rotovated straight into the soil. It is dug in at this stage because the amount of fibrous matter in the plant is still fairly small — i.e. the vegetation will rot down and provide humus relatively quickly. The process is very similar to that of digging compost in, the only difference being that the decaying of the plants will take place in the soil rather than on the compost heap.

Green manuring can be done at any time of the year when weather conditions will enable the plants to grow quickly. Obviously most gardeners will want to do it when the ground is not occupied by their vegetable crops. This often means July or August when the crops have been cleared.

Advantages of green manuring are similar to those of adding compost to the soil — the main benefit is provided by the humus formed which will improve the soil structure, especially beneficial to very light or very heavy soils. The green manure crop will also absorb any of the soluble plant foods in the soil and will prevent their being lost by the leaching of the winter rains. Again, leaching is a problem that's worst on light soils, but I'm sure that the advantages to be derived from green manuring make it worth trying on all soil types.

What to sow and when? The main crops used are mustard and rape, Italian ryegrass, plus, occasionally, vetches and tares. There is also at least one green manure mixture available from the current seed catalogues. Any such mixture or mustard or rape would be best suited to sowing in August when quick bulking of the crop is essential. The other crops require a longer period of growth and would not be ready for digging in while the soil still has some warmth in it, a vital requirement for the decaying of the green matter to be dug in.

Whatever seeds are used, broadcast them over the soil and run the rake over them (Inset A) to provide sufficient soil cover. The crop should germinate and grow very quickly and when it's 8-10 ins. high (Inset B) should be ready for digging in. Use a rotovator or just dig it in trench by trench (Inset C). If the height of the crop makes it awkward to dig, knock it or roll it down first of all. Whichever way you dig it in, a sprinkling of sulphate of ammonia or nitro-chalk on the green material will help to get it decaying quickly, so that the ground will be in good shape for sowing next year's vegetable crops on.

AUGUST
DIANTHUS
PROPAGATION

Although there are now plenty of pinks and carnations which can be raised from seed the choicest, named varieties still have to be propagated from cuttings (or pipings as they are usually called when taken from pinks) or layering, the method most successful for border carnations. Don't be put off by terms such as "piping" or "layering" though — both methods are not only easy to carry out but also likely to yield a high percentage of successful rootings.

With pinks the shoots that will make satisfactory pipings are young unflowered ones with close-jointed leaves and about three or four pairs of them, something like that shown in Inset A. These are usually pulled out of the parent plant by hand, holding down the plant with one hand and just giving a gentle pull to remove the young shoot. Remove any leaves which would touch the compost, and the pipings are ready for insertion.

They can be put straight into sandy soil in a shaded part of the garden, but I find them easier to manage if put into pots of cuttings compost or a peat and potting grit mixture. The lowest leaves should be just above the compost surface (Inset B) and the pots can be placed either in a cold frame or in a cool shaded part of the garden. Provided the compost is not allowed to dry out, rooting should take place within three or four weeks.

It is possible to propagate carnations from cuttings but layering is generally agreed to give better results. July and August are good months for the job and there's no need to worry about the plants being in flower at the same time. In order to encourage quick rooting scrape away a little of the garden soil where the layering is to be done and replace it with a good rooting medium such as the peat and sand or potting grit mixture.

Vigorous, newish growths from near the base of the plant will make the best layers. Counting from the top, leave five pairs of leaves and remove all those from lower down the stem. Then, with a sharp knife, make a cut upwards through the stem, starting just under the joint below the bottom pair of leaves remaining. The cut should pass through the joint area finishing just above it, leaving the layer attached to the parent plant by half its stem, the other half forming a tongue (Inset C).

The tongue is pressed downwards into the compost and the shoot from the parent plant held down with a hairpin, say, as in Inset D. A series of such layers can be done all round the parent plant and as long as the compost is kept moist roots should form in three or four weeks. The layers can then be severed, allowing the new plantlets a further week to establish themselves before being potted up in 3 inch pots for overwintering in a cold frame or cool greenhouse, prior to being planted out next spring.

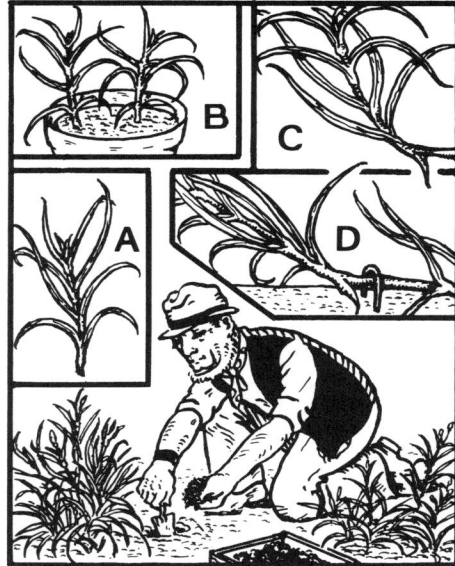

AUGUST
PRUNING AND PRUNING COMPOUNDS

Although the removal of unwanted branches on trees or large shrubs is a job that's often left until winter, it is usually better from the plant's point of view to get it done in the period from late July to September. This is because the plant will by this time have finished its period of active growth and hence there should be no risk of any wounds bleeding, but it will still be active enough for callus formation to start quickly and to be well developed before the winter dormancy. The callus is the plant's own way of protecting the wound and of shutting out water, fungal spores, etc. and obviously the sooner it develops the more useful it will be in protecting the wound from disease.

Removing branches in the winter is clearly easier on some deciduous trees because the lack of leaf cover makes it both easier to see the branches and to get at them. However, even if the wounds are painted over with a pruning compound, callus formation will not get under way satisfactorily until the warmer weather of spring.

Even in the summer, a callus cannot form immediately over any wounds created by pruning or branch removal and this is why pruning paints or compounds are so useful. In effect they provide an artificial callus while a natural one is forming underneath. They should certainly be used when large branches are removed and are useful on branches as small as an inch in diameter.

For large cuts a bitumen emulsion like Arbrex is useful. Apply it with a paintbrush, brushing well into the surface of the cut area and it will set to form a waterproof and disease-proof coat. Large wounds on trees of some species may be reluctant to heal and may need further applications of the dressing to protect them. This should be done at least once a year. Arbrex is also suitable for smaller cuts on both trees and shrubs as are products like Medo and Seal and Heal Pruning Paint. These can also be used as canker paints on fruit trees and should be applied with brushes so that they penetrate well into the plant tissues.

There are a couple of important points to remember about removing branches from trees or shrubs. The first is that if the branch is dead it must be cut back to live wood or else no callus will be formed. The second is that all cuts should be made flush with the surface of the tree trunk (Inset A) or back to a bud (Inset B). If short pieces of old stem are left projecting either from a tree trunk or beyond a bud on a branch, they will almost certainly die back and be a source of disease in the future.

The best way to remove a moderate or large branch is to cut it back in several sections, removing one at a time. This reduces the weight of the branch gradually so that when you have to cut the last section out there is no danger of the weight of the branch tearing an unsightly chunk out of the bark of the tree trunk.

AUGUST
TIP LAYERING

Layering is a fairly common method of propagation — one variation of that technique is known as tip layering and is the method by which blackberries, loganberries and other related hybrid berries are propagated.

Many gardeners will have noticed how stems of blackberry plants that come into contact with the soil often put down roots and form new plantlets without any human interference. The gardener ensures that the new plants grow where they are wanted and, by selecting healthy stock for the parent plant, that they are equally free from disease.

The canes used are the new ones that have grown during the course of the spring and summer of this year. By July and August you will find them long and flexible enough to bury their tips in the soil quite easily. As with ordinary layering, some soils, the lighter and more friable ones, are much more suitable than others. Heavy soils can be improved by the addition of some material in which roots will form readily (peat or leaf mould, for instance), or the use of the actual soil can be avoided by sinking a pot into the soil at the appropriate place and filling it with a mixture of peat and coarse sand or potting grit. The pot will need to be at least a five or six inch one

as these layers quickly form a mass of roots.

If you are going to do the layering in the ordinary soil, make a vertical cut in the soil and another at a 45° angle pointing down to the foot of the vertical cut. This is done at the position where you want the layer to be made, and will give you a hole like that shown in Inset A.

The tip of the cane is laid down along the slope and buried in the soil; about four or five inches of soil can be placed on top of the tip and firmed down. If the layer feels loose, peg it down as well to keep it in position, and keep the soil moist so that root growth can proceed quickly and without checks. Bury the tip similarly in the flower pot if you are using that method.

What will happen underground is that the tip will find itself confronted with the wall made by your first vertical cut, be unable to make any further extension growth and will start to develop a root system. It will finally send out a vigorous new young shoot growing upwards from the end of the layer (Inset B).

The rooting should take place during the course of this autumn but the new plant is best left undisturbed through the winter. By late winter or early spring it will be ready for detaching from the parent cane: cut it off leaving a 'handle' of some eight to ten inches of old cane, dig out the new plant and replant it in its permanent position as soon as possible.

The old cane can then be tied back into its position on the wire, trellis or whatever framework you are using and will bear its fruit in the usual way later in the season.

AUGUST
ONIONS

August is a busy month in the onion grower's calendar involving as it does the first stage in the harvesting of this year's crop and, for some of those gardeners who raise their own plants from seed, the sowing of next year's.

For onion harvesting the important point is to get the bulbs fully ripe because only then will they last well in storage. The plants themselves will give some indication of the approach of harvesting time when the foliage turns brown, shrivels and starts falling over. Occasional plants with thicker necks may be found whose foliage refuses to bend over — these will not make such good keepers and should therefore be used first.

When the onion foliage is definitely starting to die back, loosen the roots of the plants with a fork, partially lifting them at the same time (Inset A) — you will feel the roots loosening if you give a slight pull when the fork is underneath the plant concerned. Don't pull the plant right out of the ground at this stage, just leave it on the soil surface to continue ripening. The ripening process will have been helped by loosening the roots. The time when the foliage dies back will vary from place to place and according to the season but may be as early as mid July in a dry year in the South but can be well into the latter part of August in heavy soils in cooler areas.

With the foliage completely shrivelled complete the lifting of the bulbs by removing them from the soil. Leave them lying on the surface for a few days with what remains of the roots in full sunshine so that they too shrivel up. After this stage the bulbs must be thoroughly dried before storage. I like to dry them outdoors in the sun and air. A wire-netting tray with the netting kept clear of the ground (Inset B) is useful for this job. The onions can be moved easily and the air can circulate all around each bulb.

When the onions are completely dry they can be stored in a cool dry spot either on ropes or in old nylon stockings or any netting bags. With a good circulation of air and provided the bulbs were well-ripened to start with they should store quite satisfactorily until next spring. Any bulbs which are damaged in any way or disease affected must be kept separate from the sound ones.

Although most gardeners who grow their onions from seed prefer a winter or spring sowing, some prefer to sow some seed in August to produce an early crop the following year. Two distinct types of onion are involved — Japanese onions are sown in early August in the North, the middle of the month in the South, and are thinned out but *not* transplanted in the spring to mature in June and July. These varieties give the earliest crops of all. Ordinary onions of selected varieties such as Solidity are sown any time in August and then transplanted to their final positions in March. They will give large bulbs and a relatively early crop next summer.

AUGUST
LEAF CUTTINGS

Although only a limited number of plants can be propagated by them, leaf cuttings provide an interesting way of increasing one's stock of African violets, streptocarpus, certain peperomias, Begonia rex and sansevieria.

The cuttings from all of these are classified as leaf cuttings but the methods are not the same for each one. With the African violet and peperomia, leaf-stem cuttings would be a more accurate description as the leaves are detached from the parent plant with the stem attached, the stem being pushed into the cuttings compost (Inset A) so that the bottom of the leaf is just about level with the compost surface. Eventually after the cutting has rooted new leaves will appear by the old stem and the new plantlet will be ready for potting on.

The streptocarpus (Cape primrose) has longish leaves not unlike those of the ordinary primrose, although the two are not related. One mature leaf is all you will need for propagation. With a razor blade or sharp knife two cuts are made the length of the leaf on both sides of the mid-rib which can then be thrown away. The sections of leaf you are left with are then inserted vertically into the cuttings compost with the cut edge downwards to a depth that's just sufficient to hold the leaf section in a vertical position (Inset B). New plantlets will arise from many of the severed leaf veins.

The leaf veins are also involved when leaf cuttings of Begonia rex are taken. This begonia is the one with large heart-shaped leaves which have a variety of different markings and colourings. Take a leaf, turn it upside down and, using a sharp knife or razor blade again, make cuts across the leaf veins. Turn the leaf over again, and lay it flat on the compost. It can be held down by hairpins pushed through the leaf (Inset C) or even by pebbles resting on it. Inset C also shows another method which can be used with Begonia rex: that is to chop up the leaf into 1 inch square sections which are laid flat on the compost. With the first method new plantlets should appear from the points where the veins have been cut; the same applies to the second, only this time it will be from a vein at the edge of the chopped-up leaf section.

With sansevieria (mother-in-law's tongue) the leaf is cut into 2-3 inch sections, inserted upright into the compost to a depth sufficient to hold the cuttings in position. The new plants arising from the base of these cuttings will have a mottled green marking, not the yellow banding of the parent plant.

The compost for all leaf cuttings should be a peat/sand mixture, i.e. a combination of two parts sand to one part peat. New plantlets forming in it will soon need potting on because it's entirely without nutrient value. All leaf cuttings appreciate a close, humid, shaded atmosphere, and a temperature sustained at between 60-70°F.

AUGUST
CYCLAMEN

The cyclamen (Cyclamen persicum) is deservedly one of the most popular of all plants for house and greenhouse culture, but it's also one of the more expensive ones. So it makes sense to grow on mature corms from year to year and to raise any new plants that may be required from seed.

In fact, even raising plants from seed isn't cheap as most packets contain only 10-15 seeds, so it's advisable to sow the seeds individually in the trays of John Innes seed compost (Inset A). Cover them with a very light layer of compost and maintain a temperature of 60-65°F until they germinate, which will probably be at least four to five weeks after sowing.

The compost can be kept sufficiently moist by standing the seed-trays on trays of sand or gravel which should be watered occasionally, thus allowing the moisture to soak up into the compost. The seed-trays should be covered with glass and newspaper in the usual way until germination. Leave the seedlings to grow on until the two-leaf stage and then prick them out (Inset B) into boxes of John Innes No. 1. There they should stay until the foliage of the seedlings starts to meet — transfer them then to 3 inch pots of John Innes No. 2 and, later, to 5 inch pots of the same compost.

This growing process will occupy a lengthy period of time and the mature plant (Inset C) will not be ready until some time around the Christmas of next year; meanwhile during this winter aim to keep the seedlings growing in a temperature of 50-60°F — regard 48°F as the absolute minimum.

If you haven't done so already, now is the time to start into growth last year's corms kept dry during the summer months. The corm is removed from its old compost and pressed lightly into the surface of John Innes No. 2 in a 5 inch pot so that half the corm remains exposed. The compost is given a little water and the pot is put in a shady spot in a frame or greenhouse.

Water should continue to be given sparingly until the foliage begins to develop, when the supply may be slightly increased, but prevent any water going on to the corm itself as this may start it rotting. Keep the plants growing in a fairly dry, cool (50°F) atmosphere, and, when the flower buds begin to show, give them fortnightly feeds of a weak liquid fertiliser. This will help to strengthen their flowering season.

One other point worth mentioning about cyclamen is that ailing plants often respond well to a steam bath — a block of wood or inverted clay pot is put at the bottom of a bucket and boiling water poured in to some point *below* the top of the wood or pot. The cyclamen pot is then stood on the object in the bucket for ten minutes and the steam rising around the leaves should cause drooping foliage to perk up again.

AUGUST
HEDGES

Apart from privet and Lonicera nitida, which constantly seem to be demanding attention, most mature hedges need only be clipped once a year. August and September are the best months for this job as by this time virtually all of the annual growth will have been made and the hedges will thus retain their cut shape through the winter months.

I say mature hedges because rather different principles apply to newly-planted ones. Although no doubt they're wanted to provide an effective screen as quickly as possible, if they're allowed to grow too quickly the height they gain will be at the expense of solidity at the base. By keeping the top growth somewhat restricted in the early stages, you will be encouraging the lower branches to provide thick cover at the base of the hedge. When that has been achieved the hedge can be allowed to grow to the desired height.

During the second year, when the young plants are really well established, it pays to clip them over three or four times during the course of the summer from May onwards. That will ensure that you obtain really bushy specimens. Each clipping only needs to be a light one but will nevertheless help to stimulate new buds into growth on every branch tipped.

If you have a hedge which has become gappy at the base or is overgrown or is in some other way in need of renovation late March is the time to deal with it. Most hedging subjects can then be cut back into the old wood so that they will make new growth from lower down to fill gaps, or they can be cut back hard to make the hedge a more manageable shape. But, with the exception of yew, this does *not* apply to conifers. They will not break from old wood so they must be carefully managed every year to keep them to their desired shape.

This question of shaping a hedge is very much a matter of individual taste; some prefer rounded tops (Inset A), some flat ones (Inset B). It should be noticed, as both the insets show, that a hedge should never be wider at the top than it is at the base. Straight sides or ones tapering slightly towards the top not only look better but they will make the top much easier to cut.

When it comes to the actual cutting start with the sides so that the top will be that much more accessible when you come to do it. Although it might seem obvious, do use steps that are both secure and high enough to be able to cut the top while looking down on it. This makes it much easier to clip it to the right shape.

Keep a supply of oil and a well-oiled rag close at hand while clipping with shears or using an electric trimmer. Both function much better if kept well-oiled. Make sure the blades

of the shears are kept nice and sharp. Otherwise, not only is cutting made much more difficult but the blunt edges of the blades will tend to bruise the stems of the hedging plants instead of making a clean cut.

AUGUST
GERANIUM CUTTINGS

Although the zonal pelargoniums (or geraniums, as we usually call them) of our summer bedding schemes can be lifted in October and over-wintered in the greenhouse, it's usually much easier to obtain a supply of plants for next year by taking cuttings. It's worth the little effort required because cuttings taken at this time of year root easily and to buy replacement plants or even geranium seed has become a very expensive business.

Select non-flowering side-shoots (2½-3 inches long) that are sturdy-looking and short-jointed. Cut them out cleanly with a knife. Remove the lower leaves and the leaf stipules (Inset A) so that the plant does not have to support too much foliage while its roots are developing. Next make a neat, sharp cut through the shoot immediately below a leaf joint (Inset B) so that you are left with a cutting with just a pair of leaves at the apex. Sometimes you can also find new shoots arising from the base of the plant that it is possible to detach with a portion of root attached. Not surprisingly these make very easy cuttings.

At this stage it is advisable to leave the cuttings for an hour or so out of direct sunlight to allow a skin to form over the surface of the cut and hence prevent the possibility of the stem rotting when it is put into the pot.

The compost in which the cuttings are inserted can either be a proprietary cuttings one or a peat and grit mixture. Fill the pot, water the compost and allow any excess liquid to drain away. Insert the cuttings firmly around the outer rim of the pot, making sure the foliage is clear of the compost.

There is no need to use hormone-rooting powder with geranium cuttings, neither is there any need to enclose them in a polythene bag or put them in a propagator. Geraniums thrive in surprisingly dry conditions and the compost that the cuttings are rooting in can be allowed to stay on the dry side, although it should not be permitted to dry out altogether.

Keep the cuttings in a temperature of 60-65°F and rooting should take place within a month. When the cuttings start to grow will give you an indication of when this has happened. Pot the rooted cuttings individually into 3½ inch pots of John Innes No. 1 or its equivalent, using very little water to settle them in.

Geranium cuttings often need no stopping, but if you have any very long and leggy specimens, it will help to pinch the tops out. Because the plants are sensitive to cold temperatures it is usually easier to keep them in the house during the winter, not the greenhouse. Keep them above 45°F if possible, watering merely to keep the foliage from wilting, and in conditions where they get the maximum possible light.

AUGUST
SCHIZANTHUS

Sometimes known as the Butterfly Flower or Poor Man's Orchid, the Schizanthus is one of the easiest of flowers to raise for a fine display of blossom in the spring greenhouse. Each plant will produce a mass of beautifully marked flowers, which come in a wide range of shades, tending almost to conceal the delicate fernlike foliage. Although the Schizanthus is sometimes grown as a half-hardy annual for summer bedding, it is as a cool greenhouse plant that seeds are sown in late August and the first weeks of September.

One thing that used to discourage gardeners from growing Schizanthus was that to create magnificent bushy specimens, the plants had to be stopped several times. Nowadays there are still some of these large (2-4 ft.) varieties available but we also have a choice of two compact, bushy types which need no stopping and yet lack for nothing in flower colouring or quality. Hit Parade (Inset A) grows to a height of about 12 inches while Star Parade (Inset C) is even more suitable where space is at a premium for it only reaches 10 inches. Both can be relied upon to cover themselves with blossom in spring and early summer next year. Schizanthus are very easily raised from seed. The seeds are sown under glass —

either a greenhouse or cold frame — and the seedlings pricked out into 2½ or 3 inch pots when they are big enough to handle (Inset B). They are potted on as they grow with Hit Parade eventually needing a 5 inch pot while Star Parade will make do with a 4 inch one. Some of the other larger varieties need up to 7 or 8 inch pots, but in general one can control the size of the plant by the size of pot one chooses to grow it in.

Schizanthus do not need high winter temperatures — just keep them from being frosted. They do best in a cool atmosphere where there's sufficient light to prevent them becoming drawn. When grown in low temperatures they will develop into strong and sturdy plants but care must be taken to prevent them being overwatered. Likewise adequate ventilation is essential or else there may be attacks of botrytis (grey mould) in cool, damp, uncirculating air.

If the plants are grown in less than perfect light and do show signs of becoming long and leggy, pinching out the top of the main stem and, later, the tips of the side shoots, should help to produce a bushy specimen. If you grow the very large varieties you will need a few canes pushed in around the sides of the pots to support the extremely vigorous top growth. Both Hit Parade and Star Parade will stand up unsupported, provided they are bushy plants.

Like cinerarias, the plants will stay in bloom a lot longer when kept in really cool conditions (i.e. not indoors, or at least not in a heated room). You may find them attacked by greenfly or whitefly — spray them with an insecticide containing permethrin to kill these pests.

AUGUST
PREPARING A LAWN SITE

A lawn is one of the features of a garden most often taken for granted, yet for it to give many years of "trouble-free service" the seed must be sown or the turf laid on a site that's been thoroughly prepared beforehand.

For gardeners on low-lying or heavy soils the first problem to be considered is that of drainage; and although a network of drain tiles or pipes would be the ideal solution, a less costly one is to incorporate a 6 inch layer of material such as ashes, clinker or gravel under a 6 inch layer of topsoil.

On some sites levelling may be necessary, or at least the shifting of a certain amount of soil to achieve an even gradient on a sloping plot. The most important thing to remember with such earthworks is that when the site is finally levelled the top layer must be of topsoil, not subsoil brought to the top.

This may involve removing the topsoil, levelling the subsoil and replacing the topsoil again. An effective method of levelling is with wooden pegs driven into the ground to the required height of the eventual lawn surface — their depth in the ground being checked by means of a straight-edged board and a spirit level.

As the grass is going to be growing on the same site for many years, the soil itself must be made as fertile as possible prior to sowing. For heavy soils this may involve the incorporation of sand or rotted organic material; for light soils the organic material or peat will be of great advantage.

Any of these materials should be dug in at the same time as the whole site is being dug over to a depth of 6-9 inches. At this stage any large stones should be removed, together with all weeds plus their roots, especially if they are perennial ones.

After digging, the soil surface will be fairly rough and one simple way of breaking up the lumps of earth is by trampling over the site (Inset A). A roller will obviously do the same job if you possess one, but too heavy a roller can over-compact the soil. Obviously any such operations, whether by trampling or using a roller, should be done when the soil is dry.

At this stage a raking (Inset B) will help still further to reduce the soil to a fine tilth. This raking will to some extent help to produce an even surface, but if the soil is given, say, a week or two to settle further of its own accord, then the treading and raking process can be effectively repeated, bringing the soil surface to a fine even tilth than won't develop hollows during the months to come.

When the final raking is to be done, a light dressing (Inset C) of a general fertiliser such as

Growmore can be incorporated with the rake. This should help the seedlings to become established rapidly after sowing, which is a topic dealt with as one of the September subjects.

PLANT YOUR BULBS EARLY FOR CHRISTMAS

Mother Nature still works the miracles in gardening, but sometimes nowadays Man can achieve the seemingly impossible.

Bulbs, for instance, can be made to bloom when *we* want them. This means that we can have a perfect floral display in our homes over Christmas from bulbs planted during the next few weeks.

For sweet scent and absolute beauty the hyacinths have few equals. There are several magnificent colours to brighten any room. You can also have daffodils in flower in dark December. Such a show of gold and white fills one with optimism that perhaps spring will be a little earlier next year. And what about some tulips? There are pink, yellow and scarlet varieties which do more for a room than any Christmas decorations.

The bulbs which will bloom in late December have been specially treated, or "prepared", as the growers call the process and it is "prepared bulbs" which you should look out for. Often the suitable varieties are simply marked (P).

This is your assurance that the bulbs will flower at Christmas — provided, of course, that you follow a rigid schedule of planting and after-care.

Hyacinths

Let us start with hyacinths which should be planted within the next couple of weeks. For the bulbs need a 10-week period in a cool, dark spot where the temperature is between 45°F and 50°F if they are to flower properly.

The bulbs themselves should be planted in bowls at least 5 in. deep, containing moist bulb fibre. The bulbs should be placed so that they are neither touching one another nor the sides of the bowl.

My recommendations are: Ann Mary (rose pink), Bismarck (light blue), John Bos (rose red), L'Innocence (pure white) and Ostara (navy blue).

If you have a garden proper, the best place for the bulbs to spend their 10-week cool phase is outdoors in a special "plunge bed". This is made by digging a trench at least the depth of your spade in a convenient shady spot.

The bowls are then wrapped in several thicknesses of newspaper and placed in the bottom of the trench. The trench should then be covered with moist peat, or ordinary soil, provided that it is not too clayey.

If you have no garden, the wrapped bowls can be placed in a deep container outdoors, perhaps in a garage or on a balcony and covered with at least 6 in. of moist peat.

The bulbs will not require any further attention until the middle of November (or 10 weeks after planting) when they should be taken indoors, watered and placed in a dark cupboard where the temperature is 65°F to 70°F. The bulbs should remain in the dark until the flower bud stands well out of the neck of the bulb. Once this stage has been completed, move the bowls of bulbs into a room, but keep them away from the window and drape the bowls with newspaper for four days. The subdued light will help the flower stems to lengthen.

The hyacinths can then be moved into full light at a temperature of about 65°F. Keep the compost just moist, not soaking, and give the bulbs a little houseplant fertiliser once a week to improve the flowers.

When the hyacinths are in full bloom, just a few days before Christmas, reduce the amount of water given to make the flowers last longer. Turn the bowls every day so that the flowers receive equal light and grow with straight stems.

Should a bulb produce more than one

flower, it is best to cut away the weaker one at the base to ensure a more even display.

Tulips

Tulips are just as easy to grow, but they need a longer spell in the dark if they are to be successful.

The brown outer skins of the bulbs should be peeled off to encourage vigorous rooting. Then the bulbs should be planted by the middle of September in pots or bowls, containing moist potting compost or bulb fibre, so that half of each bulb is exposed and its flat side is towards the outside of the container.

A 6 in.-wide pot will take six to eight bulbs easily and provide a pleasing show. My recommendations are: Brilliant Star Maximus (bright red), Christmas Marvel (rosy carmine), and Marshal Joffre (yellow).

The tulips need exactly the same treatment as the hyacinths, except that they should be left in the "plunge bed" until December 1.

At the beginning of that month the bulbs should be brought indoors, watered and placed in a dark cupboard at a temperature of about 60°F for 10 days until their stems have grown a further 2 in.

At this point the bowls can be moved into the light and covered with newspaper for a few days to encourage the flower stems to lengthen.

Tulips, despite our deadline, should never be hurried. If allowed to grow slowly, we can still have them bang on target, and the flowers will last much longer.

Avoid excessive heat and draughts. At the final stage the container should be kept watered and in a light position at a temperature of no more than 70°F. Turn the bowls every day so that the tulips get even light.

Daffodils

Finally what about some daffodils? Only the "prepared" kind can be made to flower at Christmas. So you have to be very careful with your choice. My recommendations are: Barrett Browning (white and red), Jack Snipe (white and orange yellow) and Tête-a-Tête (buttercup yellow).

The bulbs can either be grown in deep pots with drainage holes using potting compost or in bowls using bulb fibre. In any case the containers should be at least 5 in. deep for best results.

The bulbs themselves are planted in exactly the same way as hyacinth bulbs. As with hyacinths and tulips the timetable is vital. Planting should be done in the first week of October, and the containers should be placed in the "plunge bed" until December 1.

At the begining of that month the daffodils in their bowls should be watered and moved to

a room where the temperature is about 60°F. Drape the container with newspaper for four days to encourage the flower stems to lengthen.

On December 5 move the containers to a well-lit, *cooler* position where the temperature is between 50°F and 55°F. The daffodils should be kept at this temperature and given plenty of water and I can promise that you will have them in full bloom by Christmas.

A higher temperature will be tolerated once the bulbs are flowering, but do remember that daffodils last longer in a cool room than in a warm one.

The beauty of a bulb is the way that it contains so much joy and happiness within its unimposing shell. Now that you have the key to unlock that treasure chest, why not get yourself some hyacinths, tulips, and daffodils? Rarely will a few pounds have been better spent.

SEPTEMBER
LETTUCE

As a salad plant, lettuce is often thought of as being suitable only for summer cultivation, yet in reality some lettuces are extremly hardy, quite capable of standing the winter weather with only minimal protection. These plants, and it is only *some* varieties that are suitable, are generally grown from seed sown in September to provide next year's earliest crop, i.e. a hearted lettuce in April or May.

Of the varieties available, the best of the cabbage lettuces is probably Valdor (Inset B), with Arctic King as an alternative, while Winter Density (Inset C) is the most suitable of the cos types. These three can in good winters survive outside without any form of protection, but their chances of success will be improved by giving them cloche cover (Inset A) which will also, of course, bring them to maturity that much earlier.

The site should be protected from cold north and east winds and must be one that is well-drained, preferably on a fairly light soil. Fresh manure or compost is the last thing you want, but if the site was manured for a previous crop there will be sufficient goodness left in the soil. Certainly, no nitrogenous fertiliser should be used at this time of year, its use being withheld until the plants begin to grow again next spring

when it should prove very effective. Alternatively, hoe in a dressing of Growmore at 2 oz per square yard in early March.

The seeds are sown in the normal way for lettuces: very shallow drills, the drills being at 12 inch intervals if more than one row is required. Thin out the seedlings to two to three inches apart first of all, and then later to five or six inches. The final thinning (9-12 ins.) is best left until the early spring to allow for winter casualties. (Winter Density, I should mention, is a very compact lettuce and needs a final spacing of only six inches.) The thinnings can be transplanted if extra plants are required. Keep a watch out for slugs and put down slug pellets at the first sign of any damage. Hoe between the rows once or twice in the winter months to keep the soil friable and the weeds down.

Finally, some ideas for those gardeners with greenhouses who want to try some lettuce under glass. If you have any heat in the house, Dandie is a useful variety to try — it can be sown from August until November. In unheated greenhouses and frames Kloek is a worthwhile cultivar but it should not be sown until the second week of October to mature at the end of March.

Varieties grown under glass are best raised from seedlings grown in seed trays. They are planted out into a greenhouse bed 8-10 inches apart when a couple of inches high. At this

stage they need very careful watering because the soil must be kept damp but the foliage of the seedlings should be kept dry. They will need ample moisture, however, when coming to maturity.

SEPTEMBER
PLANTING BULBS OUTDOORS

Winter and spring flowering bulbs are especially welcome, as they provide colour in the garden at a time when it's liable to be at its barest. For these bulbs to do well next year, some of them need to be planted in September.

Before discussing possible planting positions, it is as well to remember that the food that will enable a bulb to flower the following year is being produced by the leaves after the bulb has flowered — i.e., however unsightly they may look, the leaves should be left to die down in situ.

That is obviously a factor to consider if you're thinking of planting in lawns or borders. One way to avoid the problem is to "naturalise" the bulbs by planting them in grassy orchards or groups of shrubs, or limiting them to one corner of the lawn. Naturalised bulbs should look informal, and the traditional way of scattering a handful of them and planting them where they land is still the best way to achieve a natural-looking drift. Ideally, each drift should consist of bulbs of the same variety, so that they're all in flower at the same time.

Turning to methods of planting, the bulb-planter (Inset B) is a useful tool for grassy areas. Failing that, I like to make an H-shaped cut (Inset A), roll back the turf, do the planting and fold the turf back into position. For smaller bulbs in grass, 3-4 inch deep holes made with a crowbar are quite adequate, while for the border the trowel is the best tool.

Of the bulbs suitable for planting in grass, narcissi and daffodils are probably the most popular. Try planting them where they can be seen from the house, in ground that has been prepared with well-rotted manure or compost mixed with some leafmould. Then fork in a dressing of bonemeal at 2oz. per square yard. Plant the bulbs six to eight inches apart, because with proper treatment they will increase from year to year.

Planting depth is a subject on which it's difficult to be specific, but in general, remember the larger the bulb, the deeper the hole; and the heavier the soil, the shallower the hole (in fact, on heavy soils try setting the bulbs on sand and filling the hole with it). I would recommend covering the larger bulbs with four inches of soil, the smaller ones with two to three inches.

Other attractive bulbs to be planted now include the Chionodoxa and Scilla sibirica. Both of these make small plants (about 6ins.) and as such are useful for the rockery. They have bright blue flowers and appreciate a sunny position. Plant about 2 ins. deep and you'll find they soon increase from offsets and self-seeding. These two should come into flower in March — even earlier are the familiar white snowdrops and the Eranthis (winter aconite), with its cup-shaped yellow flowers, both of which should be planted in large groups to achieve the best effect. Again, set the bulbs about 2ins. deep and about 3ins. apart.

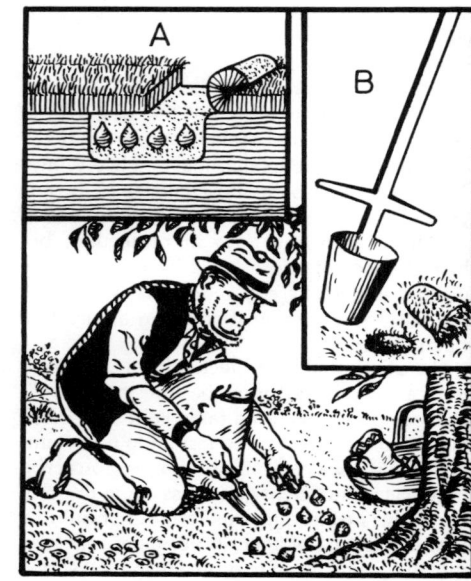

SEPTEMBER
A NEW LAWN
FROM SEED

If you want to make a new lawn and you've prepared the site as shown in the August article you must now decide whether it's to be grown from seed or created by laying turves. The latter method has obvious attractions for getting the grass established quickly, but it is considerably more expensive than growing from seed.

If seed is your choice, the middle of September is a good time for sowing, so you must decide about the type of seed mixture you want. Briefly, the more you pay the finer the quality of grasses you buy, but the qualities of the grass do not necessarily include that of durability in a much-used lawn. The luxury grasses (the bents and fescues) are subject to invasion by annual meadow grass and perennial ryegrass, etc. in any case, so you may decide to compromise and buy one of the cheaper seed mixtures which will give you a lawn more suited to hard wear, but which will also require more frequent mowing due to the more vigorous growths of the grasses in it.

Whatever seed you do choose, make sure that the site is in the best possible condition to be sown on — i.e. absolutely flat and with a fine tilth on soil that's well settled. Ideal sowing conditions require the soil to be dry on top, but with some moisture down below and as near a windless day as possible.

The main problem with sowing grass seed is to achieve even distribution. There are various ways of doing this. For instance, the lawn can be divided into strips a yard apart in each direction (Inset A) so that the whole area consists of marked out square yards. Then the sowing rate of 1½-2ozs seed per sq.yd. is quite easily managed.

Alternatively, divide the total amount of seed into two equal parts (you may care to add some sand to the mixture (Inset B) to give greater bulk and make distribution even easier) and sow half the mixture over the whole site in one direction (east-west, say). Then cover the whole site again with the other half of the mixture moving from north to south this time.

After sowing the seed, rake it in lightly but don't worry about having all the seed covered by earth. Bury it too deep and it won't germinate properly, while if it is all left on the surface it will probably prove a great attraction to the birds (although you can buy seed treated with a bird repellent). If birds do become a problem, black cotton wound round sticks about three inches high (Inset C) should help to keep them off.

Finally, a word about the treatment required during the early days of a new lawn — the seedlings should be visible within a fortnight and when they're two inches high they will be ready for their first cut. This should never be a drastic operation: set the mower blades (which should be really sharp) as high as they'll go so as just to remove the tops of the grass seedlings. The cutting height can be gradually reduced at subsequent mowings.

113

SEPTEMBER
ROSE CUTTINGS

Although not all roses are suitable for propagation from cuttings, the ones that can be successfully raised this way offer the gardener a cheap and easy way of increasing his stock.

The problem, of course, is that most of the roses bought from nurserymen are budded on to a rootstock which gives the bush its vigour. Cuttings taken from these bushes will be growing on their own roots, not the roots of the original rootstock, and might well disappoint in terms of bush size, flower production, etc., although they will certainly be free of the risk of suckering.

Therefore, although there is no harm in trying to propagate any rose from cuttings, the best chances of success come from those which either grow very vigorously in any case — the most rampant of the floribundas; climbers and ramblers — or the species roses and the closely related "shrub" varieties.

Cuttings should be taken from ripe wood of this year's growth and should eventually look like the one shown in Inset A. This will involve removing the unripe tip of the stem to just above a bud and either trimming the heel of older wood smooth or, if there is no heel of older wood, making a smooth cut at the base of the cutting just below a bud. The cutting, which should be about nine inches long and about a pencil's thickness, should be left with its two upper leaves, the lower ones being removed. Remove any thorns from the wood — these should come away easily if the wood is sufficiently ripe.

Having moistened the base of the cutting, dip it in hormone rooting powder (Inset B) before inserting it into the trench (Inset C). The trench should be in a sheltered and partially shaded spot and of a depth that will allow the lower leaf of the cutting to be just above the level of the soil.

The cuttings are placed against the vertical wall of the trench some 5-6 inches apart with their bases in a layer of coarse sand. The trench is then filled in almost to the top, incorporating some moist peat with the earth. By leaving this slight hollow at the top of the trench, the very necessary watering will be made easier. Water should always be given if there is any danger of the cuttings drying out.

Having firmed the soil around the cuttings and completed the watering, they can then be left until October or November of next year when those that have taken will be ready to be moved to their final quarters.

The earth around the cuttings will probably need firming again in the spring. Winter frosts will have loosened the soil. It is very important to have the soil firm so that the rooting portion of the cutting is always in contact with it. Continue watering next spring and summer in any dry spells and remove any flower buds that appear.

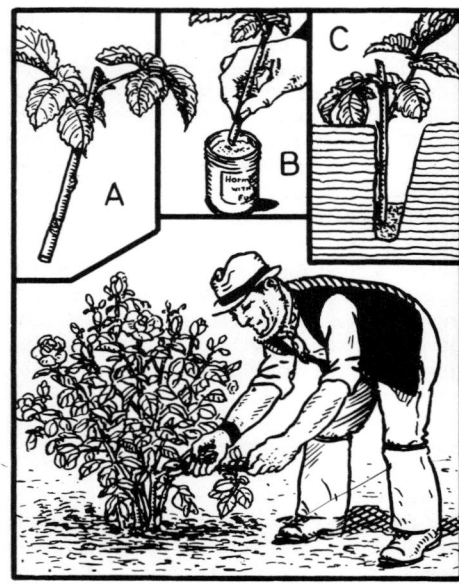

SEPTEMBER
PLANTING OUT
SPRING BEDDING

As summer bedding plants begin to die down it's a good idea to replace them as soon as possible with their spring-flowering successors such as wallflowers, pansies and violas, polyanthus, sweet williams, etc. This gives the newly set-out plants as long as possible to become established before the winter.

Wallflowers are plants for sunny spots and should be planted out about twelve to fifteen inches apart. Like many other cruciferous plants they do especially well if a little lime is applied to the soil before planting out. If you have some spare plants and an unheated greenhouse you can pot them up in five inch pots, leave them in a frame until early next year and then bring them into the greenhouse, where they will provide both scent and colour in the early spring.

Polyanthus and primroses will flower satisfactorily in full sun but the display will not last nearly as well as on those plants in some degree of shade. Where they are to be planted in a relatively sunny spot it is advisable to make sure the soil is moisture retentive. This can be done easily enough by incorporating some peat in the area where the roots are going to be. Polyanthus, with their

tremendous range of colours, make a good plant for troughs. If the removal of summer bedding leaves the soil level a bit low, top the troughs up with peat, give a dressing of Growmore and you will have a long-lasting display of colour in the spring.

Primroses and polyanthus are very easy to propagate by division and it's not too late in the year to do it now, although the resulting plants will not be as big as those divided after flowering has finished. The plants certainly benefit from being divided occasionally and you can produce very large numbers of new plants this way. Lift the plants to be divided with all their roots, using a fork, and break them up by hand. Each new plantlet will need a piece of the pink-shaded crown and a few roots (Inset A) but they will grow into new plants even if they haven't any leaves.

Pansies and violas are often treated as summer bedding and raised from spring-sown seed but you get much better plants from a June or July sowing. These are planted out at this time of year and will give a magnificent display next spring. Like polyanthus, they do best in a cool, moist soil and not in very hot, sunny spots. Plant them soon and they will provide you with occasional flowers during the winter months before their main flowering period in the spring.

Sweet Williams (Inset B) bring us back to the sun-loving category of plants. Lift the seedlings

with as much earth on the roots as possible (this is much easier if the soil is moist) and plant them out into their final quarters leaving about 1 ft. between each plant. These are not, strictly speaking, spring-flowering but will be a mass of bloom in June and July next year.

SEPTEMBER
CROCUSES

Among those bulbs that give us some really bright colours early in the new year are crocuses (Inset A). Being both small and familiar, they can easily be taken for granted; but they make a very worthwhile investment because they are still relatively inexpensive and are very obliging in their habit of spreading themselves by self-seeding.

When you buy the bulbs you may well find those on offer described as 'botanical' or 'large-flowered'. Basically, the earliest flowering crocuses are species or 'botanical' ones — these can often be seen in bloom in February, continuing into March. They are just as colourful but not quite as big as the Dutch hybrids, which are the 'large-flowering' varieties in bloom during March and April.

Like all of our familiar outdoor bulbs crocuses are very easy to grow — they are totally hardy and the only likely cause of trouble is poorly drained soil. Their size makes them much more effective when planted in groups: the groups can be at the front of borders, on the rockery, between paving stones, alongside paths or drives, around shrubs or trees or even underneath deciduous ones, in outdoor containers, etc. In fact, anywhere in full sun or partial shade and

where the foliage will be able to die down naturally after flowering. I mention that because it means that if they are grown in lawns, where they are admittedly extremely attractive, the grass around them cannot be cut until May or June.

September and early October are the best times for planting them — set them two inches deep and the same distance apart in friable well-drained soil. If the soil is on the heavy side you can improve its texture by working in generous quantities of sand or grit and leafmould or peat. Even on lighter soils the leafmould or peat would prove a very good rooting medium for the bulbs. For those gardeners not already familiar with it, the leaf of a crocus is just like a blade of grass but with a white line down its centre (Inset B): remember that so that you don't accidentally uproot all the self-sown seedlings that crop up in the garden after flowering next spring.

Crocuses also make good subjects for pots for indoor display in the early part of the New Year. Using pots with drainage holes and a good potting compost put the bulbs 1-2 inches deep and the same distance apart (Inset C). The pots are plunged into the ground outdoors for three months in a cool part of the garden and then, when they should have developed a good root system, brought indoors to a cool part of the house (50-55°F). Shade them from direct sunlight for at least

their first week inside and give them a regular supply of water, even after they've finished flowering. The bulbs can later be replanted in the garden.

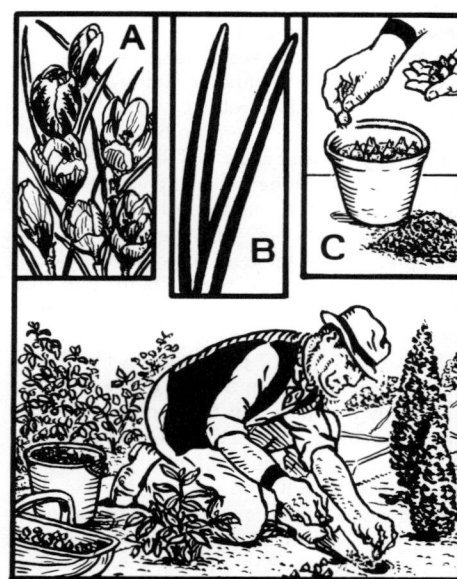

SEPTEMBER
FRUIT PICKING AND STORING

Apples and pears of different varieties and in different parts of the country will obviously ripen at widely differing times; picking them, therefore, is not something that can be done by the calendar. The colouring of the fruit and the appearance of windfalls on the ground are useful pointers, but the best test of ripeness is to lift the fruit in the palm of the hand and give it a slight twist. If it parts easily from the spur you can be sure the fruit is ready for picking.

Not all of the fruit on the tree will ripen at the same time, so be prepared to make two or three pickings. Fruits on the top and sides of the tree are likely to ripen before those in the middle. Pears, especially, bruise very easily, so pick them gently, using the palm of the hand rather than between finger and thumb; and remember that both apples and pears should be picked with the stalk still attached to the fruit. Never pick apples before they are fully ripe, but some pears of the earlier-ripening cultivars should be picked while still fairly green and hard — they will then ripen while in storage.

As far as storage is concerned, the late-maturing varieties are almost always the ones that will store best although mid-season apples will keep for a couple of months. Apples and pears need slightly different conditions, but there are points that apply to both of them: try to keep different varieties separated, and store the individual fruits so that they are not touching one another. Wooden trays are ideal — those whitewood boxes with corner posts that are to be seen in greengrocers' shops are very useful. They can be stacked easily and allow air to circulate around the fruits.

To lengthen the storage life of apples, they can be individually wrapped in squared pieces of oiled paper sold for the purpose (Inset A). If you cannot get hold of these you can use pieces of newspaper instead. Both of these have the added benefit of helping to prevent any rot spreading from fruit to fruit. Apples appreciate a moist atmosphere without which their skins tend to shrivel. The ideal storage temperature is just below 40°F and although most gardeners can't meet this requirement, the nearer you get to it, the longer will be the storage life of the fruit.

Pears, on the other hand, like a dry atmosphere and should not be wrapped at all (Inset B). Being unwrapped means that they can be easily inspected, which is necessary to make sure you get them when they're at their best. Again, their ideal storage temperature (just above freezing point) is impracticably low, but keep them as cool as possible and, for their final ripening, bring them into the warmth of the house a couple of days before their intended use.

A final word of warning — take care not to store the fruit near containers of petrol or paraffin, creosote, paint, etc., or anything with a strong smell. Any of these can ruin the fruit you've carefully put into storage.

SEPTEMBER
LAWN REPAIRS

Because September and early October usually offer a combination of reasonably high soil temperatures and adequate moisture they make a good time to carry out "repair" jobs on the lawn: mending broken edges, eliminating bumps and hollows, reseeding or returfing bare patches, etc. The moisture and relative warmth enable the grass to make a quick recovery before the onset of winter.

Bare patches may be due to constant wear, the elimination of weeds or coarse grasses, cutting too close over bumps with the mower, etc. Once the cause of the trouble has been decided on and put right, the grass can be made to grow again either by putting in fresh turves over the affected area or by sowing fresh seed. For the former method remove a square of turf that includes the bare patch and loosen the soil underneath. Replace with fresh turves that have been cut to fill the square and fill in the cracks with sifted soil.

Reseeding involves breaking up the soil over the affected area and raking it flat to form a fine tilth for sowing. Grass seed is applied at roughly 1 oz. per sq. yd. and raked over again to cover it. Firming can be done by pressing down with a board after which measures should be taken to prevent the birds removing all the seed — black cotton wound round twigs is one way, a piece of netting draped over the area is another.

Bumps and hollows are other common minor defects in a lawn. Where the hollow is a small one it can be filled up with fine sifted soil or one of the proprietary autumn top dressings (Inset A). For larger hollows and also for bumps make an H-shaped cut in the lawn over the affected spot using a sharp spade or edging iron, push the spade under the turf to loosen it, roll it back (Inset B) and then either add soil to fill a hollow or remove it in the case of a bump. Rake over the soil when this has been done, check that it's level and then roll the turf back into position again, filling any cracks with sifted soil.

Where a broken edge is causing annoyance, it's a good idea to cut a square piece of turf that includes the offending indentation, remove it by putting a sharp spade under it and replace it facing the other way (Inset C), so that the edge of the lawn is made straight but with the hole where the indentation was in the actual lawn. This hole can then be filled with soil and seeded or a suitable piece of turf found that will fill the hole.

If you find shrubs or other perennials have grown to the extent that they impede your progress with the lawnmower because they have grown out over the grass, it's sometimes possible to alter the lawn edge slightly so that the plants are no longer covering the turf. This will save you constantly having to prune back the offending plants and will also give you some spare pieces of turf that might come in handy with other lawn repairs.

SEPTEMBER
PLANTING A HEDGE

Now that new gardens are seemingly getting smaller and smaller, the question of whether to have hedges or not becomes more of a problem. Personally, I think a well-trimmed hedge adds a note of distinction to any garden, but against this it must be said that groups of closely planted shrubs or trees, which is all hedges are, tend to take a lot out of the soil without putting anything back in.

Anyway, if you've been thinking of planting a hedge this is a good time of year to get the job under way. The first consideration must be clearing and preparing the site. Remember that the hedging plants might well be serving their purpose for the next fifty years or so and that the only time you're going to be able to dig the ground is now.

Having decided on the line of the hedge, mark out a strip of ground for it at least a yard wide, preferably a bit wider. Then dig over the land, carefully removing all the perennial weeds plus their roots and at the same time incorporating as much humus-enriching material as you can. This could be well-rotted manure or compost, or peat, perhaps.

Inset A shows the best way of doing this: namely, taking out a trench a spit deep, loosening the soil at the foot of the trench (i.e the second spit) with a fork, then adding the humus and filling in the trench. That way you have the soil easily penetrable to roots, the sub-soil kept in its place and the humus-bearing material in the topsoil which is where you want it.

This prepared ground should be given a week or two to settle and then planting can begin. This is usually done in a straight line down the centre of the dug strip, but if an especially thick hedge is required, the plants may be staggered in parellel lines (Inset B). The plants should be put in firmly and if possible before the middle of October so that they have a chance to establish themselves before the winter. This applies to container-grown specimens still in leaf. Bare root specimens of deciduous plants can be left till a month later — mid-October to mid-November.

Planting distances vary with different specimens but some of the more popular hedging subjects are Lonicera nitida, hawthorn and privet — 12 ins.; beech, holly and box (Buxus sempervirens) — 18 ins.; yew and chamaecyparis (false cypress) — 2 ft.; Leyland cypress — 3 ft.

Next spring keep the ground around the plants free of weeds, give them a dressing of a balanced fertiliser like Growmore and when they seem to be growing away well cut them back so that they quickly develop the bushy shape that will make a solid hedge. This does *not* apply to the conifers (apart from yew) for they will not break from lower down; but all other hedging subjects will need this attention repeatedly in early life so that the final shape of the hedge will be solid right down to the ground level.

SEPTEMBER
STORING VEGETABLES

After all the effort put into raising vegetable crops in the summer it's well worth taking the trouble to ensure they're given ideal storage conditions to make them last as long as possible into the winter.

With potatoes this involves lifting the crop a fortnight after the haulm has either died down or been cut off. As they must be completely dry to be stored, do the lifting on a sunny day with a drying wind if possible. That way the tubers can be dug, laid on a dry surface and turned occasionally until completely dry, and then put away all on the same day. Put them in sacks — the double or treble thickness paper ones are good for the job — and keep them cool but frost-free in a dark place. The darkness is essential to stop them turning green. If any are damaged or show signs of disease keep them separately and use them first.

For onions to store well they must be fully ripened and kept in a dry atmosphere with a good circulation of air. They should be lifted in September and dried off, under cover if the weather is bad outside. If looking for an easy method of storage, have you thought of using old nylon stockings? Hung up as in Inset A with a small hole cut below the knot to allow the onions to be removed, they get plenty of air, can be easily inspected for signs of disease and will occupy a minimum of space.

Like onions, marrows need to be fully ripe to store satisfactorily. This involves leaving them on the plants longer than one normally would — in fact they are left until they have reached their full size, at which point the skin should change colour somewhat and harden. Pick them before the first frosts and store them in a cool room in the house at a temperature of about 50°F. Hanging them up in nets (Inset B) is a good way of keeping them but if that's not practicable just keep them on a shelf so that they're not touching one another.

Storable winter cabbages of the Dutch Winter White type (Hidena, Holland Late Winter, etc.) are best dug up when they mature in November or December to prevent them suffering frost damage. Remove a few of the outer leaves but otherwise leave the plants intact, roots, stem and all. Hanging them in a shed or garage (Inset C) can be quite a good way of utilising storage space that would otherwise be unoccupied.

Of the root vegetables, parsnips are very hardy and can be left in the ground without protection; carrots, too, needn't be lifted but will require some protection with leaves, straw, etc. in cold, frosty weather plus some slug-bait scattered around them if slugs are a problem. Beetroot, turnip and swedes I like to leave outside as long as possible — with the later sowings this means until use, but earlier sowings which are in danger of becoming hard and woody can be lifted, have their tops twisted off and be put into boxes of sand for storage in a frost-proof shed.

RASPBERRIES — SERVE WITH THICK CREAM

Do you have a favourite fruit? What about the greengage with its honeyed, syrupy flavour? Or the peach? The sweet perfume and soft, succulent flesh of a garden peach is magnificent. Perhaps you would prefer a pear with its soft texture and delicious fragrance?

Yet I would be prepared to forgo all such pleasures so long as I could have my raspberries.

Raspberries are by far the best of British high summer and later summer fruits. When it comes to growing raspberries, there is not another country to touch us.

The modern varieties, which you can plant in your garden over the next month or two, yield huge crops of excellent fruit suitable for everything from jam to dessert. A mere 20 plants for instance gives me at least 40 lb. of berries annually.

My perfect fresh raspberries are eaten with a little castor sugar and thick cream.

The remainder of the crop provides superb desserts like raspberry pavlova, a marvellous concoction of meringue, cream and fresh raspberries.

The smaller, and perhaps damaged, fruits are useful for making a raspberry soufflé, or there is the delight of a raspberry fool, which can be flavoured with a tablespoon of cognac.

The modern raspberries are excellent for freezing. Some of mine are fast frozen on trays before being stored in waxed cartons. The raspberries preserved in this way can be used to produce the best of summer desserts in the depth of winter. Think of the thrill of being able to serve perfect "fresh" raspberries at Christmas.

What is left of my raspberry crop is used for jam. And can there be a child, or an adult, who does not like raspberry jam for tea?

I said raspberries were the best of British fruits. To be more precise, Scottish raspberries are unbeatable. Yet even if you do not live in Scotland, you can get first-class crops by growing the Scottish variety Glen Clova.

In fact, in Southern England, unlike in Scotland, Glen Clova will produce its first fruits in the second week in July and will continue to produce an abundance of berries well into August.

In Scotland, Glen Clova normally does not give of its best until August.

The beauty of this variety for impatient gardeners is that it will give a moderate crop the year after planting. Most summer fruiting raspberries keep you waiting for two years before you get a decent crop.

There are good English raspberries too, many of which are also grown with great success in Scotland, Wales and Ireland.

There is the variety Delight, for example, which outyields Glen Clova and which produces very large, although rather soft, well-flavoured fruits. Delight is resistant to certain raspberry viruses which seem to be prevalent in the warmer parts of England. Delight's season is similar to that of Glen Clova.

Then there is Admiral, also a very heavy cropper, which in Southern England produces fruit from the last week of July to September. It is resistant to virus diseases and also to mildew, which can lead to substantial fruit losses. The snag with this variety is that it may not ripen completely in the colder parts of Scotland.

By choosing two varieties and by planting 10 canes (as the plants are called) of each, you can have fresh fruit for two whole months. Twenty canes should cost you no more than a fiver, and you will be able to harvest a crop from them for up to 15 years.

Raspberries will grow well in partial shade, but they are much better in a sunny position with a good circulation of air. The soil does not particularly matter, provided that it does not become waterlogged in winter.

The soil should be prepared by forking it over to remove all perennial weeds. At the same time you can incorporate generous quantities of well-rotted garden compost or moist peat if the soil is poor.

Each raspberry plant should be set in the soil so that its root system is about 3 in. deep. The plants themselves should be spaced 15 in. to 18 in. apart in a single row.

Subsequent rows should be 4 ft. to 6 ft. apart. The new varieties produce very vigorous canes which will benefit from whatever space you can give them.

The plants will need wires for support once they have begun to produce new canes. I have oak posts about 6 ft. apart with two single, thick galvanised wires at 3 ft. and 5 ft. from the ground. All the canes are lightly tied to the wires as it becomes necessary.

Once the plants have been put into the ground, they should be cut down to 12 in. if this has not been done for you already by the nursery. No further major pruning will be required until the second year after planting.

The routine with the summer fruiting raspberries is to cut away all the old canes once they have finished producing fruit. Then tie up to six of the best new canes from each plant on to the wires to take their place. Annually in February, once you have sufficient *established* canes, the canes can be reduced in height to 5½ ft. to encourage them to develop fruit-producing side-shoots.

In order to get my heavy crop I feed the plants every March with general fertiliser at the rate of 4 oz. to a yard of row. Then in April I put down a thick layer of well-rotted compost or moist peat to keep the roots moist and to cut out the need to do any weeding.

The most troublesome pest is the greenfly, thought by experts to be responsible for the spread of virus disease. So do spray your plants, beginning in April, with a systemic insecticide such as one containing dimethoate.

In early May a spray of contact insecticide such as fenitrothion, derris or pyrethrum will eliminate the raspberry-cane midge which is responsible for blight. The same sort of insecticide should also be used again when the first fruits are turning pink to kill the raspberry beetle which is the cause of maggoty fruit.

The canes should be draped with plastic netting to protect the fruit from birds as the berries start to colour.

Finally, what if you are short of room for raspberry growing? Why not have the Swiss *autumn fruiting* variety Zeva which can be grown in a tub on a balcony or patio? Five plants can be accommodated in a tub 18 in. in diameter. The canes themselves grow to a mere 4½ ft. and need no support. They are also ideal for small gardens as they can be planted 1 ft. apart.

Other autumn-fruiting raspberries worth considering for a September and October crop in Southern areas are Heritage, an American red fruited variety, and Fallgold, also from America, but with sweet apricot yellow berries. Both of these grow to at least 6 ft. tall and should be planted like other raspberries.

Autumn raspberries are pruned annually *in spring* and *all the canes* are cut down to ground level. Apart from that, the cultivation is exactly the same as for the summer kinds.

With these splendid raspberries and such tempting desserts, can there be anyone who doesn't rate the raspberry a favourite fruit?

OCTOBER
DAHLIAS

As dahlia tubers are subject to rotting and frost damage in the winter, they must be lifted and kept in frost-free conditions, ready to be planted out again next spring.

Don't cut down dahlia plants until they're affected by frost. Then, when the evidence of the blackened foliage is very obvious, you can cut through the stems, with a pair of secateurs, about six inches above the ground. Leave the cut-down plants in the ground for a further fortnight before lifting them. Remember that the tubers are the food-stores of next year's plants, so be careful not to damage them when digging them out. Use the garden fork and loosen the soil around the plant, and then, holding the stem with one hand, ease the plant out by inserting the fork as deeply as possible underneath it.

With the plant out, put a label on it (Inset A) before you forget which variety it is. Make a note of the flower colour, and more important, how tall it grows. Now the plant is ready for drying prior to being put into storage. The object of the exercise is to make sure there's no sap remaining in the stems. Stand the plants upside down for a week or ten days in a dry spot under cover. At the end of this time, any large lumps of soil still attached to the tubers can be taken off, but there's no need to be too particular about this as a little soil on the tubers themselves will do them no harm.

For storage, the important things are to prevent the tubers from becoming shrivelled and to prevent the crowns (the swollen area where the tuber joins the stem) from rotting. One way to do this is to stand the tubers in shallow boxes of peat (Inset B), where the peat is covering most of the tubers but the crown is left exposed. If you're worried about rotting in storage, you can try spraying with a benomyl fungicide before putting the plants into store, but in most cases allowing plenty of air to circulate around the threatened parts should be sufficient.

Where to store is the other problem, and one to which different gardeners will find different solutions. The tubers must be kept frost-free, but they should also be kept cool (about 40°F) or else they will tend to shrivel. An unheated greenhouse, garage or shed will do, remembering to give them a bit of extra protection if there's any severe weather in the winter. The moist atmosphere in such a building will also help to prevent the tubers shrivelling.

Finally, a word to those gardening on light, well-drained soils, particularly in the South of England. If you don't mind taking a slight risk, and you want to save yourselves work, cut down the foliage when it's frosted, but leave the plants in the ground just giving them a covering of peat or ashes. In most cases this will be sufficient protection to see them through the winter.

OCTOBER
BROWN ROT

An all too frequent cause of wastage in the apple crop is the brown rot disease in which a fungus infection produces symptoms like those illustrated in Inset A. The infection starts with just a small brown patch appearing on the fruit, but this spreads very rapidly and soon the whole fruit will be rotten; yellowish growths appear through the by-now brown skin of the apple and it is from these that spores are released to spread the disease. Although apples are the principal fruit to be affected, the fungus will also attack plums, pears, cherries and peaches.

Brown rot is the sort of disease that you'd be very unlikely to eliminate from your garden simply because the spores are so light and easily spread that reinfection from outside sources is quite possible, however careful you may be with your own fruit; but you *can*, by regular inspection and removal of diseased fruits, reduce the losses from the fungus quite substantially.

The disease spreads so quickly because any apple with any sort of surface wound (caused by wasp damage, bird pecks, apple scab, earwigs, codling moth larvae, etc.) is liable to attack and an infected apple soon passes on the infection to any others with which it is in contact.

This makes it sensible during the growing season to inspect the trees weekly and remove any apples showing signs of the rot. Some varieties are even affected by the fungus spreading along the stalk of the diseased apple into the fruiting spur: if that happens cut out the spur as well.

At this particular time of year care should be taken to remove all of the infected fruits from the tree. Although most of these diseased ones will have fallen to the ground (whence they should have been removed to the bonfire) some will have remained on the tree but shrunk in size so that eventually they would appear like the mummified one in Inset B. These, if left on the tree, would still be there next summer and would be the first source of infection on next year's crop.

One of the reasons why apples are always picked with their stalks attached is that any wound where a stalk has been torn out from the fruit is a very likely point of entry for the brown rot fungus.

Just as trees should be inspected regularly to remove diseased fruit, stored fruit needs a similar weekly examination because a week is quite long enough for the rot to spread through the whole of an apple. Remove the infected ones (some varieties merely go black when affected in store with no exterior fungus growths, but this is still caused by the brown rot fungus) and burn them, and clean up the wood which they will probably have become stuck to if stored in wooden boxes. To avoid greater losses than necessary store apples so that they are not touching one another.

OCTOBER
AFRICAN VIOLETS

One of the most popular of all house-plants is the Saintpaulia, the African violet. Its foliage is always attractive but what really makes it outstanding is its ability to flower for such long periods of each year. However, getting it to flower in the winter is more of a challenge and it really needs a room where the temperature does not fall much at night.

In fact, although African violets should always be kept out of very strong sunshine, a south-facing windowsill is probably the best place for them in the winter so that they benefit from all the limited light available. Ideally, the temperature should be within the 60-70°F range, without wide fluctuations. Night minima much below 60°F will probably prevent winter flowering — minima much below 50°F will probably kill the plant altogether. Kitchen windowsills are often good places for African violets: the high humidity there is good for the plants and I suspect the extra light they receive from artificial illumination due to the kitchen's being a much used room must help to promote winter flowering. Fluorescent strip lighting is more effective in this way than ordinary bulb lighting.

Another way of satisfying the high humidity requirements of the plants is to create a moist atmosphere for each one by standing the pots on some moisture-retaining substance like peat, giving the peat sufficient water to keep it perpetually moist. If plastic flowerpots are being used and are in intimate contact with the layer of peat at the bottom of the container, the water applied to keep the peat moist will also be sufficient to keep the compost in the pots moist.

If this method is not being used, keep the water off the leaves, because they quickly get marked and spoilt when splashed. Although African violets like plenty of moisture, if you are in doubt about whether you can maintain the proper minimum temperature levels in winter, your plants will stand a better chance of survival if kept slightly on the dry side.

If you want to propagate an African violet, leaf cuttings are the method to use. Take a mature leaf with 1-1½ inches of stalk (Inset A) cut off cleanly from the parent plant with a sharp knife. These can be rooted by sticking them in a cuttings compost or even in water. Keep the leaves just clear of the compost or the water. Eventually roots will form and the cuttings can be potted up in individual small pots. After this stage you will see the new plantlets that have formed on the old stalk push their way up and appear through the compost (Inset B). These can be carefully separated if several appear in the same pot.

African violets grow well in peat-based soil-less potting composts. If you are using John Innes, No. 1 is quite sufficient but will give better results if mixed with some extra peat.

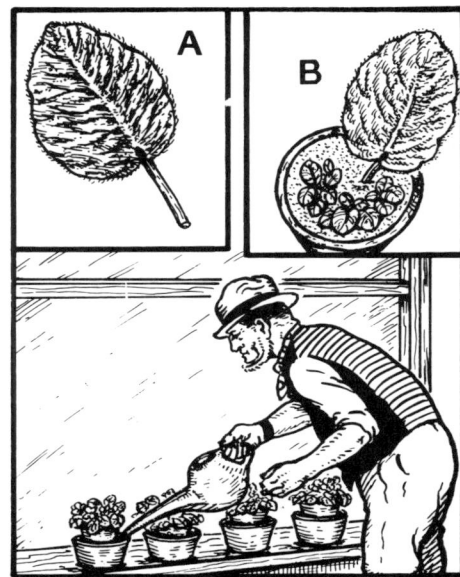

OCTOBER
TURFING A LAWN

Despite the relatively high cost compared with a lawn grown from seed, laying turves will provide a "finished product" in such a short space of time that it continues to be a popular method of lawn making. Although turf can be laid at most times of the year, October is a particularly good month for the job because the soil still retains sufficient warmth to encourage root growth and there are unlikely to be any of the problems associated with water shortage, i.e. turves shrinking and curling up at the edges.

When buying the turves, have a good look at some samples if possible. Make sure they are free of weeds, of uniform depth and have plenty of root material visible underneath. Try to get them delivered as near as possible to the date you wish to lay them.

It is just as important to have the site properly prepared for laying turves as it is for sowing grass seed. In fact, the requirements are similar — a completely flat surface with a fine tilth of soil that contains plenty of moisture and has been allowed to settle for a couple of weeks after any previous digging. Again, a light dressing of Growmore (1-2 ozs per sq.yd.) raked into the surface of the soil will help the newly laid turves to become established quickly.

Having finished preparing the site, the laying can begin. Start at one side of the area and work outwards and across it so that at no stage are you treading on the soil you've raked to a fine tilth. The work will be easier if the turves are laid in straight lines and arranged in a similar sort of pattern to a brick wall (Inset A). They should be packed tightly together thus keeping to an absolute minimum any gaps that may appear between them.

If you work with a couple of boards on which to kneel or stand, you will avoid leaving footmarks on the newly laid turves and the pressure of the boards as you stand on them will be sufficient to ensure adequate contact between turves and soil surface. Don't go in for beating the turves or rolling them — neither will be necessary if the soil was adequately settled and levelled beforehand. Check that the turves you have laid are level: if they aren't, lift them and either add or take away soil until the surface is flat.

When all the turves are in position, the job can be finished off by preparing a mixture of sand and sifted soil, spreading it over the whole area and brushing it into the cracks between the turves (Inset B). The grass roots will soon grow into this mixture and any noticeable gaps quickly disappear as the turves are bound together.

Finally, when it comes to mowing the newly-turfed lawn next spring, begin with the blades set very high and only gradually reduce the cutting height over a period of months.

OCTOBER
HARDWOOD CUTTINGS

The soft and semi-hard cuttings taken during the summer and early autumn always need some form of cover to cut down the moisture lost through the leaves before the new roots have begun to form. But hardwood cuttings, which form an excellent way of propagating many deciduous trees and shrubs, don't suffer from this problem. The cuttings are taken about the time of leaf-fall, thereby eliminating the source of moisture loss and consequently can be rooted in the open ground without any sort of protection.

They will, however, be occupying the ground until this time next year when they should be ready for transfer to their final quarters. A suitable site might be at the foot of a north wall or anywhere that has partial shade and well-drained soil.

Hardwood cuttings are taken from ripe wood of the current year's growth and are usually somewhere between 10-14 inches long. They should be cut just below a bud at the base and with the soft wood at the tip cut back to just above a bud (Inset A) thus leaving a shoot some twelve inches long.

The shoots are inserted into the ground to about half their length, i.e., six inches above ground, six inches below, in a small trench with one vertical side to it (Inset B). The cuttings are lined up against this vertical side and spaced about six inches apart, the soil is put back in the trench, firmed down thoroughly and the job is complete.

Two useful refinements which will help to improve results are the use of hormone rooting powder and the filling in of the bottom of the trench with a good rooting medium such as sand or a sand/peat mixture. The rooting powder is very simple to use: dip the base of the cutting in water and then dip it in the powder so that a layer of powder adheres to the base of the cutting.

The use of sand, etc., in the trench is advisable on heavy soils which have tendencies towards being either very wet and sticky or, in the summer, formed of impenetrable clods of earth. A two-inch layer of anything like sharp sand or potting grit which roots will form in readily should increase one's chances of success. Put the chosen material at the foot of the trench, push the cuttings into it and then replace the soil. Next spring you will find the cuttings have been pushed up by frost action during the winter and you will have to press them down again so that their bases are once more in contact with the soil.

A list which gives some idea of the shrubs and trees which can be propagated this way includes Cornus, Forsythia, Buddleia, Philadelphus, Deutzia, Weigela, Lilac, Jasmine, Willow, Flowering currant plus, of course, fruits such as red and blackcurrants and gooseberries.

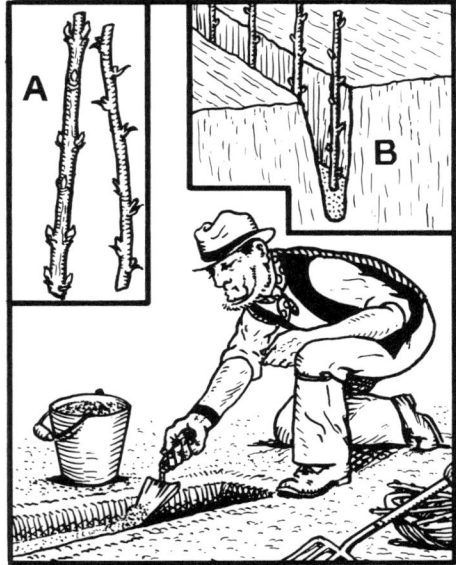

OCTOBER
STAKING AND TYING

A plant's root system is important not only to help it take up water and nutrients from the soil but also to anchor it in the ground: the bigger the plant the stronger the root system required. With large plants such as trees the importance of this anchoring function is at its most obvious; it's equally obvious that trees being planted after delivery from the nurseryman won't at first have roots capable of holding the top growth stable. Only when the roots begin to grow through the soil will they come into their own as "stabilisers". Until that occurs the trees need to be made fast in their planted positions — this is usually done with the aid of stakes.

Some trees such as apples grown on dwarfing rootstocks will need stake support for the whole of their lives as their root systems are brittle. Others won't require such extended assistance but will still benefit from having a strong stake. The ideal stake (Inset A) for a standard or bush tree needs to be 2-3 inches in diameter, with a pointed end to facilitate insertion in the soil and of sufficient height to bring it up to the crotch of the tree. Treat the bottom third with a wood preservative so that it doesn't rot away in the soil.

The stake is best inserted in the planting hole before the tree is put in, so that there is no possibility of damaging the tree roots while hammering the stake in. Put the stake near to the centre of the hole and drive it in so that approximately one third will be below soil level. This job is best done with one person holding the stake, another knocking it in. The tree can then be put into the planting hole with its roots well spread out and the soil gradually replaced. Give the tree an occasional shake while returning the soil so that the earth falls all around the roots leaving no underground air pockets. Firm the soil well and the tree will be ready for tying to its stake.

There are various tree ties that can be bought, or one can devise one's own. The important points to watch out for are that the tie won't cut into the bark of the tree but will nevertheless hold it completely firm, while at the same time making sure that there's some distancing material to prevent the tree chafing against the stake. Good bought ties should offer all these features; if you make your own you could do it in the way shown in Inset B. Put a piece of durable cloth or sacking round the tree and then wind some soft but strong string round the tree and stake in a series of figures of eights, finishing off with a couple of turns round the centre of the figure of eight to keep the tree and stake apart.

Ties are best positioned at the top of the stake just below the crotch of the tree, but with tall specimens a second tie about half way up the stake may be required as well (Inset C). Tree ties should be inspected annually to make sure that they're still tight enough to be doing their job properly but not too tight to be constricting the tree's growth.

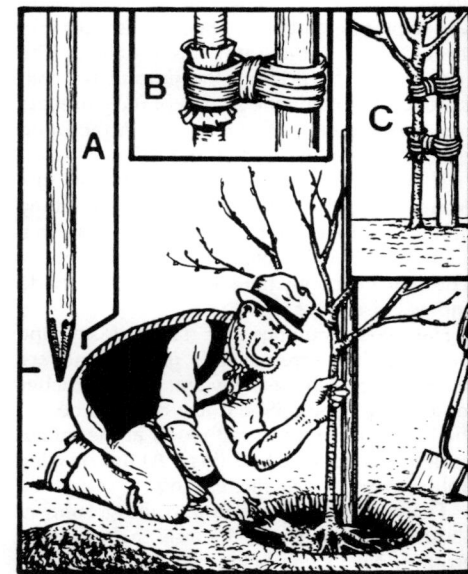

OCTOBER
GREENHOUSE WORK

In the winter months light, every bit as much as heat, is needed by those plants still active in the greenhouse — the effects of the lack of it are very obvious: spindly growth, pale and unhealthy foliage, etc. The best way to maximise the amount of light available is to remove all the shadings, etc. used in the summer and then to clean all the glass thoroughly inside and out.

Turning to heat, and how to keep fuel bills to a minimum: the cheapest and simplest method is by introducing what is, in effect, a form of double-glazing using clear polythene as the inner liner. This will cause only a very slight reduction in the amount of light entering the house but should have a big effect in preventing heat escaping from it. With wooden greenhouses, the polythene is easily fixed with the aid of drawing pins (Inset A); in metal houses it may be necessary to stick wooden bars to the metal with an adhesive and then fasten the polythene to them or use the special plugs or suction pads sold for greenhouse insulation purposes.

Whichever type of greenhouse you have, it is important to remember that it is a layer of static air trapped between polythene and glass that is the insulator. This layer is most effective if the polythene is about an inch from the glass and fixed firmly enough to prevent the layer of air being affected by the general greenhouse circulation.

Another useful tip to help plants survive very cold weather is to cover them at night with sheets of newspaper (Inset B), which must of course be removed during the daytime.

Two other points requiring very careful attention during the winter months are ventilation and watering. Mismanaging either of them can very soon result in plant fatalities. With watering it's a case of don't do too much and do what you're going to early in the day, before noon preferably and keeping the water off the foliage of the plants. Never feed any plants that aren't in active growth.

Adequate ventilation is another must in the fight to keep plants as healthy as possible. The secret is to find a compromise between a gentle flow of air and the devastating cold draughts that can occur with winter winds. On mild days the greenhouse will always benefit from being opened up to allow fresh air to penetrate, but it should be shut again early enough to make full use of the warmth of the sun's radiation, which can be sufficient to keep the temperature just a degree or two higher overnight.

If insect pests become a problem, fumigation with one of the smoke cones or pellets available is often an easy way of dealing with it. If the house is made as airtight as possible and the pellet lit on an upturned clay-pot or brick (Inset C) with the smoke left to do its work overnight, the problem should be greatly reduced.

OCTOBER

TULIPS

The later flowering bulbs, such as tulips, can be planted from October until well into November. In fact, tulips offer the gardener enormous scope — they have the widest colour range of all the spring bulbs, they can be in flower from March to the end of May, and they lend themselves to both formal and informal plantings.

There's nothing to be gained from planting tulips too early — their leaves may well appear above ground prematurely and be damaged by severe frosts. But when you do plant, use the trowel and set the bulbs about four inches deep and six inches apart. Tulips respond well to organic matter such as leaf-mould or compost, but it must be incorporated in the soil at a level lower than that at which the bulbs are to be planted. Otherwise, work in a dressing of bonemeal at 2 ozs. to the square yard.

Tulips are seen at their best in group plantings, restricting each group to the same variety to ensure that they flower simultaneously and are of uniform height. If you want to create a formal bed interspersing tulips with forget-me-nots or wallflowers, use the later-flowering tulips (Darwin or Cottage, say) to make certain that all of the flowers in the bed are blooming together. Also, check to see how high your tulips will grow — it's a waste if their blooms are lost among the foliage of the other plants in the bed. Remember that the late-flowering bulbs (Late Double and Parrot types) will occupy the ground until early June, which will influence your choice of summer bedding plants to follow.

The classification of tulips relates to the shape of the flower, the time of flowering and the parentage of the plant. The first to flower (in March) are the species tulips and Kaufmannianas (Inset A). These are valuable not only for their early flowering but also for their short stems which make them ideal candidates for the rockery. They, in turn, are followed by the Early Singles (Inset B) and the brilliantly coloured Fosterianas in April, both of which grow to a height of 12-15 ins. This makes them more able to withstand adverse weather than their taller May-flowering successors. After the Early Doubles and Greigiis at the end of April come the larger-flowered and longer-stemmed types. Darwins have very rich colours, Parrots (Inset C) exotically-shaped flowers but they need a sheltered spot to avoid wind damage.

Lastly, remember to remove flower heads after the blooms have finished and, if possible, allow the foliage to die down naturally. If, however, you need the space for other plants, lift the tulips before the leaves have turned yellow and replant them in some odd corner where they will stay until the leaves have died down. Then the bulbs can be lifted, dried and stored in the normal way until replanting the following autumn.

OCTOBER
REDCURRANTS

Although not quite as useful as blackcurrants or gooseberries, one or two redcurrant (Inset C) bushes make a welcome addition to any fruit garden. They're relatively undemanding and easy to cultivate and their fruits are always appreciated for pies, jellies and other preserves. In their cultural requirements they're very similar to gooseberries — if you can grow those satisfactorily you should be sure of good results with redcurrants.

The bushes will tolerate a certain amount of shade and are basically very hardy and fairly resistant to spring frost damage, but like most fruiting subjects they do appreciate being given a site with some protection from cold winds. The chosen site needs to be fairly deeply dug, removing any perennial weeds as the digging's in progress and incorporating some rotted manure or compost at the same time. Where space is really limited, it might be worth considering growing a couple of bushes as cordons.

Grown as bushes redcurrants need a spacing of 5ft apart each way; single cordons can be planted at 15 inch intervals, doubles at 21 ins. and triples at 27 ins. Planting can be done at any time between October and the early spring of the following year but autumn-planted bushes have a much better chance of making really strong growth in their first season.

When you buy a bush from a nurseryman you will find it has been formed with a "leg" (Inset A), a clear length of stem between the roots and the point where the stem breaks into the radiating structure of branches. The bush must be planted with this leg clear of the soil, i.e. at the same depth it was planted in the nursery. Otherwise new shoots will grow out from soil level which, although in no way harming the bush, will make it much more difficult to keep in easily manageable shape.

So planting is done with the bush not too deep in the ground and with the roots well spread out in the generously-sized planting hole. After replacing and firming down the soil, the bush is ready for its initial pruning. This pruning is particularly important in that it encourages the plant to grow vigorously during next summer, leading to the establishment of a well-sized bush as soon as possible.

All that needs to be done is to cut back each of the branches by about half its length to an outward pointing bud (Inset B). Weaker growths may be cut back further still. The wood that's pruned in this way usually makes good material for hardwood cuttings.

Of the varieties of redcurrant commonly available, Red Lake would be my choice for a reliable, high-quality heavy cropper. Other good varieties include the early Laxton's No. 1 and Jonkheer van Tets, and the late-season Stanza.

OCTOBER
AUTUMN LAWN CARE

The grass in our lawns has almost finished its season of growth and although many lawns will get their last mowing of the year this month, some further treatment in the way of raking, aerating and the applying of top dressings will help to ensure a healthy lawn again next year.

Cutting will obviously continue while the grass is still growing, but the cutting height of the mower should be raised as the interval between cuts lengthens. Before the final cut give the lawn a thorough raking with a wire rake. This has the effect of reducing the surface "mat" of dead vegetation, old grass cuttings, etc. and will also help the penetration of any top dressings or fertilisers.

The next task is to aerate the lawn and thereby counteract the compaction of the soil by mowers and all the feet that have walked over it in the summer months. Proper aeration will both improve drainage and stimulate root development, and is normally carried out with a normal garden fork, a hollow-tined fork or a spiking machine (Inset A).

The spiking machine obviously makes the work easier, but if you haven't got one or access to one, use the garden fork and push it straight down into the grass to a depth of four inches and repeat this process at six inch intervals. Hollow-tined forks are best used on heavy soils where drainage is poor. They take out small cores of earth, and once the spiking is complete, a dressing of coarse sand is applied. This, in turn, is brushed in so that much of the sand will go down the holes made by the hollow tines and thereby improve the drainage.

After raking and aerating, most lawns will benefit from the application of a top dressing (Inset B) which should promote a denser growth of grass next year, as well as filling in minor hollows in the surface of the lawn. If you want to make up your own top dressing the ingredients are peat, sand and clean sifted top-soil or loam.

For the average soil, two parts by bulk of soil should be mixed with one each of peat and sand. For heavy soils increase the sand content; for light ones increase the content of peat (or any other well-rotted organic matter). All top dressings should be brushed well into the grass immediately after they have been applied.

Lastly, remember the lawn can be mown during the winter months to keep it looking tidy. Whether it will be necessary or not depends on how mild the weather is, but, should you wish to mow, make sure the blades are set high and the grass is not too wet. A good brushing an hour or so before cutting will knock any drops of water off the grass itself, and you can at the same time gather up any fallen tree leaves which will spoil the lawn if not cleared up.

OCTOBER
LEAFMOULD

An all-too-common sight at this time of the year is the smoke from a bonfire consisting of a huge pile of fallen leaves. It's an especially distressing sight to the resourceful gardener who likes to find a use for all the naturally-produced materials in the garden. Leaves are, in fact, one of his most valuable assets, for in their rotted-down state, known as leafmould, they are a rich source of humus, which is useful for giving bulk to light soils and making heavy ones more friable. Leafmould has the added attraction of requiring no attention while it is decaying.

The best policy for collecting leaves is to gather them as they fall. It's easier, of course, to collect them from the lawn where they will quickly get trodden into the grass if not swept up, as well as making the garden look untidy. I like to use a wire or rubber rake to gather them up and then transfer them into a sack using a couple of short boards to pick them up. Another useful tip is to use a piece of netting as a cover for any rockery that frequently gets covered with fallen leaves. Lightly drape it over the plants and you can easily remove all the leaves once a week.

The problem of storage is not one of what to do to the leaves, but of finding sufficient space for them. The ideal container (A) need be no more than an enclosure made of four posts surrounded by wire netting. Tip the leaves in and allow them to decay in their own time. This may well take from one to two years, but, naturally if you make this a regular annual practice, you will always have a supply of mature leafmould ready to use. There is no need to use an 'activator', such as is used on the compost heap, to get leaves to decay.

One of the questions that is often asked concerns the best leaves to use for leafmould. The short answer is that beech and oak are ideal; but that doesn't mean that other types shouldn't be considered. The larger leaves (plane, chestnut, sycamore, poplar, etc.) take longer to decay but they will eventually do so especially if mixed in with oak and beech. An alternative method with large, coarse leaves is to mix them in with other garden refuse on the compost, where the heat of the heap will enable them to decay quicker.

Finally, a little advice on what use to make of leafmould. I've already mentioned its properties as a soil conditioner, but remember that its value lies in its humus content and not as a source of plant food. It's also a highly beneficial surface mulch for rhododendrons, azaleas, etc., and, when well decayed and sifted (B) it's an excellent top dressing for lawns, an ideal additive to mix into the soil when preparing for shrub and tree planting, and one of the vital ingredients if you're preparing your own potting compost. If you have a damp, shady part of the garden for plants like ferns and primulas, leafmould added to the soil will really help them to thrive.

OCTOBER
BORDER WORK

The 'back-end' of the year is a good time for both tidying up the herbaceous border and carrying out any alterations in its layout, planting hardy perennials and shrubs, etc.

The obvious way to start is by cutting down all the old topgrowth of herbaceous plants to near ground level, leaving just enough showing to remind you of where each of the plants is. Much of this topgrowth is likely to be too woody to be composted and will have to be burnt.

Having finished this clearing and also the lifting of any tender plants to be overwintered in the greenhouse, etc., you can get down to the job of weeding and turning the soil over in the spaces between the plants. If the ground is made weed-free at this time of year, it is comparatively easy to keep it so for the rest of the winter.

By all means use the hoe if the soil is still friable enough to make its use easy, but by November most gardeners will find a small long-handled fork the best tool for the job. Don't try and dig deeply, especially if you come into contact with plant roots. Avoid disturbing any bulbs you have planted in the border.

The only exception to that rule should be if you suddenly find yourself with an area of the border free of plants after removing a shrub, say. Then digging in some rotted manure or compost to restore the soil's fertility is certainly a good idea, as herbaceous borders, when compared with the vegetable garden, often get neglected in this respect.

Many border plants are very easily propagated by division and this is a simple way of increasing one's stock of plants and filling in any gaps in the border. Michaelmas daisies, rudbeckias, golden rod, erigerons, achilleas, some chrysanthemums, heleniums, etc. can be lifted out of the ground altogether and split into sections, either by hand (Inset B) or by using two forks as shown in Inset A. The best parts of the plant to keep and replant are the outer sections which are the youngest and will consequently grow with the greatest vigour.

It's perhaps as well to mention here some plants which resent being disturbed and should *not* be dug up in any border work. Japanese anemones, paeonies, delphiniums, lupins, eryngiums, oriental poppies and hellebores all come into this category.

If you have trouble with slugs in your garden, you might care to try and protect the very susceptible plants such as delphiniums by the following method. Scrape away the soil around the crowns of the plants to a depth of about two inches and in its place put the same depth of a fine, sharp sand. The young shoots next spring should avoid slug damage this way. Inset C illustrates in cross-section how this is done.

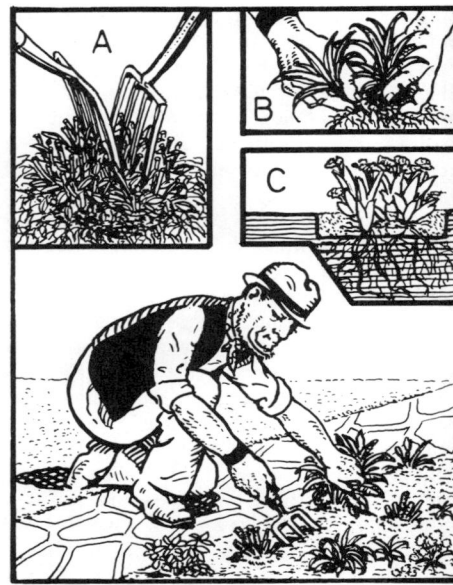

TULIPS — PLANT NOW FOR A MAGIC CARPET OF COLOUR

From Izmir to Baku there stretches a land of magic carpets. Can you picture in your mind's eye the many shades of red and pink, cream, yellow and purple?

These "living" carpets are at their best in March and April when the snows are newly gone and whole valleys in Turkey are filled with flashing colours.

It is here that some of the world's finest tulips were found growing wild some 300 years ago. Indeed, the word tulip itself comes from the Turkish *tulbant,* meaning a turban, and from the neatly overlapping petals of the flowers it is easy to see why.

Although Turkish tulips have been popular in European gardens for centuries, it was not until 80-odd years ago that botanists travelled eastwards to Central Asia in search of other species. There in the valleys around Samarkand, Tashkent and Turkestan they found exquisitely beautiful dwarf tulips with stems often no more than 6 in. high.

Superior

These new tulips were used to breed better flowers, far superior for most garden purposes than the Mendels, Triumphs and Darwins, which are generally between 20 in. and 30 in.

high.

Tall tulips look magnificent in massed beds in public parks, stately homes or in the right situation in a shrub and herbaceous border, but most of the time you are far better off with some of the little tulips which are more resistant to wind and rain.

Short in stature they may be, but their flowers are usually just as large as their taller cousins. Some species even produce several flowers on a single stem; and dwarf tulips usually have attractively blotched foliage to complement the beauty of the flower.

These shorter tulip species and their hybrids are ideal for planting in tubs and window boxes and for mass planting in the garden, either among shrubs or alongside a path.

Ten bulbs of a single variety planted in November will give you a splendid show next March and April.

That is another good reason why I grow so many of these little tulips; they give me the brightest possible show of colour often when winter is lingering into spring. And their flowers last so very much longer than the majority of tulips which bloom in late April and May and which rapidly become exhausted under a hot sun.

A further point in praise of little tulips is that the foliage has always died back by June when the time comes to fill my tubs and gaps in borders with summer annuals.

Unlike the May-flowering tulips (Darwins, Cottage, Parrot, Doubles, etc.) dwarf tulips do not have to be lifted and are best left in their tubs or in the ground. This is a useful saving in work, particularly at one of the busiest times of the gardening year.

Best of all, these dwarf tulips multiply quite astonishingly. So the ten bulbs you planted this year will be producing the equivalent of 30 in two years' time.

Of the dwarf tulips Tarda is the smallest and one of the earliest to flower. It is 3 in. high, but it produces up to six purple, white and yellow flowers on a single stem. This tiny tulip would be ideal for a window box or rockery.

Tulipa praestans Fusilier, a native of Central Asia, bears out what I said earlier about the size of the flowers. In March and April it produces a cluster of two to four 2 in. long flowers the brilliant scarlet of a guardsman's tunic on 6 in. high stems.

From the Caucasus mountains there is Tulipa eichleri, relatively tall at 12 in., with shiny, waxed scarlet flowers which measure up to 5 in. wide when they open up in even the weakest rays of spring sunshine.

However it is the hybrids Fosteriana, Greigii and Kaumanniana to which you should direct your attention if you are in search of the spectacular.

In my own garden the Fosteriana hybrids are represented by Madam Lefeber which produces 15 in. tall tulips in early April. The bright scarlet flowers open up to a remarkable 9 in. wide.

The Greigii hybrids have given me some of my most colourful and most highly prized flowers. I have Plaisir, just 6 in. high with petals in red, feathered with gold. The leaves, like all Greigii tulips, are heavily veined with maroon or brownish purple. There is also Red Riding Hood, a mere 5 in. tall with large, bright red flowers.

Many of the leaves of the Kaufmanniana tulips are also marked with brown or purple which adds to the attraction of the flowers.

Of this group I strongly recommend the 7 in. tall gold and scarlet Ancilla, the 6 in. tall Shakespeare in salmon, apricot and orange, and the 10 in. tall Stressa, a delightful mixture of crimson, scarlet and gold.

All of these hybrid tulips will flower in March and April in any part of the British Isles.

Compost

Tubs and window boxes can be filled with good garden soil, John Innes No. 3 compost or a peat-based compost.

Tulips grow best in alkaline soil, which is good news for the vast majority of gardeners in Britain. However in acid soils the bulbs are seldom known to fail.

In containers and light soils the bulbs can be planted up to 12 in. deep, which is a considerable advantage if like me you wish to plant annuals on top of them in summer. In heavy clay do not plant more than 6 in. deep.

The deepest possible planting is essential if the bulbs are not to produce too much foliage above ground too soon. This is also the reason why tulips should not be planted outdoors before early November in their first year.

The bulbs should be spaced 4 in. to 6 in. apart to get the best possible display. My tip is to plant no fewer than five of a single variety in a group if you want to get a proper eye-catching patch of colour among the leafless shrubs and other still dormant plants.

Should you wish to fill in around the bulbs with other spring-flowering plants, forget-me-nots are your best bet. The brilliant blue looks marvellous against the reds of the tulips.

The one pest to be prepared for is the slug. It can give even the most expensive magic carpet a rather moth-eaten appearance. The remedy is to bury some slug pellets with the bulbs and to put down slug pellets regularly throughout the winter to give protection.

Once the tulips have finished flowering, remove the dead heads and any fallen petals, but leave the foliage to feed the bulbs. In just two weeks or so the leaves will turn straw yellow, wither and be easy to take away.

So why not get your own magic carpet? From the moment you see those first green shoots breaking through the still cold earth, the very idea of rich reds and glistening gold will whisk you off to a land of dreams.

NOVEMBER
BROAD BEANS AND PEAS

For the earliest crops of broad beans and peas it is possible to make sowings at the beginning of November. Both vegetables are hardy and should stand up to the rigours of the winter provided they are grown in well-drained ground, but there can be problems caused by mice taking away the seed, for example, which might make one prefer to wait for a March sowing. The great benefit of early crops, especially in small gardens, is that when they have been cleared next summer they allow plenty of time for other vegetables to be sown or planted out on the same ground.

Broad beans will grow satisfactorily in most types of soil — an area that has been manured or composted for a previous crop should bring good results, especially if it is not prone to waterlogging. Fork the ground over to make sure the soil is not compacted and, if you have any, apply a ½ oz. per square yard dressing of sulphate of potash. This helps to promote winter hardiness. Otherwise leave the application of fertilisers until the plants begin to grow rapidly in the spring when a dressing of Growmore at 2-3 ozs. per square yard will help them to make vigorous growth.

The broad bean for sowing in November is the variety called Aquadulce or, if you can give the seedlings cloche protection, one of the dwarf types such as the Sutton (A). This has smaller beans and pods than the normal broad beans but crops quite heavily and only grows to about 15 ins. high so that it can be kept under cloches for a large part of its life to produce a very early crop. The Sutton is usually grown in single rows about 15 inches apart but Aquadulce is treated like other broad beans, being grown in double rows nine inches apart, leaving 2ft. between the double rows and growing the beans at six inch intervals in the rows.

The same remarks about choice of site apply to peas, which are not quite so commonly grown from November sowings. The reason for this is that the varieties that are winter-hardy are known as round-seeded, and they do not have the same flavour as the wrinkle-seeded types that constitute most of the peas we grow. The round-seeded lack in sugar content, although they do of course provide much earlier crops. Two varieties especially suitable for November sowing are Feltham First and Meteor. Both are dwarf cultivars and may be grown under cloches to produce an early crop. Feltham First has the added merit of being able to be grown without peasticks.

Probably the easiest method of sowing peas is to take out three parallel drills about 1-1½ inches deep and 3-4 inches apart and to sow the peas along these at 2-3 inch intervals (Inset B). However, with sowings that have to survive the winter it would be a good idea to sow a little more thickly to allow for casualties.

NOVEMBER
SHRUB PLANTING

November to March is the planting season for deciduous trees and shrubs which like to be set out whilst dormant, thus allowing their roots to start into growth before the leaves appear next spring. As trees and shrubs may be expected to remain in the ground for an indefinite period, it's obviously well worthwhile taking trouble to prepare the soil beforehand and planting carefully afterwards.

If your plants are bought or delivered before you are ready to plant them, their roots must be kept moist. With container grown or balled plants this simply entails watering them. Bare-root specimens should be heeled in, using a deep-slit trench in which the roots will be covered by soil.

Soil preparation consists largely of breaking up hard subsoils and incorporating quantities of peat or leafmould, decayed manure or compost into the soil. Any of these will help new roots to develop and thus give the plant the good start it needs. Deep preparation also encourages deep rooting, which will make the plant better able to withstand high winds and drought conditions in hot summers.

Having prepared the soil, we can now move on to the planting procedure. If the shrub is container-grown, this is very simple: the container is removed (unless it's of the peat-type that doesn't need removal), the roots at the bottom of the container loosened a little if they look constricted, and the shrub set in the soil. Other shrubs may be bought in a ball of soil, or with loose roots wrapped in sacking, etc. These will need rather more attention in planting.

Dig a generously-proportioned hole in ground that has been prepared beforehand, bearing in mind that the correct planting depth is that which will leave the soil mark on the stem level with the surface of your soil. Have a look at the roots and use the secateurs to cut back any damaged ones. Stand the shrub in the hole and spread the roots out (Inset A), so that they don't have to be bent to get them into the hole. Spreading them out will help give the plant stability and allow it to draw its food from a wide area. At this juncture it is as well to put in a stake, if one is needed, (Inset B). Hammering it in afterwards might very well result in root damage.

With the stake in position, the soil, which can be mixed with a little peat, leafmould or compost, should be put back into the hole. Having made sure the soil is crumbly, put it back gradually, giving the plant an occasional shake so that the soil falls all round the roots. To make sure the plant is firm in the ground, tread down the soil as you're putting it back — don't be afraid to do this fairly vigorously as the roots need to be in close contact with the soil, but stamping it down too hard will damage the soil structure. One final point — remember that frost will loosen the soil around the roots again, so be prepared to firm it down after any severe weather.

NOVEMBER
SLUGS

Although more of a nuisance on heavy soils and in areas of high rainfall, slugs are usually responsible for some damage in most gardens at some stage in the year. You might be aware of the damage without being aware of the culprit, because slugs spend the greater part of their lives underground, or under surface debris and when they do emerge it's usually at night.

To know how to control them, it's useful to know that normally slugs have to keep their surfaces moist and thus like to live in a saturated environment. Evidence of slugs in gardens often consists of seeing their mucus trails. The mucus is a secretion which is connected with the slug's method of locomotion. Slugs which are forced to crawl any distance to seek shelter in a dry atmosphere rapidly suffer dehydration and die.

So the conditions that will prove uncongenial to slugs are obvious. A clean and tidy garden, without weeds or decaying vegetation but with a well cultivated soil surface, lessens their scope for above ground activity. At this time of year that means removing old, yellowed leaves from brassicas, including turnips and swedes, and keeping the whole of the vegetable plot, in particular, weed-free.

Keeping the garden clean is an effective way of controlling the slug population, but there are occasions when, perhaps, seedlings are being attacked and prompt action is needed to save them. In such a case some form of bait would help.

If the weather's damp enough to encourage soil surface activity the following seedlings are particularly at risk, especially with early sowings: brassicas, carrots, lettuce, celery and certain flowers such as pansies, sweet peas and chrysanthemums. The first foliage of broad, French and runner beans may be attacked, as may that of many herbaceous plants. Potatoes, both foliage and tubers (Inset B), may suffer — most at risk are King Edward, Pentland Crown and Maris Piper. The characteristic damage to leaves is shown in Inset A — note that the succulent parts of the leaves between veins are eaten, giving them a ragged appearance.

If a bait is required, those available contain either *metaldehyde* or *methiocarb*. Metaldehyde is less toxic — it may merely paralyse the slugs so that they cannot reach shelter. This is satisfactory in dry and windy conditions when the slugs will become dehydrated and die, but in moist weather they may recover. Methiocarb is more poisonous and is effective even in damp weather and when the plants cover a lot of the ground. Scatter the pellets thinly around plants at risk; when there is a risk of birds or pet animals eating them, set them under a propped-up tile so that only the slugs can get at them.

NOVEMBER
ROOT CUTTINGS

One easy but relatively unfamiliar method of plant propagation is by root cuttings, its unfamiliarity probably being because only a limited range of plants can be grown this way. But for those which are suitable the technique is simple and the success rate high. Unlike leafy cuttings, root cuttings are best taken during the dormant period of the plant concerned. This usually means the winter.

The type of plant which lends itself to root cutting propagation usually has thick fleshy roots — examples of flowers are Anchusa italica, Acanthus, Eryngium (sea holly), Echinops (globe thistle), Phlox, Oriental poppies, Cynoglossum (hound's tongue), Romneya (Californian tree poppy); seakale is a good vegetable example, while amongst shrubs and trees certain kinds of Rhus such as the staghorn sumach (R. typhina), Ailanthus (tree of heaven), Cydonia (quince) and various poplars should all succeed.

It's worth noting that suckers on trees and shrubs are often the result of accidental root cuttings in the literal sense! That is, they appear from a portion of root that has been sliced through in the course of digging around the parent plant. Remove the whole root of weeds like dock or any portions left behind will

in effect be root cuttings and the weed will grow again.

For those plants whose roots are thick enough take portions of root about two inches long and, in order to remember which way up to insert them, make a horizontal cut across the top and a sloping cut at the bottom (Inset A). The cuttings are then put into pots or boxes (Inset B) an inch apart so that their tops (with the horizontal cuts) are just below the surface of the compost. Putting a thin layer of grit on top of the compost helps to keep the new shoot that develops from the top of the cutting well-drained. If the compost is well-moistened before the cuttings are inserted, no further watering will be needed until the cuttings develop their own roots, provided they are kept in a humid atmosphere.

An ideal medium for growing them in is a half and half mixture of peat and potting grit. For those plants which have thinner roots the cuttings (just chopped-off two inch sections of root) are merely laid on the surface of the compost (Inset C) and lightly covered. Generally, however, vertically grown cuttings are more successful.

Keep the pots or boxes in either a cold frame or cold greenhouse. If you have a propagator in which a temperature of 70°F can be maintained you can use shorter cuttings (1 inch long) because the greater warmth will enable them to develop new roots

and shoots quicker. Once any new stem appears keep the cuttings in a light position. When the cuttings can be seen to have rooted, pot them up individually so that they develop really good root systems prior to being planted out.

NOVEMBER
ANIMAL MANURES

The way to develop a really fertile soil in any garden is to make sure that it has a plentiful supply of organic matter in it. Organic matter means simply the remains of either plant life (in the form of garden compost, say) or the remains or by-products of animal life, in the form of animal manures.

Whether from animal or vegetable sources, organic matter decomposes to form humus which is what has such a beneficial effect on the soil structure. In heavy clay soils, plentiful supplies of humus reduce the tendency of the soil to form itself into large, dense clods; on light soils the water-holding capacity is much increased. On any soil humus encourages better root development, facilitates movement of water through the soil and supports all the biological and earthworm activity which help to make soil fertile.

The compost heap is the gardener's main source of humus, but may need to be supplemented by animal manures. These are not so easy to get hold of as once they were, but can be valuable to gardeners if plentiful supplies are available at a reasonable price.

Horse manure shouldn't be too difficult to buy (try ringing round riding stables listed in yellow pages). It is a fibrous manure which rots quickly and is the best manure for clay soils or for making hotbeds. Try to make sure it's based on straw, not wood shavings or sawdust because all woody materials take much longer to decompose.

Farmyard manure may be from cows or pigs or a mixture of the two. Both these manures are wetter and colder than horse manure and take longer to rot down. However, if you can find a source of supply, you will usually have to buy a load and will at least get the stuff delivered. If enquiring about how well-rotted a manure is, you may be told it's either a long or short manure — long indicates a lot of fresh strawy material, short means fairly well-rotted.

Poultry manure may come as battery manure, i.e. fresh hen droppings, or broiler and deep litter manure. Battery manure contains some useful nutrients but to make it into an effective soil conditioner it should be composted with other garden waste. Broiler and deep litter manures may contain wood shavings but are much easier materials to deal with than battery manure.

If manures are dug into the soil in too fresh a state, their decomposing will have to be done underground by bacteria which will in fact be removing nitrogen from the soil to continue the conversion to humus process. It's therefore best to rot the manure before incorporating it into the soil. This should be done by building it into a heap (Inset A) which should be kept moist and turned periodically (Inset B) to let in air and expose the outer parts of the heap to the heat which should be building up in the middle.

NOVEMBER
GROUND COVER SHRUBS

One effective method of dealing with dry, sunny banks, shady spots under trees and other 'difficult' parts of the garden is to find a strong-growing adaptable plant that will soon carpet the area concerned, its canopy of foliage preventing the growth of any weeds underneath. The ground-cover plants described here are all low-growing evergreen shrubs.

As these shrubs are required to produce strong, fast growth it's worth giving them every encouragement by making sure that the site where they are to be planted is (a) weed-free, especially of perennial weeds like couch grass, and (b) not terribly undernourished, as sites where ground cover is required often are. Incorporate some peat or rotted compost, etc, in the soil and a slow-acting long-lasting fertiliser like bonemeal.

Hypericum, St. John's Wort, despite its invasive tendencies when well established, is a reliable plant both for sun and shade. Plant at 3ft. apart, Hypericum calycinum, the most commonly grown St. John's Wort and one which can be raised from seed, will soon provide good cover as well as attractive yellow flowers throughout the summer.

The periwinkles are also familiar plants, but no less good for being so. They spread by means of their stems rooting as they come into contact with the soil and they perform well in the shade as well as more open conditions. Their glossy green foliage is pleasing throughout the year and one variety of Vinca major called 'Elegantissima' has an attractive variegation. Their names Vinca major and Vinca minor are self-explanatory as to size, with the major form being more rampant.

Of the many different Cotoneasters, dammeri (Inset A) is best suited for ground cover. It hugs the ground, growing no more than 4-6 ins. tall, has the bright red berries typical of cotoneasters and is suitable for banks, ground cover between and around other shrubs, etc. Plant it at 3ft. spacings.

Although the Ceanothus family, the Californian lilacs, normally provide quite tall shrubs, one called C.thyrsiflorus repens (Inset B) has the characteristic dark green, shiny foliage but spreads quickly whilst growing no more than 1½-2ft. high. Quite hardy, it has lovely pale blue flowers in spring and early summer and can be spaced at 4ft. intervals.

Lonicera pileata (Inset C) is a useful evergreen shrub with small bright green leaves and violet berries and is another good shade plant which will grow some 2ft. high and 3-4ft. across; Genista hispanica, the Spanish gorse,

on the other hand, is a very good shrub for a hot, dry spot. It and its slightly smaller companion, G.lydia, aren't in fact evergreens although they appear to be. Smothered with yellow flowers in May and June, they form dense bushes that will make admirable ground cover if planted 2ft. apart.

NOVEMBER
RHUBARB

There are not many food plants in the garden which are as productive as rhubarb but require as little work in cultivating. Indeed, for those with established plants grown for cropping in spring and early summer, a late-winter dressing of thickly-applied manure all over the rhubarb bed will prove quite adequate for feeding and will help to conserve soil moisture as well.

If you are thinking of growing rhubarb for the first time, you can either buy roots or raise your own seedlings. The latter method entails a longer wait before the first pickings may be made, but will be cheaper. If buying roots, they can be planted out now if the soil is still workable, but otherwise defer planting until February or early March.

Rhubarb appreciates a sunny site and a rich soil and will repay deep cultivation: work in plenty of manure, compost etc., when preparing the soil, and apply a dressing of general fertiliser around the plants when the crowns break into growth. The roots should be set out at 3ft. apart each way, with the crowns just showing above the surface of the soil. Don't pick any of the first season's growth and pick that of the second year sparingly to encourage root development.

One of the natural advantages of rhubarb is the earliness of its maturing. It can, however, be forced in various ways to provide a crop even earlier than normal. Outdoor forcing, much the simplest method, is accomplished by covering well-established roots with tea-chests, barrels, etc. to exclude the light. Both top and bottom of the barrel should be removed. Cover the plants from December onwards.

Put a mulch of manure around each plant, place the barrel etc. in position and then use straw, strawy manure, bracken, etc., packed around the outside of the box to provide a layer of insulation. Cover the top as well but in a way that will allow easy removal, so that you can inspect the progress of the plants without disturbing the straw, etc. round the outside of the box. Plants forced in this way should be left for two years before being picked from again.

For an even earlier crop, lift the required number of two or three-year-old roots and leave them standing on the surface of the soil until well-exposed to frost. Then bring them in and pack them into boxes of sifted soil mixed with a little compost (Inset A). Keep them dark by hanging black polythene down from the greenhouse staging (Inset B), or by putting them in a cellar, and fairly warm (55-60°F). Make sure the soil never dries out and you'll have rhubarb far in advance of an outdoor crop. Remember, however, that such forced roots will require at least a two-year recovery period before they are brought back into normal use. In most instances it is more sensible to start off with new plants, rather than replant those that have been forced.

NOVEMBER
FRUIT TREE ROOTSTOCKS

Nearly all the fruit trees sold are not growing on their own roots. Instead they are budded or grafted on to selected rootstocks (leading to the typical shape shown in the inset) which effectively control the pattern of growth of the variety concerned. This is particularly useful for anyone with a small garden. It means that by selecting a dwarfing rootstock, say, one knows that the tree will not grow beyond a certain size, but that it will start bearing fruit early in its life and its smaller size will enable more trees to be planted within a given area.

Giving a few details about the rootstocks that are available should make it easier for fruit tree buyers to select the one that's right for their purpose. Some nurserymen don't say which rootstocks their trees are on, but they should be able to tell you if asked.

Before describing individual rootstocks it's as well to point out that figures for growth can only be a rough guide because vigorous growers like Bramley will always make more growth than weaker ones such as Cox when on the same rootstock. Soil conditions play a part as well: on poor soils a rootstock of medium vigour will produce a tree equivalent to a dwarfing rootstock growing on really good soil.

For apples the rootstocks commonly used are, in ascending order of size, known as M9, M26, MM106 and MM111. M9 needs good soil, secure permanent staking and careful cultivation but given these will make a tree, as in the main picture, some 8ft. high and 10-12ft. across (i.e. leave that amount, at least, between planted trees) M26 is rather stronger growing (to 10-15ft. in height and spread) while MM106, probably the most commonly available, provides a medium-sized tree in good soils but a rather smaller one in poorer conditions. It is probably the best rootstock for a general recommendation. Types 9, 26 and 106 all begin to fruit quite early in their lives. MM111 will grow much too big for the average garden.

Pears are usually grown on quince rootstocks. Two common ones are Quince A and Quince C. Quince C is more dwarfing but is also more particular about its soil requirements. Quince A, making a moderately-sized tree, is the one most widely sold.

For anyone wanting a small plum tree a new rootstock called Pixy is now available. In a small garden this is more useful than the only relatively small St. Julien A and the vigorous Brompton.

Sweet cherries used to be out of the question for most gardens because the trees grew so large and were thus impossible to protect from birds. Now a new rootstock called Colt is available and although it doesn't produce really dwarf trees, it does produce trees of high quality and a definitely smaller size than the old rootstock, F12/1.

NOVEMBER
VARIEGATED EVERGREENS

It's around this time of year that evergreen trees and shrubs begin to demonstrate their special worth in the garden by providing us with their foliage to admire while much around them is bare. It therefore seems an added bonus that quite a few of our evergreens can also be obtained as varieties with variegated foliage, making them even more attractive in the eyes of many gardeners.

The planting season extends from October to March but one must use one's discretion about when, within that period, the soil is friable enough to make planting feasible. Remember that the tree or shrub has a long life expectancy and prepare thoroughly beforehand. Make the hole for the plant generously large and break up the subsoil at the foot of the hole, at the same time enriching it with well-rotted compost or manure or dampened peat.

When the new plant is put in the hole the nursery soil mark should be level with your soil surface. If the plant has a root ball, try to preserve the ball intact; if the roots are loose, spread them out in the hole and replace the soil around them, shaking the plant gently to make sure the soil is in contact with all parts of the root system. Firm the soil to make the plant secure and repeat this operation after frosts or strong winds have loosened the soil.

Turning to the individual shrubs, Elaeagnus pungens 'Maculata' (Inset A) is a hardy plant with very striking yellow leaves, each edged with green. It will eventually grow to a moderate size, but can be pruned to keep it within bounds and will not lose its bushy shape. Its colour makes it especially effective in the winter months.

The common holly (Ilex aquifolium) has quite a few variegated varieties, Golden King and Golden Queen (Inset B) being two of the best. Paradoxically, Golden Queen is a male plant, Golden King a female (only female plants can produce berries). They both have dark green leaves with very noticeable yellow margins and will over the years grow into small trees. They too are hardy.

Often mistaken for a holly because of its leaf shape is Osmanthus heterophyllus. Not quite so hardy (i.e. needing to be planted with some shelter in the coldest districts) it is of more use to small gardens as it is slower-growing and much smaller when fully grown. The variety "Variegatus" has creamy white borders to the dark green, shining leaves.

Finally, to a shrub that's eminently suited to the small garden. Euonymus fortunei never grows much more than 1ft.-1ft.6ins. in height but does spread nicely over the ground, making a good ground cover shrub. Quite hardy and extremely attractive for their variegation are Silver Queen (cream and green), Emerald Gaiety (brilliant white and green) and Emerald 'n Gold (Inset C) whose name is self explanatory.

NOVEMBER
SEED STRATIFICATION

Many seeds from plants of the temperate or colder zones, especially trees, shrubs and herbaceous perennials, are produced in the autumn. Examples are nuts like acorns, chestnuts, etc., berries such as holly, cotoneaster and berberis, stones in stone fruit such as peach and plum, pips in apples, etc. But because the cold of our winters would not offer good conditions for seedling growth, nature has so arranged it that many seeds of this type require a period of cold followed by warmer conditions to induce germination.

The seeds have a natural dormancy to prevent autumn germination, a dormancy gradually broken by exposure to the chilling and moisture characteristic of winter weather. Later, warmer conditions in spring signal to the seed that conditions are right for germination to take place and growth will then start.

For gardeners this means that certain seeds must first be given a cold-period treatment in order to get satisfactory germination. One method devised to do this is by putting the seeds, interspersed in layers of sand, in pots which are then buried in the ground in the winter. The alternate layers of seed and sand give rise to the term seed stratification.

This method is illustrated in Inset A. The bottom layer of sand needs to be 1½ins. thick followed by a layer of berries ½in. thick followed by another 1½ins. of sand etc. carried on up to the top of the pot. Use some sort of wire mesh to prevent mice entering the pot either from the top or bottom. Berries which can be stratified this way include berberis, cotoneaster, holly, hawthorn, rowan and rose hips, although germination times will be widely different. The pots are buried in some free-draining medium like sand or ashes or even stood at the foot of a north wall until the spring, when the berries, or the seeds from them, are sown in drills in the open ground or in moderate (60-70°F) warmth under glass.

The temperatures at which many fridges operate coincide with the ideal cold-period temperature for seeds requiring stratification, namely 35-45°F. For this reason, stratification is often now displaced by what's known as moisture-chilling. This merely involves putting the seeds in *moist* sand in, say, glass jars or polythene bags (Inset B) and standing these containers in the fridge with the sand kept moist and the mixture kept exposed to air (i.e. no lids on glass jars) for between one and four months. Treat them after this like the stratified seeds.

When buying seeds for which moisture-chilling or stratification is recommended (Bergenia, Clematis, hardy Cyclamen, flowering Quince and quite a few different trees) you may find it easier to sow the seeds straightaway into the seed compost and then give them the cold treatment. That way the same container can be used, merely transferring it from fridge to warmer location without the need to separate seeds from sand.

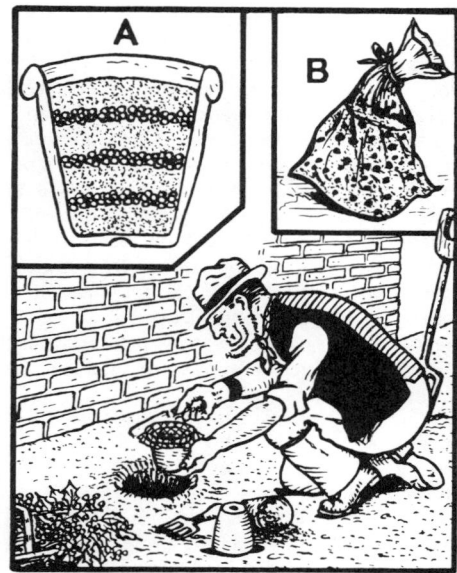

CAMELLIAS — BEAUTY THAT IS MORE THAN JUST SKIN DEEP

When you see a well-cut diamond sparkle, the fragile-looking facets give the impression that just like crystal the stone might easily shatter.

With the camellia the delicate petals, almost paper thin and with the texture of silk, would lead one to believe that a shrub producing such seemingly exotic flowers would need a great deal of loving care.

Yet that self-same shrub is capable of producing its blossom during the darkest and coldest months of the year.

Camellias are excellent evergreen shrubs which are suitable for every garden from the grandest of stately homes to the smallest city backyard and balcony.

One of the many marvellous things about the glossy green-leaved camellia is the way it will flourish in partial shade and in particular in the shelter of a north facing wall.

In cities, where gardens are often shaded, such a shrub is invaluable, especially as it can be grown very successfully in a variety of containers from 6 in. to 8 in. diameter plastic pots to tubs 12 in. or more wide.

In the garden a camellia can easily be 10 ft. tall with a 6 ft. spread, but in a pot you can limit it to a mere 3 ft.

The most common camellia originated in Japan, which is why its full name is Camellia japonica. There are numerous varieties which flower between February and May.

This type of camellia has been in Britain for the past 240 years. It can be grown successfully outdoors as far north in England as the Lake District and in mild areas of the West of Scotland and Ireland. Elsewhere it is best grown in pots which should be placed during the winter in the shelter of a greenhouse, porch or conservatory.

But what if you live in a cold eastern county? Does that mean that you cannot grow camellias outdoors? Not in the slightest. About 50 years ago a new group of hybrid camellias were produced in Cornwall by crossing a Japanese camellia with a species from China. The new camellias were called Camellia williamsii after their raiser.

These camellias are extremely hardy. In fact, I have seen a particularly lovely variety called Donation growing sturdily in Tayside, where snow and frost in winter are common .

In the most favoured areas of Southern England and Ireland these "British" camellias will flower as early as November and continue until April. In colder districts and in most of Scotland the first flowers are generally produced in February and appear at intervals until May.

The ideal position for a camellia is in partial shade (perhaps under a tree) and in a spot which is sheltered from both east winds and the early morning sun. The latter point is very important. Open flowers are likely to be damaged if sudden warm sunshine melts the overnight frost on the petals too quickly.

Camellias have to be grown in a lime-free soil. Chalk soils cause the leaves to yellow and die. However the majority of soils can be made suitable by the addition of plenty of peat or leaf mould. In extreme alkaline soil conditions the camellias are best grown in pots and tubs containing John Innes No. 3 compost.

Camellias can be grown as free-standing shrubs or they can be trained against a north or west-facing wall. South facing aspects should be avoided as the shrubs have many of the roots close to the soil surface.

Camellia flowers are extremely handsome and they can be single, semi-double or double. Those of the Japanese camellia are usually 3 in. to 5 in. across. My recommendations are Alba Simplex (single, white), Adolphe Audusson (semi-double, scarlet) and

Contessa Lavinia Maggi (double, pink).

There are actually several thousand varieties of the Japanese camellia grown in the world. Apart from the rose no other flower commands such popular support nor can be obtained in such a diversity of colours and forms.

The "British" camellia does not offer such a wide choice, but that is sure to change. For this type of hardy camellia has found considerable favour in Australia and the United States and already superb varieties have been introduced from these countries.

Without doubt my favourite camellia is Donation. The large, semi-double orchid pink flowers gradually fade to peach. If you have room for only one camellia, this is the one to choose. It will cost you around a fiver. I also recommend Francis Hanger (single, white), St Ewe (single, rose pink) and J. C. Williams (single, pink).

Most of the flowers of the hybrid camellias are 2 in. to 3 in. wide, half the size of the Japanese varieties. But what they lack in size they make up in their ability to go on flowering come snow, hail or prolonged heavy rain.

Once camellias are established, they need very little attention. But for the first year or two it is worth giving them some special care. After planting, if the shrub is likely to be exposed to icy winds, surround it on the windward side with a piece of polythene held between stakes.

Every April the root area should be covered with a 2 in. layer of well-rotted garden compost, leaf mould, farmyard manure or moist peat to provide the right sort of humus-rich cool soil conditions which camellias like.

Pruning is generally unnecessary, but if you want to remove any straggling shoots, April is also the month to do so.

The dead heads of all camellias should be removed by hand, except those of the hybrid camellias which should be allowed to fall.

The secret of getting plenty of flowers on a camellia is to ensure that it always has plenty of water in June and July when the following year's buds are forming.

Camellias in pots and tubs should have the top 1 in. of compost renewed annually in April, and so far as possible should always be watered with rainwater. If yellowed leaves should appear, due to your having to use tap water, the damage can be corrected by giving the shrub some sequestered iron which is available in sachets from garden shops.

Liquid feeds can be given between spring and summer, according to the vigour of the particular shrub.

Japanese camellias for greenhouses are best stood in a cool, shaded position outdoors from May to October and then put into the greenhouse (or porch) during the winter and spring. In the coldest districts it is simply necessary to provide sufficient heat to keep the temperature just above freezing point.

Camellias are generally free from pests and diseases. The problems that do arise are usually due to something we gardeners are doing wrong. For instance, buds drop off due to lack of moisture: leaves become distorted and flowers turn brown when they are exposed to freezing winds.

Yet with the right sort of care a camellia will provide you with flowers over several months, particularly at a time when colour in the garden is limited.

There is a great deal indeed to be said for growing camellias: their beauty is much more than skin deep.

DECEMBER
PLANT PROTECTION

So many of the shrubs and flowers we grow in our gardens are not natives of the British Isles that it's not surprising that they don't all seem to appreciate the winter weather conditions we provide for them. It's not always a question of excessive cold; too much moisture, very high winds and in particular the *combination* of cold air and strong winds, all share in the responsibility for garden casualties.

Plants at risk obviously vary very much from area to area, but new plantings that have not had a chance to establish themselves should come high on any gardener's list of priorities.

Most vulnerable are evergreens and conifers whose browned leaves usually indicate that the roots are not taking up water from the soil, while the leaves are losing water in cold, dry often easterly winds. Also in need of protection in severe weather are those tender shrubs against walls, walls which make the job of protecting them that much easier.

With all of these trees and shrubs, there's plenty of choice available in suitable protective materials. An arrangement of sacking or polythene and sticks (Inset A) or even fine-meshed netting or spare branches cut off evergreens and pushed into the ground around the plant — any of these should give adequate protection. A really thorough job can be done by erecting a barrier of wire netting around the plant and stuffing it with straw or bracken (Inset B).

Straw, bracken and even leaves are also useful materials to use around newly planted herbaceous perennials, especially those on the borderline of hardiness. A layer six to eight inches deep around the crowns of the plants will give useful protection but shouldn't be left in position after the middle of March or else new growth will start earlier than usual and will thus be more susceptible to damage from late spring frosts.

Plants growing in pots outside should ideally be moved under cover in very frosty weather, but if this isn't possible, burying them up to their rims in a sheltered spot should help. Cold frames can be given extra protection on very cold nights by covering them with old mats or carpets, sacking etc. Cloches, too, are another obvious form of protection, useful for early pea and broad bean sowings or to cover any plants of doubtful hardiness.

Cloches are effective not least because they keep excessive moisture off plants. Many rock garden plants, for instance, can easily withstand very cold conditions but cannot cope with a waterlogged soil. A layer of stone chippings around them (Inset C) improves drainage considerably, while for really prized specimens a sheet of glass supported by four wire pins, or an open-ended cloche should see them through the wettest of winters.

DECEMBER
CORDON APPLES

One effective way to grow apples in small gardens is to train them as cordons, i.e. single-stemmed plants grown at a 45° angle, which prompts all the buds along the stem to break into growth and thus become potential fruit-bearing branches. This means that a maximum amount of fruit can be produced in a minimum area. The trees are grown on dwarfing rootstocks and they start fruiting whilst young; their close spacing enables a good selection of cultivars to be grown, thus promoting good cross-pollination, and their controlled growth means that pruning, spraying, picking, etc. may be done from the ground without having to use step-ladders.

Cordons may be grown against a fence or out in the open — either way they are going to need strong wires and posts to support them. The posts should be firmly secured in the ground at 10ft. intervals with about 6½ft. of post above ground level. Three parallel wires should be fixed up at 2,4, and 6ft. from the ground. Bamboo canes are then tied to the wires at the 45° angle of the trees and the trees will in turn be tied to these canes.

The best trees to buy will be maidens (i.e., one-year-olds) and they must be on rootstocks that will achieve a dwarfing effect. The three

most suitable are called M9, M26 and MM106. They are listed in order of ascending vigour — i.e., M9 is suitable for good soils while M26 and MM106, because they make more growth, are better for poorer soils.

The trees are planted at 2½ft. intervals with the scion (the join between rootstock and grafted or budded wood) uppermost (A). This avoids any risk of cracking at the point of the join. The trees are set at a 45° angle in rows that should run north-south, with the trees pointing north.

After planting, the plants are pruned to encourage growth during their first year and discourage any premature fruiting before the tree is established. If the tree is a maiden, it will either be just a straight stem or have a few short branches coming off the stem (a "feathered" maiden). With the former, cut back to a bud about 2ft.6ins. from the ground (B1); with the latter, the "feathers" (side shoots) should be cut back to two or three buds from the main stem and the leader (the terminal extension of the main stem) cut back by half (B2).

Next year, remember to keep the new growth of the leading shoot tied down to the cane and start the pruning which will be necessary in subsequent years. This consists of cutting back the leading shoot by up to half if growth is very poor or leaving it unpruned if growth is very vigorous. Side-shoots should be

treated as shown in Inset C (this pruning should be done in late July to early August when of course there are leaves on the branches): the main side-shoots are shortened to three leaves from the basal leaves, the new side-shoots (those growing from existing side-shoots) are cut back to one leaf.

DECEMBER
CONIFERS AND HEATHS AS GROUND COVER

Included amongst the plants which provide good ground cover in our gardens are the heaths and conifers. Contrary to popular belief, some of these will grow well on soils other than acid ones and these tolerant ones include the juniper, whose various prostrate forms account for most of the ground-cover conifers available. Even some of the heathers such as Erica carnea are lime tolerant and should succeed on any soil which has a high humus content and good drainage.

One of the best ways to provide conifers and heaths with a humus-rich soil is to incorporate plenty of peat into the ground before planting. These plants are generally relatively slow growing, and keeping the area around and under them weed-free in their first years is very important; otherwise their growth will be made slower still.

The Juniper genus is remarkable for the wide range of shapes and sizes of its members. These include quite a variety of spreading but very low-growing forms which, because of their pleasing colours and dense evergreen foliage, function very well as ground cover. Although tolerant of most different soil types they do best in sunny positions where they can be used to grow over manhole covers, provide a thick carpet over awkward banks, drape themselves over rocks, etc. Being such good spreaders, they're usually grown as solitary plants rather than in groups.

Among ones that should be easy to find are Juniperus communis depressa (also in a golden form 'Aurea', Inset A) and J.c. Hornibrookii; Juniperus horizontalis (Bar Harbor and Prostrata are good forms) tends to have more grey-green foliage compared with the deep green of J.communis. All these junipers are low in height and very spreading in habit.

A useful conifer of slightly greater height (18 ins.), but equally good as a spreader and good for shade as well, is the yew, Taxus baccata Repandens. With its dark green leaves it's a slow grower but will do well on all soils.

Heaths are traditionally good ground cover plants, but some are better than others as spreaders. Erica carnea (Inset B) and Erica darleyensis are both lime tolerant; they are also among the best for our particular purpose if planted at 18-24 inch spacings in a sunny, open spot. They may not blend too well with plants of other species, but a bed containing a mixture of heaths with, say, a few dwarf conifers can produce a lovely effect.

Erica carnea varieties are winter and early spring flowering. Good ones include Springwood White and Springwood Pink and two golden-leaved cultivars, Aurea and Foxhollow. E. darleyensis is somewhat taller than carnea (18 ins. as opposed to 9) but just as good from the ground cover point of view. Arthur Johnson (rose pink) and Silberschmelze (white) are both reliable long-flowering varieties.

DECEMBER
PEAT

In wet tracts of land, where the vegetation consists of mosses and marsh grasses, the abundance of water can inhibit the decomposition of plant remains so that they stay in an only partially decayed state for great lengths of time. These plant remains are in fact peat which, as can readily be imagined, is virtually all organic matter and hence a rich source of humus.

This humus-forming capacity is not the only quality that will appeal to the gardener though. The fine, fibrous structure of the decomposing aquatic plants also has remarkable characteristics as an absorbent of water. It can hold up to ten times its own dry weight of water and its light, open texture makes it similarly good at holding air, both of which qualities are fundamental attributes of any soil conditioner.

Peat comes in a variety of colours and stages of decomposition. Moss peat is normally brown in colour and the least decaying of all the peats. It is usually sold in bales consisting of peat that has been dried, granulated and compressed, which of course makes it relatively easy to transport, but it *must* be thoroughly rewetted before use.

It's no good pouring a can of water on dried peat — the water runs straight through, leaving the peat quite dry. Put it into a bucket in a crumbled state, add the water and leave it to soak in (A). Moss peat will continue to decompose only slowly in the soil and has a long-lasting effect when used in the garden as a soil conditioner or put into the planting holes of shrubs and trees.

Sedge peat is a mixture of the remains of sedges, reeds and various forms of pond vegetation which is usually sold in a more decomposed state than moss peat. Black and crumbly but not compressed, it absorbs water readily enough although it does not have quite the same capacity for water-holding as moss peat. Being more decomposed already, it won't last in the soil for quite such a long time but there are cases where the greater degree of decomposition can be an advantage. Because it absorbs water easily, has excellent drainage qualities and is a relatively sterile medium, sedge peat is very attractive for use in potting and seed tray work. Used with modern plastic pots or trays and one of the peat, sand, loam composts like John Innes, a layer of peat at the bottom of the container (B) will save on the volume of the compost required. It will also be more than adequate for drainage purposes, thus obviating the need for crocks, not to mention its being a material in which roots develop quickly and well.

Used as a soil additive sedge peat is ideal where a rapidly available source of humus is required and may be dug into the topsoil in the same way as moss peat. But however good any peat is at improving soil structure, it contains little or no *nutrient* so that it cannot be used as a substitute for fertiliser to feed the plants themselves.

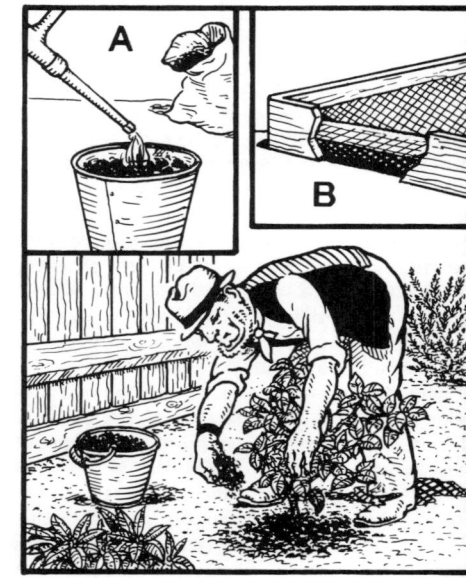

DECEMBER
CHAFER GRUBS AND CUTWORMS

Two common examples of soil pests often encountered while digging are chafer grubs and cutworms. They are both easily identifiable and large enough to be spotted without difficulty, and should, for the sake of next year's vegetable crops, be destroyed whenever found.

The most destructive of the chafer grubs is that of the cockchafer, shown in Inset A. They have long, whitish, fleshy bodies, characteristically seen curled up, the bodies contrasting markedly with their brown heads. These grubs spend three years in the soil living on a diet of plant roots and eventually grow some two inches long.

In the garden their damage may affect potatoes where the tubers are eaten into over a wide surface area (in contrast with wireworms and slugs which make holes in and then eat the insides of the tubers); strawberries and lettuce are also liable to attack, as are young trees, the above ground symptoms usually being a sudden wilting of the leaves.

Chafer grubs frequently live fairly deep down in the soil which means that one only comes across them when cultivating the soil deeply, as in winter digging. Cutworms, on the other hand, live much nearer the soil surface and although their bodies are dull in colour (normally shades of grey or brown) they are sufficiently large to be noticeable either as caterpillars or pupae (Inset B).

Cutworms are in fact merely soil-living caterpillars of various species of moth. Their name derives from their nasty habit of eating through the stems of seedlings and young plants at soil level, often moving along a row from night to night, which is when all the harm is done.

In the summer months, which is when most of the seedling damage occurs, cutworms can be controlled by looking for them in the soil by day near a seedling attacked the previous night. But they will also eat roots such as potatoes, turnips and swedes, occasionally continuing to feed when the weather is suitable during the winter months.

A very effective method of dealing with both chafer grubs and cutworms is to destroy them as and when you come across them while digging. Even if you miss them, by uncovering them you'll leave them exposed for birds to eat. If you want to use a garden chemical, one such as bromophos or diazinon would be appropriate, worked into the soil before sowing the crop; but really the most sensible practice is to keep the vegetable garden well-cultivated at all times of the year.

Weedy ground provides plants for the moths to lay eggs on and food for the young caterpillars; any old vegetable crops which could have been dug up are a similar sort of attraction to pests. Keep the ground well-weeded and clean even in the winter months and trouble from chafer grubs and cutworms, not to mention slugs, should be minimal.

DECEMBER
WOOD PRESERVATION

Careful treatment with a wood preservative can greatly extend the life expectancy of garden timbers but it is important to use the right type of preservative as some, notably creosote, are very harmful to living plants.

If wood rots in the garden, (a wooden post, say, breaking off at the soil surface is a common example) the cause will almost always be some sort of fungal attack; knowing this, it's possible to define where wood is most at risk and hence where applications of preservative will have greatest effect.

Fungi, like other plants, need both *air* and *water* to grow; when these are present around a suitable source of food (in our case timber), then, if the temperatures are right, they can grow very rapidly, sustaining themselves upon the wood or, in other words, causing it to rot. However, in the instance of our wooden post, the water will readily drain off its above ground sections leaving it merely exposed to the air, while that part of it that's buried deeply in the soil will be perpetually moist but have little or no air around it. Hence the danger zone lies in the surface layers of the soil where a combination of air and moisture provide ideal growing conditions for fungi. In general this area at risk may be said to extend from some six inches above soil level to about a foot below it (as the Inset shows).

Of the many different wood preservatives available the only ones that can be recommended for use on wood that is going to be in intimate contact with plants are those based on a chemical called *copper naphthenate*. This chemical is distinctively green in colour and the preservatives based on it usually contain the word 'green' somewhere in their names thus helping to identify them.

The greenness of the preservative makes it inappropriate for use on fencing panels but wherever the question of colour doesn't matter it should be applied so that as much of the wood as possible is penetrated by the preservative. That means steeping the wood in the preservative wherever possible or applying several coats if brushing it on, the second and subsequent coats being put on after the previous ones have soaked in but before they have dried. It's perhaps worth mentioning that although copper naphthenate is quite harmless to plants, the solvents used with it are not, so that it is important to let the preservative become quite dry before it comes into contact with any growing material.

Fencing panels and posts can be bought pre-treated with preservative but if you decide to apply one of the *brown*-coloured exterior preservatives yourself, you must leave the fencing to weather thoroughly before growing plants against it. That can mean 6-9 months where creosote is involved, although with posts coated with such preservative around and *below* ground level, its effect will only be to harm the fibrous roots in the immediate vicinity of the post.

DECEMBER
CHRISTMAS CACTUS

It started out as an Epiphyllum, was re-classified as Zygocactus and is now called Schlumbergera truncata; however, most of us know it as the Christmas cactus.

To describe it as a cactus may be misleading because it belongs to a small group of epiphytic cacti which grow in a completely different environment to that normally associated with cacti. An epiphyte is a plant found growing on another plant, but non-parasitically, and this gives a good guide to the sort of conditions the Christmas cactus appreciates. A small patch of rotting vegetable matter on a tree in tropical America would be a typical growing medium for the plants from which our Christmas cactus has been derived as a hybrid.

We obviously can't simulate those growing conditions in our own homes but we can do the next best thing which is to provide them with a potting compost that has a relatively open texture — i.e. to, say, John Innes No. 1 should be added some coarse peat or sifted leafmould and potting grit. Such a compost will of course have better drainage than would the John Innes by itself.

This brings us on to the subject of watering — in the forests of Brazil the epiphytes receive plenty of rainwater but their growing conditions ensure that it drains away very rapidly but with the tree cover maintaining a humid atmosphere. Similarly, when grown here as a houseplant the Christmas cactus likes a humid environment and the soil must never be allowed to dry out in the flowering period or the buds will drop without opening. To prolong this flowering period use a weak liquid feed once a fortnight.

Temperature also has some influence on flowering: the plants will in fact survive temperatures down to as low as 35°F but for flowering purposes, which is the whole point of growing them, a minimum of 50-55°F is recommended. It's also advisable to avoid large temperature fluctuations and to keep the plants out of draughts. Although plenty of light is needed, strong sunlight will do more harm than good.

Because its stems have a natural tendency to hang downwards, the Christmas cactus can look very effective in a hanging basket (Inset B) or on a pot raised by standing it on another pot, perhaps (Inset A). After flowering has finished give the plants a rest for a few weeks in a cool spot with no fertiliser and very little water. When the compost is quite dry start them into growth again by renewed watering before taking them outside and leaving them in a shady spot during the summer months.

The summer is a good time to take cuttings consisting of stem portions of one or more joints: a peat and sand compost is quite suitable with a well-balanced effect being achieved by setting two cuttings in a pot (Inset C) and growing them on together after rooting.

DECEMBER
HOUSEPLANTS

When looking after houseplants in the winter, watering can often be a problem: the golden rule is underwatering does far less harm than overwatering, especially at this time of year. For those plants that are virtually dormant, the soil should be allowed almost to dry out before any water is given, and then only a little will be needed, to moisten the soil rather than saturate it. Other plants with life cycles that involve autumn growth followed by winter flowering need more water, though not necessarily a lot more. One of the best ways to apply this is by standing the pots in pails of water, so that the water is absorbed from the bottom upwards. This is especially useful with plants like cyclamen whose corms are susceptible to rot from water applied from on top. However, do allow time for the pot to drain when removing it from the pail.

Associated with the problem of watering, especially in rooms that are regularly given some sort of heating, is the problem of humidity. Radiators, gas and electric fires not only provide heat, but they also tend to create drier atmospheres. Plants, however, should be kept away from direct heat sources and should ideally be given a continual source of moist air. This can be done by packing peat around pots standing in troughs or fairly deep trays and then making sure the peat stays moist. The plants should respond by putting out a cover of leaves over the peat to help prevent the moisture evaporating. Alternatively, stand the pots on a tray on a layer of small pebbles or chippings (Inset A) and bring the water level to just below the surface of the pebbles so that the pots are not actually standing in water.

One of the other key factors in whether you have healthy-looking house plants or weak, drawn ones is the amount of light they receive. This is very important during the winter months, when the days are short in any case. Window-sills are obviously the best place, but remember that they can be very cold at night, so that delicate plants may have then to be moved to the centre of the room. Large fluctuations of temperature will do plants no good at all. Turning the plants occasionally will help to prevent uneven growth caused by the plants' natural tendency to grow towards the light.

Finally, if you want your pot-plants to be as healthy again this time next year, in the late spring, when they are making plenty of growth, take the plant as shown in Inset B, give the rim of the pot a sharp tap and the plant together with its ball of soil should come out intact. If the roots show signs of being over-crowded, re-pot into a pot one size larger than the old one. Otherwise put it back in its old pot first removing some of the compost from around the top of the soil mass and then replacing this with some fresh potting compost well firmed down in the pot.

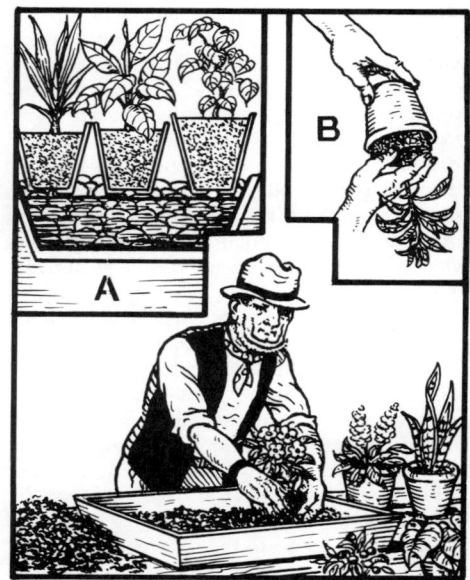

DECEMBER
CHRISTMAS DECORATIONS

Despite the quantities of artificial leaves, flowers and berries that are always on offer to the pre-Christmas shopper, there's nothing quite as good as the real thing and it's surprising how much of it can be obtained, free of charge, from our gardens.

Holly is such a traditional part of the Christmas scene that one hardly needs to mention it, but have you thought of using even just a few sprays of one of the variegated varietes to add a touch of gold to a seasonal display? The same gold is obtainable from the fairly commonly grown Elaeagnus pungens 'Maculata' or one could go for the different forms of variegation found in the cultivars of Euonymus fortunei. The light green foliage of pittosporums can look very attractive in arrangements as can the grey green of the eucalyptus, although this tends not to last too well when cut.

Box is sometimes used as a substitute for holly and its smooth-edged leaves have no doubt saved many sore hands. Mahonias have fine glossy foliage (plus their share of prickles, of course) but the deep green periwinkles have no such drawback.

Conifers are obvious choices for Christmas arrangements. Almost all are suitable, from the dark yew to the golden shades of some of the cupressus and junipers. Their cones are also invaluable both for dotting around in displays of greenery or for more prominent positioning in table pieces, etc.

Berries have their own special place in festive decorations and if you've no holly ones to hand, perhaps the birds have left you some on a cotoneaster or pyracantha. Even pieces of bark can be used effectively in Christmas creations while on a slightly larger scale silver birch logs are most attractive bases for a display.

Ways of making Christmas arrangements are many and varied but some quite attractive decorations such as the one illustrated in Inset A can be constructed with the simplest of materials. Basically one wants some moisture-retaining substance to be concealed in the interior and many lawns, I suspect, can supply some moss for this purpose or one could use the spongy flower-arranger's material known as Oasis. Whatever you use, the moisture will be retained better if the Oasis or moss is enclosed in a polythene bag and the whole will keep its shape well if some wire netting is crumpled around it (Inset B).

The greenery can then be arranged by sticking the stems through the wire-netting and polythene bag into the moist centre material. If you want to incorporate cones or berries into such a display, these can first be attached to a florist's wire (Inset C) which is then pushed in in a similar way to the foliage material. The wire netting will prove useful if you want to hang the decoration up or fasten it to anything.

DECEMBER
CROP ROTATION

Now we're at the end of the year, it's as good a moment as any to look ahead to the coming season and make a few plans for the arrangement of crops in the vegetable garden. Given a little thought, careful planning will enable you to make maximum use of what's very often a limited area available for vegetable growing.

One of the most elementary rules for gardeners is never to continue growing the same crop year after year on the same piece of land. The reasons for this are fairly obvious — the pests and diseases associated with that particular crop will build up in the soil, and the soil will also suffer from continued extraction of the plant foods required by the crop concerned.

From this has arisen the idea of crop rotation, which is designed to ensure that the same crops are grown on a piece of ground only once in three years. As is shown in the inset, it requires the plot to be divided into three sections, each of which requires different treatment in the application of fertilisers and compost or manures.

Thus, section A in the first year will be ground into which manure or compost has been dug, and to which a light dressing of fertiliser can be added before sowing or planting time. This ground is for peas, beans, potatoes, celery, onions and lettuce.

Section B is for greens (cabbages, sprouts, cauliflowers, etc.) and will benefit from some manure or compost on poor soils, although this is not essential. What is recommended though is an application of lime during the winter, followed by a dressing of fertiliser before planting time.

Section C does not require manure or compost, but relies on an application of fertiliser before sowing. Into this section come carrots, parsnips and beetroot, and also turnips and swedes. (These last two will also benefit from some lime in the soil.) As the inset shows, in the second year greens follow peas, beans and potatoes, roots follow greens, and so on until at the end of the third year the cycle is complete.

This type of plan has to be adapted to suit the needs of individual gardens, because in most cases the plot doesn't lend itself to being subdivided into three sections, or one grows much more in one section than another, but the principle of avoiding successions of the same crop should be observed, especially with regard to potatoes and brassicas.

In certain cases, we can allow for one crop to follow another in the same season — thus it's usually possible to plant out leeks and sow winter spinach on ground that's been cleared of a crop of peas or broad beans, and the same applies to spring cabbages which will be planted out in September and October.

INDEX